ACCLAIM FOR
TO THE EDGE

"A splendid adventure, splendidly told, and one more proof that the further you go outside, the further you go inside."

—**Bill McKibben, author of**
The End of Nature **and** *Long Distance*

"Fascinating . . . lovely passages. . . . Johnson deftly blends excitement, tension, grief, and humor."

—*Publishers Weekly*

"A terrific story, beautifully written, which provides yet more proof that the best sportswriting is about events at which the fewest people are present. A wonderful piece of reportage."

—**Dick Schaap, coauthor of** *Bo Knows Bo*,
Montana, **and** *Instant Replay*

"Pleasing authenticity."

—*New York Times Book Review*

"I marveled at how very, very far Johnson went and I marveled more at how deep. Johnson has returned out of the wilderness with a story so vivid and right and profound that he made me gasp at the real meaning of victory."

—**Kenny Moore, author of** *Best Efforts*,
former senior writer at *Sports Illustrated*, **costar of** *Personal Best*,
and executive producer and cowriter of *Without Limits*

"Evocative. . . . A nice job: Like all good sports narratives, this is more about meeting challenges than winning titles."

—*Kirkus Reviews*

re . . .

"A thoroughly absorbing book. . . . The narrative gathers momentum, until we are completely riveted by this portrait of one small man struggling to discover himself."

—Amby Burfoot, editor of
Runner's World and Boston Marathon winner

"A superb book."

—*Rockland Courier-Gazette* (ME)

"A compelling story of survival and triumph in one of the world's most grueling physical challenges."

—Joshua Piven, coauthor of
The Worst-Case Scenario Survival Handbook

"Essential reading for anyone who cares about pushing personal limits . . . thoughtful, emotional, and entertaining."

—Martin Dugard, author of
Surviving the Toughest Race on Earth

"A reminder of the extraordinary feats even ordinary people are capable of."
—Alberto Salazar, former marathon world record
holder and three-time New York Marathon winner

"Johnson, by lowering himself into the soul-scouring cauldron that is Death Valley as a journalist, reemerged as a devotee. . . . He used his blood as the ink, and the dedication to his subject drips from every page."
—Rich Benyo, editor of *Marathon and Beyond*

to the *EDGE*

A MAN, DEATH VALLEY, AND THE MYSTERY OF ENDURANCE

KIRK JOHNSON

WARNER BOOKS

An AOL Time Warner Company

Copyright © 2001 by Kirk Johnson
All rights reserved.

Warner Books, Inc., 1271 Avenue of the Americas, New York, NY 10020
Visit our Web site at www.twbookmark.com.

W An AOL Time Warner Company

Printed in the United States of America
Originally published in hardcover by Warner Books, Inc.
First Trade Printing: July 2002
10 9 8 7 6 5 4 3 2 1

The Library of Congress has cataloged the hardcover edition as follows:
Johnson, Kirk
To the edge / by Kirk Johnson.
p. cm.
ISBN 0-446-52617-7
1. Death Valley Marathon (1999 : Death Valley, Calif., and Nev., and Whitney, Mount, Calif.) 2. Marathon running—United States. 3. Johnson, Kirk I. Title.
GV1065.22.D42 J64 2001
796.42'52'0979487—dc21   00-042346

ISBN 0-446-67902-X (pbk.)

Book design by Giorgetta Bell McRee
Cover design by Tom Tafuri
Cover photo by Masakatsu Yamazaki / Photonica

For Gary, who made me run
For Pat and Wayne, who helped me run
And for Fran and the boys, who brought me home

Acknowledgments

Special thanks to the Network—Alice and Eri Golembo, Bob and Julia Greifeld, Sharon and Herb Lurie, Rod Granger and Susan Obrecht—for their unflagging if not always comprehending support and encouragement, to my running buddy Jim Colvin for the breadth of his spirit, and to my many friends at the *New York Times*.

In a dark time, the eye begins to see,
I meet my shadow in the deepening shade;
I hear my echo in the echoing wood—
A lord of nature weeping to a tree.
I live between the heron and wren,
Beasts of the hill and serpents of the den.

What's madness but nobility of soul
At odds with circumstance? The day's on fire!
I know the purity of pure despair,
My shadow pinned against a sweating wall
That place among the rocks—is it a cave,
Or winding path? The edge is what I have . . .

—Theodore Roethke, "In a Dark Time"

PART ONE

"The reasoned argument is but a surface exhibition.
Instinct leads, intelligence does but follow."

—WILLIAM JAMES,
The Varieties of Religious Experience

The Boogie

At 4:30 A.M. on a Sunday in mid-June 1999, I was sitting on the shoulder of a two-lane road near Ellerbe, North Carolina, flat-assed on the blacktop, legs stretched out in front of me, staring into the dark woods that pressed up to the lip of the pavement. I was beaten and about as alone as I've ever been in my life.

I was trying to tell myself that what had happened was a good thing. I should get acquainted with the bottom. I should touch the walls of it and think of it as a learning experience, because I would surely be back, in circumstances worse than this. I turned off my flashlight and let the night swallow up the bubble of illumination in which I'd been running. In the predawn stillness, even the birds and frogs that had been keeping me company clammed up.

It didn't work. As much as I tried to tell myself that what I was experiencing was somehow edifying—a landmark on the road I'd begun six months earlier—the truth is that I was scared to death. I'd gone, by that point, about 43 miles in an oddball footrace called the Bethel Hill Moonlight Boogie, a 50-mile ultramarathon that loops all night long around the towns of Rockingham and Ellerbe near the South Carolina border.

Forty-three miles! The number clanged and clattered in my head as I sat there. *Forty-three miles!* Only a few months earlier, it would have been an unimaginable achievement for me—a distance beyond the furthest margins of belief. But that night I could only see it as a crushing defeat and a portent of failures to come. I felt exposed for the fraud that I was—an imposter and a pretender. I'd gotten into something that was far, far beyond me.

"Who am I kidding?" I called into the darkness, though there was no one to hear. "Who am I kidding?"

Up until that year of my life, I'd been a runner and athlete of the most casual and modest sort. I seldom ran much farther than five miles, never participated in races and had no real goals except fitness and the flush of well-being that I felt from exercise. I came from a nonsports—or even, you might say, anti-sports—background. One of the most humiliating images from my childhood was a photograph of my Cub Scout troop, taken behind our house by the big old black walnut tree that dominated the yard. Every other boy was up in the branches—clowning, grinning and hanging upside down in his silly blue uniform—except me. I lived there and I couldn't climb my own damn tree. I was the chubby little failure left to stand and smile bravely but pitifully beside my mom, the troop's den mother.

By high school, I'd slimmed down physically, but in my head I was still the angry, frustrated fat boy. I'd also become a self-cast radical, tilting against whatever injustice I thought I saw, and my school's sports program loomed as the perfect target. In its hierarchy of brawn over brain, I saw a celebration of mediocrity. In the rah-rah cheering of school spirit, I perceived a cynical calculation by administrators seeking to control the student body by manipulating our emotions. And in the barriers to participation, I felt the sting of a biased reward system that favored children of the pampered middle class over working-class types like me who had to get part-time jobs after school. Underneath all that rage I was just jealous. Athletics was for others and therefore it sucked.

I carried pieces of that hoary old critique inside me for years, rattling around like spare parts. Every time I read about some prima donna professional sports star sulking over his plush contract, the old revulsion would flare up. But in the summer of 1997, it all began to crumble. An ambush of odd and unexpected changes in my life, especially the sudden and shattering death of my oldest brother, Gary, triggered a need somewhere inside me that I hadn't even known I had. By the time of my crisis that morning in North Carolina, I'd become—though I still couldn't quite say the word aloud—an athlete in a way I never would have imagined possible. I was exactly one month away from attempting what many veteran runners consider the most extreme footrace on earth—135 miles across Death Valley, California, in the middle of the summer. I'd entered a race called Badwater.

Most people have probably never heard of Badwater; few runners who have heard of it ever try it. The idea that I would be one of those runners was, on its face, ridiculous. I'd run my first regular 26-mile marathon only seven months prior to the Boogie, in late 1998. I was, in real life, a forty-one-year-old reporter for the *New York Times* who'd written an article about Death Valley and its bizarre desert ultramarathon and then, through some error of cosmic miscasting, fallen under its spell. I was not the real deal. But Badwater was the hardest thing I'd ever heard of, and for this one season of my life, that was enough. In ways that made perfect sense and no sense at all, the race had dragged me into its orbit.

In truth, I'd wormed my way into Badwater without amassing the record of running achievement generally required to secure an invitation. I'd promised the race organizers that I'd only go as far as my limited ability and training would let me, and that I wasn't trying to be a hero, but rather a kind of participant/observer. I wanted to experience the race from inside for a book about the perverse, confounding, paradoxical world of the ultramarathon. I'd drop out when and if medical authorities deemed my continued participation unwise. I'd almost certainly not be able to finish, I said.

All that was still true. I was going to Death Valley more as reporter than runner, more a stowaway than a participant—trying to grab just enough of a tailwind to understand a phenomenon that left me in utter and complete awe. Any small piece of the Badwater experience I could take home with me, I told myself, would be enough to say I'd touched the mysterious edge of human possibility.

In many ways, the mysterious edge was the goal itself. Pushing myself to the outer limits of endurance, I believed, would burn away the old shell of my life, exposing a place where I might find something—though I hadn't a clue what it would be—about my family and brother's life and death. Through the ferocity of its physical challenge, Death Valley beckoned to me as a portal into another world: If there was a place where life's forces and sources of power could come to the surface or flicker into view, this should be one of them. If there was a place where human limitation—but also the limits of explanation and reason and science—

should hit the wall, this was it. Badwater was a perch from which I could look for the definitions of what we are—what makes us stop, and what makes us go.

Maybe spirituality wasn't quite the word for what I sought. But I was enough of a believer, or a seeker at least, to think that there might be a way—through the unfathomable postapocalyptic wildness of racing across Death Valley—to reach through the veil and touch something beyond me and my life. A place where misery and transcendence were so deeply intertwined could not be without meaning.

By the time of the Boogie, though, my goals had become even more complicated. Just six months earlier, saying that I'd attempt Badwater had seemed like the wildest, most absurd concept I could imagine. I was embarrassed even telling my friends I planned to do it; to colleagues at the *Times* I mostly mumbled and fudged and changed the subject. The race just sounded too crazy: 135 miles of desert, mountains and blowing sand, from the bottom of the Western Hemisphere in Death Valley National Park—the hottest, driest place on the planet—to the trailhead of Mount Whitney, 8,300 feet up in the Sierra Nevada.

But over the months, through a regimen of training that had become a journey in itself, simply "trying Badwater" came to seem like no goal at all. I never consciously changed my mind. One day I simply realized that it had happened. The only thing that made sense now for me was to try and finish the race and go the whole distance within the time allowed.

Committing myself to this new path meant that I'd fallen all the way inside the looking glass. I'd become an arrow in flight and I was also the archer, standing there helpless to correct or alter what I'd released.

To simply "try Badwater," I'd realized, would be to perpetrate a fraud. It would be completely contrary to the spirit of all I was trying to explore—the limits of endurance, the borderlines of human possibility, the edge of physical effort. A halfhearted journalist's attempt wouldn't demand enough in a race that demands everything. I had to surrender to that spirit or I had no business in Death Valley.

But I wasn't at all sure where that left me. I'd taken a year off from real life—a leave of absence from my job, a flight from all the rules and rhythms of ordinary existence. And by the time of the Moonlight Boogie, which was to be my last long training run before the race itself, I felt like a man without a country. I didn't belong to the only club that would fully understand me—the universe of ultramarathoners—and yet by attempting to get there I was distancing myself, day by day, from the world in which I'd lived before.

One morning that June, not long before the Boogie, I'd been sitting on the edge of our bed, lacing up my shoes for another full day of training. I was visualizing the block of work I faced—a 20-mile run, followed by a weight-training session at the gym and then an hour or so in the sauna to push my heat tolerance. Picturing my day made it easier, like a movie that would go past frame by frame, piece by piece. My wife, Fran, lay there beside me in bed, still sleepy and cuddled under the sheets. She reached out and touched me lightly on the arm.

"You're far away," she said quietly.

I looked down, startled at the intrusion into my preworkout reverie. Her words and her touch had come to me as through a curtain—muffled and distorted.

"Yeah, I guess I am—I'm sorry," I said. I touched her cheek, but the distance between us was still there. In my head, I was already out the door and down the road on my run. I *was* far away, in all the ways that matter. I sometimes felt in those months that I'd become simply a lonely figure on the road, chasing something only I could understand. Sharing it felt risky. Maybe the doubters were right and what I was doing was just craziness. If I kept it all inside, my uncertainties could be restrained. But then it would all come full circle and I'd think, well, if I can't articulate it even to my wife, maybe I *should* have doubts and maybe it really is crazy.

"I want to be a part of this," she said. "I want to share what you're going through."

I promised to try, but I knew, even as I said it, that I'd fail and disappoint her again. I couldn't even tell her why I couldn't open up, because that would mean admitting how lost I was. I'd be all the more terrified then. Far better, I thought, to swallow hard and keep it bottled.

And that's partly what made my crash and burn at the Boogie so devastating. I'd glimpsed, for the first time, the dark edge of the sport I'd stumbled into, the bleak and desolate places of the soul that it can reveal, and the loneliness that was at its heart.

Anyone who has attempted or attended a big urban marathon, with its product expos, pasta dinners and cheering crowds, would be shocked at the average ultramarathon, which offers none of those things. You get a medal for finishing a marathon these days. By comparison, the typical ultramarathon—technically defined as any race beyond the traditional 26.2-mile marathon distance—prides itself on giving you nothing. Marathons have glamour and publicity and attention and money. They've become the Holy Grail for casual runners who want to become serious runners, and cash cows for cities all over the world that have seen how hosting a race can boost tourism and showcase a city's attractions. They're polished and commercialized—an extended archipelago of the big-business fitness-leisure-tourism industry.

Ultramarathons exist in the shadows, sustaining themselves on different sorts of energy and competition, and offering very different kinds of rewards. They're anti-marathons in a very real way—secret and cultlike and exulting in their separation. The New York City Marathon alone enrolls more than 30,000 runners each year, with tens of thousands more turned away. By contrast, the entire universe of 100-mile-or-more races—about 21 events in the United States each year—draws less than 2,000 athletes. I typed the word *marathon* into Amazon.com and Barnes & Noble.com on the Internet one day that spring and got hundreds of hits—training manuals, inspirational tracts, reminiscences and biographies of the greats. Then I typed in *ultramarathon* and got nothing. The computer search engines that were designed to take me to the last possible remotely connected tangent of my inquiry in the hopes of selling me a book didn't even know to recognize the word, because in the mainstream vocabulary of America it simply doesn't exist. Marathons are urban. Ultramarathons are mostly rural. Marathons take themselves very seriously and tend to glorify any and all who participate. Ultramarathons have names like the Fat Ass and the Big Buns, the Quivering Quads and the Mountain Masochist.

The Boogie was a classic example of the genre in that it had no budget, no media attention, no prestige for competing and hardly any more for winning. For finishing the Boogie—50 of the hardest miles I'd ever attempted on foot—I was supposed to get a coffee mug, if any were left. All of 26 souls—22 men and 4 women—had registered to run it. The directions to the starting line were marked by a single crude hand-lettered sign about the size of a license plate that had been taped to a telephone pole: BOOGIE was all it said, with an arrow pointing to the right road. When you got there, all you found were a couple of guys in baseball caps sitting on lawn chairs in front of a card table. Even in the town of Ellerbe, the race was all but invisible. It began at 6 P.M. on a Saturday, when most people were sitting down to dinner, and was gone without a trace by the time they woke the next morning. And in the odd, self-deprecating style of the ultramarathon, the Boogie's difficulty was also fiercely and deliberately understated. The jokey one-page announcement on the Internet, with its warnings about course hazards like drunken rednecks and snakes, described its five repeated ten-mile loops as being "not mountainous, but definitely not flat." But the Boogie was all hills, many of which had to be walked, at least by me. By the time I hit bottom, after 10 and a half hours on the course, I'd been delivered to a new place entirely.

The mental mine shaft into which I stumbled shortly before dawn that day has no parallel in the real world, at least in my experience. People in the running community talk about "hitting the wall," by which they usually mean that moment when energy supplies in the muscles, called glycogen, are depleted, and the body starts poisoning itself with lactic acid and waste products. When you hit the wall, you can feel confused, exhausted, nauseous or delirious. To all that, the mine shaft of the Boogie added a fillip of hopelessness. I felt, sitting there on the road, like I'd fallen to the very center of the earth and every direction was up. There might be a tiny dot of light out there somewhere in the endless blackness, but I couldn't reach it or draw strength from it. Everything had become menacing. The pines that pressed up to the roadside, which had provided a cool and comforting embrace of nature when the race began, now seemed like something from a Grimm Brothers tale—twisted and tortured, forbidding and frightening, oozing with a sense of doom. There were things that would reach out and grab me if they could. I was defenseless, a tiny candle standing up against the vastness of everything that was bent on defeating me.

In daylight, it's always possible to feel, if only in a vague and subconscious way, in command of things, no matter how much trouble the world throws at you or how exhausted you become. If nothing else, you can see the horizon and the limitless vista of the sky, with their combined illusions of possibility or escape.

The night closes all that off. When the body and the mind are crashing out in darkness, all the things of the world that we fear but can't see—the phantoms and failures and half-forgotten nightmares—join forces. Then they begin to circle and press in toward you tighter and tighter with a whispered chant that chills the blood: *It's just you and me now, bub, and no one to save you.*

And that's how I first realized I'd begun to understand the ultramarathon. By breaking down, I'd broken through. By hitting the bottom at 4:30 A.M. and 43 miles, I saw how fundamentally different super-distance endurance really was. Running these races didn't just mean running longer, it meant running deeper into the places in yourself that had to be found and conquered. For most of us, sports is defined by what we see on television or in the newspaper—a big business of spectators and fans and money. The ultramarathon turns the mirror inside out and backward. It lives at the margins, coming to life while most of us are blinking or sleeping or looking away. It's sports under a rock. And the rock that must be turned over to find it is inside each of us.

*   *   *

What would Ulrich do?

I tried asking myself that question as I sat there in the road, and it made me laugh. There was no answer anyway because Ulrich—or at least the Ulrich I'd created in my head during my months of training—would never face such a situation as this. *What would Ulrich do?* had become one of my little mantras. I could repeat it in whatever singsong melody or rhythm happened into my head to match the rhythms of my feet hitting the ground or my breathing, and the answer was always the same. *He Wouldn't Stop . . . He Wouldn't Stop.* It was a kind of call and response. When my endurance would begin to falter on a long run, I'd ask the question and be rewarded with my own programmed answer. Now it became one more symbol of my desperation.

Marshall Ulrich is a real person, and in fact I knew quite a bit about him. He owned a pet supply store in Fort Morgan, Colorado. He was forty-eight years old. He'd completed more than 90 ultramarathons, including the so-called grand slam of ultramarathoning—four of the biggest 100-mile trail races in the country, all in a single summer. His best time for a regular 26-mile marathon was 2 hours and 58 minutes— far from a world-class pace—but his best performance in running for 24 continuous hours was 142 miles, which made him one of the top super-distance runners in the world. More to the point, he'd finished Badwater an incredible seven times—more than anyone on earth. And he'd won it four of those times, including the 1992 race in which he'd set the record for the fastest Death Valley crossing ever recorded: 26 hours and 18 minutes.

And that spring, it was whispered, he'd raised the bar yet again: He was planning to pull a handcart across Death Valley, all alone, carrying his water, food and spare clothes in a kind of rickshaw device that he'd built himself. He planned to take no help along the way—a pure solo, unassisted Badwater run of a type that had never been done. *Ulrich was going to pull a rickshaw across Death Valley.*

I'd been stunned by the idea when one of the Badwater organizers had described it to me in a phone conversation a couple of months before the Boogie, and frightened by it, too. As a reporter, I knew I should call Ulrich then and there and get the scoop. As a runner in that summer's race, I was terrified of the idea and couldn't bring myself to do it. Ulrich was larger than life, an unapproachable, forbidding giant. He and his plan had become a psychotic image that I could see and imagine somehow all too well. At any time, a vision of his lonely quest—one man alone in the desert under that blazing sun in defiance of all the world and its comforts—was liable to pop into my head and produce a shiver.

Now, sitting flummoxed on my fanny in North Carolina, trying to figure out how to get going again, Ulrich once again strode imperiously into my thoughts, resplendent in his real and imagined detail.

What would Ulrich do?

I had no idea.

The Bethel Baptist Church sits at the top of Bethel Hill, which was the Moonlight Boogie's focal point. Through the course of 50 miles, we had to climb the hill 10 times—five times from each side as we went through the race's 10-mile loops. But it wasn't until about midnight—30 miles through the course, the sixth time past the church—that I heard the music. A friend of one of the runners had positioned himself there on the roadside, illuminated from behind by the church lights. He'd become a silhouette and nothing more—featureless and anonymous—and then, magically, as I went by, he began to play a flute. The melodies were random but warm and rich and with enough of the minor key in them that I felt lifted right out of my skin. The whole hilltop seemed to undulate as the notes rippled out, so sweet and pure that you wanted to swallow them.

I wasn't sure whether I'd been changed in the course of 30 miles, or whether the rules of music and beauty had evolved toward some new plane of perfection, but I was transported. I wanted to cry and float off the hillside, and almost felt that I could, buoyed by the notes themselves. Mostly I was thankful that I could be there at just that moment. And as I went by, the thought struck me how singular and unrepeatable the moment was. It could only occur there and then—and in just that state of fatigue that made me so susceptible. Like falling in love, there was a chemistry that could never be reproduced.

Around me, the other runners had become disembodied shadows, anonymous and almost invisible if they ran without flashlights, as many did. And if their lights were on, then they were just bouncing beams that floated by and disappeared, utterly without form. The human family that surrounds and supports us most of the time had stepped to the sidelines or gone to bed, leaving only this tiny collection of individuals struggling through the night, each with his or her own agenda.

Even my flashlight took on new meaning. There were long stretches when my light was the only illumination in an otherwise black and enveloping darkness. The beam, not terribly powerful, would only extend perhaps 10 feet, and gradually it came to seem as if that pool of light—the frontier of the observable universe—had become a kind of floating bubble. I moved forward and it moved forward, and I was trapped within it—never able to see or move past it. There was no horizon—no long-term view to temper the relentless sense of enclosure. And that meant I often had no visible cues at all as to whether I was climbing or descending. I had to rely on how my legs felt—whether it *seemed* like uphill or downhill—and that barometer became increasingly unreliable as the night wore on and every step, in my fatigue, came to feel like a climb.

The same sort of blind momentum had defined this whole year of my life. I was pushing my mind and body through uncharted territory. Every step was an exploration and often a milestone as well, as I surpassed, again and again, my own supposed limits. All I knew was that I was moving forward, and where I ended up was a question that would have to answer itself. There was no stopping, no turning back and no flinching—only motion, and thus, in its own sweetly brutal way, hope.

I don't know how long I sat there in the dark. Long enough, in any case, that it became pretty uncomfortable, and that standing up—hell, even running—began to sound better. And I began to think about home, too. I thought about Fran and my twelve-year-old twin boys, Anthony and Paul. It seemed like I'd been gone for so long, though it had really only been 24 hours. I needed to hug them and have them yank me back from this place. And I began to think about the responsibilities I had, all the tasks still left to be completed before the race. I didn't have time to be sitting here. I'd made too many promises. I clicked my light back on, grunted and groaned and tried to holler some pale and pallid encouragement to myself, scraped off the road pebbles and shuffled down the road.

I arrived back at the Boogie's card-table finish line at dawn—in fifteenth place out of the 20 people who went the full distance. It took me 12 hours and 20 minutes. And I guess they were out of coffee mugs by the time I got in just after dawn, because I never got one.

Red Square

Early one afternoon in August 1997, Fran and I were cleaning out the garage. I was sweeping. The telephone rang, and Fran stepped into the house to answer it. The mind tends to freeze moments like that into bookmarks of memory: I can still see and smell the clouds of acrid dust that I was stirring up with my push broom, and the angle of the sun through the garage window. When Fran came back she was in tears. My brother Gary, she'd been told, had taken his own life earlier that day in the mountains outside Salt Lake City.

Gary left no apologies. He'd simply gotten up that morning and driven away, never to return, leaving everyone who loved him staggered and grasping for explanation, and throwing my belief in the order and predictability of the universe into a place of dark and groaning uncertainty. Gary was the most gentle and stable and decent of men. If he could take such a course, then what *was* stable? What could be counted on?

What was worse, most people in our family thought that Gary, the oldest of five children, and I, the youngest, were most alike. More than 15 years separated us in age, and for many years most of a continent as well, but we'd stayed connected. For a long time that was a gift—suddenly it became a threat: Was the sense of stability I felt in my own life a fragile facade as well, as Gary's seemed to have been? What could I trust, even in myself?

My response to his death, rational or not, was to put on my running shoes and take off. I returned from Gary's funeral a marathoner—in spirit if not yet in fact—bound and determined by forces I could neither fully describe nor control to run the 26.2-mile New York City Marathon in November 1998, then 15 months away. I needed to run, or run away, as I never had before.

Gary wasn't a marathoner himself, though everyone told him he should be. We all knew he had it in him. He'd run for two hours in the morning to warm up for an all-day bike ride through the mountains. He ran in the dark and in the snow and in the blazing desert heat. He pushed his body hard to see where he could take it.

And Lord knows he had the right temperament. His whole being radiated with the deep mellow alpha wave of a natural endurance athlete. He seemed enfolded in what I thought of as a kind of Zen-like pocket of inner peace—a permanent runner's high for which I envied him. He even ate like a man with one eye on the 1000-yard horizon, slowly chewing and savoring every bite until eventually, after the rest of us in the family had gobbled like sprinters, he'd be left alone, a man with his own unalterable pace. And there'd be nothing left for us to do but to sit there in fascination and watch him finish.

But he never took the step of actually committing to do

a marathon. He always waved the idea off as something he didn't have time for. I think the larger reason, though, was that he believed it would be too selfish, too pretentious, too great a claim on the spotlight that he always felt should be directed at someone else. Undertaking a marathon is an act of hubris, a statement of bald self-assertion and ego that a modest, self-effacing man like Gary couldn't quite bring himself to make.

And maybe, it occurred to me, it was the mark of some egoistic flaw in me that I so immediately *could* take on the marathon as a goal, along with all the enfolded commitments of time and energy and selfishness that it entailed. I told myself I was running for Gary, but in truth, I really wasn't sure why I ran except that somehow it helped.

Grief running is probably not very wise for the body. I severely overtrained in the first months after the funeral, through the fall of 1997—doubling my old weekly mileage, then tripling and quadrupling it until I was hobbled and limping every morning with plantar fasciitis, a straining of the tendon that connects the heel to the ball of the foot. So I iced and limped and popped ibuprofen. And when it started to act up, I'd stop everything and do stretching exercises right there on the sidewalk, in New York or wherever I happened to be. But I kept going, and slowly over the months my feet mostly healed.

I was already running, even then, toward a new place within myself: Pushing the envelope into longer distances seemed to open a door, somehow, into a kind of undiscovered country of the mind and body that I'd never known about or imagined. And as my old physical limits faded behind me, I began to wonder if the boundaries I'd perceived and believed about thought and consciousness might be elastic as well.

What makes a human being go? What makes a person

run, climb, try hard or even get up in the morning, and what makes him stop? I realized one morning with a blinding flash on a long run through New Jersey that those questions—the central defining topics of all motion and effort—were what still bound Gary and me: He'd stopped short, and I'd accelerated. We were still linked. It was simple Newtonian physics—inertia and momentum.

Most of us, most of the time, occupy our lives in a river that carries us along, for better or for worse, in rhythms that are outside our control. The flow of jobs and commitments and family life and friends rolls on—it's natural and easy to let the march of days push us forward as it will. We all match our own stride, in varying degrees, to the pace around us because we're social animals.

Gary broke his stride and stopped the machine. He halted the momentum of life and asserted his will to stop, and in a way I didn't fully understand, that triggered my will to go. Does one connect directly to the other? Did Gary's death lead directly to Badwater? I can't honestly say. The path was not so clearly marked as that. I was also on the edge of turning forty when he died, and there's no doubt that his actions compounded everything about the symbolic corner of time I was approaching. It wasn't just midlife anymore, but real life-and-death mortality that I was wrestling with—what really keeps us alive and kicking, not just how many more years I'll need a comb for my thinning hair. Without Gary, I might have been pushed to some ridiculousness of midlife behavior, the kind that gets resolved by a sports car or a bottle of Rogaine.

Gary made it serious. That's the difference. Gary made it more than a pang of aging, but a dark shadow.

And yet it was not so much his death that put me on the road, but rather the questions that it raised about everything. This least likely of men, so full of compassion and warmth and humor and love for his family and especially his grandchildren, had challenged and refuted everything I thought I knew. At age fifty-five, retired and financially comfortable, he'd simply turned and walked off the field. Some people in our family settled on the idea that he'd suffered a sudden mental breakdown that destroyed his reason. Others, looking back at hints and clues he left over the years, saw a pattern of long-term depression and poor self-image that he carefully hid from everyone. I didn't find myself fully satisfied with any of those explanations. I became unbalanced, like a mathematician who wakes up one day after a lifetime of work to find that 1 plus 1 does not equal 2 after all.

About six months after Gary's death, in the spring of 1998, I became, to my utter surprise and astonishment, a sportswriter. I'd been at the *New York Times* for nearly 17 years, mostly covering things like politics and real estate and crime and economics—matters of the intellect and analysis and interpretation. I'd never wanted to write about sports—never even thought of it. In truth, I didn't even read the sports section. I hadn't sat through a whole Super Bowl since I was twelve. I told all this to the editor who'd approached me about the job over a cup of coffee upstairs in the *Times* cafeteria.

"Uh, I don't follow sports all that much," I said. That was a huge understatement, but then, I didn't want to sound like a complete dweeb, either. He was a guy, after all.

"Well, that's okay," he said, "If you'd said, 'Who are the New York Yankees?' that'd be a problem, but—"

"I know at least that much," I said.

We rambled on a bit after that, finished our coffee and went back to work. I figured I'd talked my way out of a job that it wouldn't have occurred to me, before that morning, to want anyway. But it turned out the paper wasn't looking for another sportswriter—they already had plenty of great ones who really, truly liked sports. They wanted, in a way, an outsider, which is what they got.

What I did wasn't sportswriting at all as most fans would think of it. I didn't cover games or leagues or teams or any specific sports. I didn't go into locker rooms much and I never once visited a press box. I did investigative pieces and features and profiles and projects. I wrote about small-time club boxers and the sociology of professional wrestling and the demise of high school sports in the New York City public schools. But it all seemed to fit somehow, and I found myself loving it more and more: I was training for the New York City Marathon, and I'd become, well, almost *athletic*. There was a parallel in my working life to what I was looking for every morning out on the road, and what I found on the road was in turn, I felt, making me a better reporter.

And then one day, after about three months on the job, I met a woman named Lisa Smith and heard for the first time the word that would come to dominate my life: *Badwater*. My editor hadn't told me much about Smith. She was a runner about to do some ungodly thing in Death Valley—that was about it.

"Check it out," he'd said. "See if you think there's a story."

By the time I pulled into Smith's driveway for our interview a few days later, I still wasn't sure she'd make a good story, but I'd learned enough to feel pretty apprehensive and skeptical about her—though in truth, *scared* is probably closer to it. I'd read her résumé. Inside this modest condominium complex in an anonymous strip of northern New Jersey suburbia was a woman who'd run 150 miles across the Sahara Desert carrying her own food and water—*and done it voluntarily*. She'd completed a seven-day, 400-mile wilderness race on bikes and snowshoes in the freezing mountains of Montana—*and afterward claimed to have enjoyed it.* And now here she was packing her bags for what she'd told me in our one brief telephone conversation was the hardest of the hard.

Something about Badwater nagged me from the beginning—an over-the-top quality both piqued my interest and annoyed me. The race quietly claimed a space for itself as the most extreme event of its kind on the planet; but did that mean it was too difficult to comprehend, or too masochistic and sick to comprehend? It produced an itch I couldn't scratch.

The race, formally known as Hi-Tec Badwater, starts at the lowest point in the Western Hemisphere, 282 feet below sea level, in mid-July at the heat-etched, wind-blasted nadir of Death Valley's annual weather pattern. It then stretches out across the desert for the length of more than five regular marathons, finishing in the Sierra Nevada at the trailhead to Mount Whitney, which is the highest point in the lower 48 states.

Air temperatures typically reach 120 degrees or more for the first 50 miles or so, dropping to freezing or below at higher elevations. Forty- to 50-mile-per-hour headwinds and sandstorms are not uncommon, nor, in the final miles continuing on to Whitney's summit, are lightning, hail and snow. Over the 12 years of its running there'd been incidents with scorpions, rattlesnakes, coyotes, mountain lions, bats, bears, flash floods, even a roadside autopsy on a mysterious corpse. Race officials, I read, pulled the plug on anyone still on the course after 60 hours.

And Badwater had been just as tough on its one and only ever corporate sponsor—Hi-Tec Sports, a Modesto, California–based shoe company that had first become involved with the race in the 1980s, and then hung on like some grimly determined ultradistance runner who couldn't give up.[*] In one of the first races as a sponsor, Hi-Tec distributed a new line of adventure racing shoes to all the participating runners.

The shoes melted before the end of the first marathon.

Of course they did! It only made sense in a place where holding a race made no sense at all. At Badwater, the blacktop in July radiates up into the runners' feet at temperatures approaching 200 degrees Fahrenheit by midafternoon. Whole flocks of birds have been known to plummet to earth, baked to death by the superheated updrafts that surge from the valley floor. (I'd considered that to be a particularly nice Hitchcockian element for my article—precooked wildlife.) A sputtering car engine can become a matter of life-and-death concern in just a few short hours if a person has ventured out with no extra water. Under extreme exertion in extreme heat, the lining of the stomach also has a perverse tendency to slough itself off. That was something I not only couldn't quite imagine, but didn't want to try.

The more I dug into Badwater, the more absurd it started to sound—but not entirely absurd, either, and on that subtle distinction was to hang a year of my life. I was susceptible. I was looking for endurance every day as I trained for the New York City Marathon. I was primed for Badwater's disturbing, unfathomable, nth-degree vision of what endurance could really mean.

I was also probably already flirting with obsession that spring, pushing my marathon goal through long runs every weekend, pouring my energies into getting where I felt I had to be. In such a state of mind, Badwater loomed like a colossus—a monster camped on the outskirts of the very place I

*Hi-Tec withdrew after the 1999 running; the race is now simply the Badwater Ultramarathon.

was desperately trying to reach. It was alien, but I under-stood it as I never would have before that year. I had to learn everything I could about it. This was not a matter of being a good reporter. I simply had no other choice.

By the time I walked up to Smith's duplex, though, my imagination had taken over. Behind her front door I imag-ined a brooding, Teutonic countenance, a storm-cloud vis-age of intensity and top-heavy determination, a seeker after the unearthly. I predicted that in some way—perhaps a tic or a compulsion to leap up during the interview and break into wind sprints or calisthenics or self-mutilation with the odd kitchen utensil—the word *weird* would be stamped across her forehead. I was more or less prepared, in other words, for a nut, an uberwoman who disdained all normal human activity or small talk, a Frankenstein's monster of the age of fitness. I was prepared not to like her at all.

But she was none of those things. If she had been, I wouldn't be writing this now. I wouldn't have begun the journey that took me down the road to Badwater myself. I wouldn't have fallen into the bottomless mystery of Death Valley.

The thing is, plain-vanilla crazy is forgettable and boring. The raving psychotic in the street shouting free verse at the fire hydrant is compelling only as long as it takes you to pass. Then you forget. It's the unpredictable, indecipherable ones that get you, the ones you don't expect.

Smith wasn't plain-vanilla crazy and seemed, in fact, to be fairly ordinary. She taught spin classes at her local YMCA and had her own one-woman company, Dream Chasers, which helped people achieve whatever goal they'd set their minds to. If you wanted to run a marathon, Dream Chasers would get you there—and Smith would even run the race with you, step for step. She was trim and attractive, with no knotted musculature or compulsions anywhere in evidence. She had a yellow Labrador named Beau and a simple house full of tasteful furnishings in wicker and blond wood. She didn't look incredibly . . . well, incredibly anything. She seemed more or less within the spectrum of normal.

And that, in retrospect, was the scariest thing she could possibly have been.

If this thirty-six-year-old woman—married and divorced and wanting someday to have children, a dream chaser herself after the mainstream things of life—could compete in the most arduous and audacious sporting event that I'd ever remotely heard of, what did that mean? What was the missing piece of the puzzle? What part of her couldn't be seen or felt in her cheerful little home? Was there a darker side to her sunny, upbeat determination? Or was she entirely what she seemed?

Certainly she was not driven by a quest for fame or fortune. There was precious little of that in her world. In an event like Badwater, where typically only about two-thirds of the runners ever make it to the end, just finishing the damn thing, I came to understand in talking with her, was the victory. Getting there fast got you a belt buckle. *A belt buckle, for God's sakes.*

And if Smith was representative of the breed, then the other participants of Badwater weren't ordinary athletes, either. They weren't the kinds of people we read about on the sports pages who are motivated by the things of this world. Badwater was off the grid. It existed outside the media culture, in the realm of doing the extraordinary simply for the sake of doing it: no money, no glory, no recognition.

I was utterly dumbfounded by this because it so instantly and decisively trashed the last of the old assumptions about sports that I'd been lugging around since high school—that athletic participation was mainly about status. Smith, sitting there across from me, semi-lotus-style with one leg tucked beneath her—anonymous to most of the world, and even to most of the running world—was a throwback. She belonged to an earlier time in sports, before the money and the marketing all transformed it. I'm not sure I could have even defined the word *ultramarathon* before I met Smith, and I certainly hadn't ever heard of her. I knocked on her door a blank slate, a vacuum of information. And she defined everything for me there at her kitchen table: an event I'd never imagined and the kind of person who would do it.

And that's how my seduction began. Certainly, I didn't leave her apartment thinking that I'd be standing with her only a year later at the Badwater starting line. But in a way, I was already hooked. I'd glimpsed something that I'd never known about, a terra incognita glistening out there on the endurance frontier—secret and powerful and fearful. It offered a promise and a threat that I couldn't get out of my head.

It's from such a mixture that you find yourself actually thinking, well, could I maybe do this thing myself? And how, one night when you're lying in bed, turning it all over in your mind, you turn to your wife and say, well, maybe I could, what do you think? And she gets that narrow, suspicious look of hers that says, uh-oh what now?

What is possible? Where *are* the boundaries? It's the kind of thought that makes you want to hide the kitchen utensils just in case your little experiment goes too far.

I continued to train for the New York City Marathon as summer turned toward fall 1998, and though I kept telling myself my goal was simply to finish, I was beginning to feel confident or cocky enough that I started to fantasize about breaking four hours. Or faster, who knew?

But Badwater never went away, either. After my article

about Smith appeared in the *Times*, I'd received a lot of calls from literary agents and book editors who encouraged me to think about a larger story. And I'd also discovered a whole subgenre of literature about Death Valley, which I'd begun poring through with an unquenchable thirst. I checked out every book I could find in the *Times* library, including musty old volumes from the Depression-era Writers Project—many of them uncirculated for decades—and the published diaries of some of the 1849 pioneers who'd given Death Valley its bitter reputation and name. And I began to write, mostly just doodling on my computer in the evenings and before work, and I found, to my surprise, that I was writing about Gary, and my own running journey, and how the two had led me to Badwater. When an editor who was considering the project casually suggested over the phone one day in mid-October that it sounded like I was halfway to wanting to try Badwater myself and why didn't I just go for it, I barely even hesitated.

"Why not?" I said.

Why not? After I hung up the phone that day, I felt like I wanted to write the words down to save for my epitaph. It's precisely because of such rash impulses and thoughtless decisions that epitaphs are needed in the first place. I'd never been to Death Valley. I hadn't even run a whole marathon yet, and I'd given a casual "why not?" to the idea of running 135 miles through Death Valley. I didn't have the thinnest wafer of credibility as someone who had any business trying to get into an event like this. *Why not?* There was a whole universe of reasons why not—a whole bookful, in fact.

But gradually I began to see that my answer hadn't really been an impulse at all. I'd wanted and needed to get deeply inside Badwater, and now, with a halfway flip answer over the phone, I was. I'd dived off the highest platform I could find without first learning how to swim.

*   *   *

As the nature of my plans about Badwater and Death Valley became known around the *Times* that fall, I felt as if I were having the same conversation over and over, always and invariably punctuated by what I came to think of as The Question: Why are you doing this?

Often, I felt that The Question was accompanied as well by a certain definitive body language. The eyebrows arch and the voice takes on a slight edge, conveying just the tiniest filigree of annoyance, as though attempting a thing like Badwater were not just foolhardy for me, but a personal affront to the questioner's sense of propriety and decorum. And I knew exactly where that feeling came from, because I'd had it myself. It was the itch you couldn't scratch.

But while The Question invariably put me on the spot, the difficulty of articulating an answer also gradually became part of Badwater's grip. The inchoate, fuzzy, nonrational mystery of it told me somehow that I was on the right track. Fuzzy is a hard thing to defend, though, especially at a place like the *New York Times*. Hard, clear, accurate, incisive—those things are good. Fuzzy is bad.

In the profession of journalism that I have inhabited for most of the past two decades, and especially at the *Times*, the world we live in can always be understood and, with enough thought and hard reporting, explained. A reporter sent out to cover a story who came back and told his or her boss that something was too deep or profound or mysterious to describe in a newspaper article would soon be in another line of work. Journalism perches on the shoulders of logic and science and is terrified to look down for risk of falling, and so, to a reporter, that makes everything explainable. But I've always believed that there *are* forces larger than logic, powers of the mind and body that go beyond the Western scientific methods of experimentation and proof

29

and physical law. There are worlds that cannot be imagined, I think, because our imaginations are simply too limited. I've always felt a hunger—for something larger, something more, something beyond the accelerated, complicated, maddening, commercial-saturated, numbered, ordered, bought-and-sold world we live in.

"I hope you're not planning on running it," one editor and marathon runner volunteered, leaning hard into my cubicle one day with a complicated smile on his face. Other variations carried the same basic whiff: You're not thinking of doing any of it, are you?

My basic response to those sentiments, whatever their intention or subconscious message, was to shrug and mumble. Ultimately, I suppose, I was afraid that what I'd embarked upon was fundamentally stupid, irrational and pointless and that I'd wake up one day screaming in horror at the realization of it. Could a majority of the world's population—or at least most of my friends and colleagues—be wrong?

"I want to run *some* of it," I'd say, with heavy emphasis on the *some*, so as to communicate that I was still sane, still in control, still the reporter who'd plotted it all it out quite thoroughly, and was only out there to bag the Big Story. Another variation that communicated a little more of my real intention and state of mind was this one: "Oh, I'll probably not go very far [shrug], just, you know [mumble], to see how far I can get. I certainly don't think I'll finish or anything."

But even that response seemed to raise suspicion in the office that I'd lost my professional bearings. I'd committed the cardinal journalistic sin of becoming so close to a subject I'd written about that I'd painted myself right into the picture. I'd come to fantasize that I was as strong and tough and brave as the people I'd described. It happens all the time in journalism. Reporters who write about politicians sometimes start to think they're better than their subjects—as of course sometimes they are. Reporters who write about movies start to think they can bang out a better screenplay than the bilge being pumped out of Hollywood. Reporters who write about book publishing start scribbling novels in the morning.

At the *Times*, the line between reporter and subject is much more than just a hoary old cliché of objective journalism. It's the core of a deep rumbling institutional wisdom that defines and shapes what I believe is the greatest newspaper in the world. If you stay aloof from your subject, then you can be brave in describing it, and honest. If you get too close, then you lose the ability to see the truth. Worse still, you lose the courage to step back and denounce phoniness, fraud and frippery even when it hits you in the face because then you'd be denouncing a part of yourself. That's the creed, and I believed it.

When I first started at the paper as a news clerk in 1981, an old warhorse of a reporter—40 years on the job, an unlit pipe anchored to the corner of his jaw, a thousand crusty stories pinned to his cuff about the life of a foreign correspondent—invited me to lunch one day. He had two pieces of advice for a twenty-three-year-old newsroom rookie.

"Go out and report, then come back and forget everything except to write the truest thing you can, without fear or favor," he said, quoting a maxim handed down by Adolph Ochs, who'd bought the paper in the 1890s and created the dynasty that it became. The old reporter paused for a long time and ate his lunch while I sat there waiting for the other shoe to drop. Finally, when he sensed, in good storyteller fashion, that my tension level was at its peak, he stopped and looked down at me severely from his sandwich.

"The second thing is, don't screw up," he said.

Now I did risk screwing up. Just as I risked failure and injury and who knew what else at Badwater, I realized that I risked being wrong about it. I needed Badwater to be certain things for me. I'd fallen under its spell in part because of what it was, but also because of what I wanted it to represent—a place where doors might open, where truth might emerge, where perhaps I'd find the insight I'd been struggling for about what happened to Gary.

In my moments of purest *Timesian* objectivity, I had to concede that Badwater might be no more than a race. The doors that opened might be mere delusions, heat mirages and flutters of physical exhaustion—a contrivance of exertion.

But I must have communicated at least something about my deep need to go there, fuzzy as it was. The leave of absence I'd applied for to train and run the race and write about it was granted. The momentum toward Badwater, for better or worse, was growing.

But I still had no answer to the question my editors had asked me: Why? Why does Badwater exist, and why does it persist? Why does it capture the imagination, and why do people like Smith and Ulrich come back to try it year after year? Why do people push themselves to places where they're barely able to keep going? Why had it grabbed me?

There are dozens of sporting events around the world that can reasonably claim to be the toughest, hardest, longest or most extreme. But like the frontiers of science that get pushed back all the time by every new discovery, the limits of human endurance have yet to be found, or even defined. The so-called Ironman—a 2.4-mile swim in open ocean followed by a 112-mile bike ride and then a 26.2-mile marathon—once seemed to hold unquestioned claim to the title. Then came double Ironman competitions, with twice the distance on everything, then triples.

Now there's an event that's 15 times an old-fashioned and comparatively wimpy regular Ironman. People have run across the United States. People have run the length of the Western Hemisphere and rowed boats across the Atlantic.

Certainly, some elements of human performance are limited by physiology. Records for the fastest 100 meters or mile or marathon are certainly there to be broken—and they will be, over and over, in years to come—but eventually we'll begin to bump up against a more or less finite boundary. The increments by which a record is broken inevitably grow smaller and narrower each time. Someone, someday might eventually break a two-hour marathon. But no one will ever do it in five minutes.

Going long, on the other hand, has no boundary whatsoever. The limits of *how far* a human being can go, as opposed to *how fast*, haven't even been glimpsed. There's no science that can measure the human ability to endure and persevere.

Badwater's claim to the pinnacle of endurance is the combination of its distance, its weather and its minimalist wilderness-adventure style. There are races longer than 135 miles, but most are run in stages, usually no more than 40 to 50 miles a day. Badwater clings to an old-fashioned format once called "Go as you please," which means that the course is run straight through, with no breaks for rest or sleep except as determined by the runner. There are races that have more and higher mountains to climb, but there are none that do so in what climatologists agree is the hottest, driest place on earth. And there are races where volunteers are scarce and aid stations are far apart, but there are very few that, like Badwater, have no services or aid stations at all. Many of the runners I'd begun interviewing that fall—people who'd done dozens or in some cases hundreds of ultramarathons—told me that Badwater had taken them closer to the frontier of the possible than anything they'd ever done. And it had beaten or intimidated some of the greatest distance runners in the world in the process. Eric Clifton, a living legend of the ultramarathon cult who at one time held the course record for eight of the biggest 100-mile races in the United States and was believed to have won more ultramarathons than anybody in history, with 48 victories to his name, had attempted Badwater twice before that year *and never finished it.* No genuinely famous marathoner of the caliber of a Salazar or a Shorter, I was told, had ever even tried.

Impossible or seemingly impossible things are everywhere, of course, once you start looking. Most things, in fact, are impossible. You can't knock down the Empire State Building by smacking your head against it over and over, or swim across the Pacific Ocean on a single breath of air, or leap from the roof of your house onto the moon. It'll never happen, however many times you try. But pure difficulty was also not the key measure, either. Badwater seized me for reasons that were not particularly noble or heroic or perhaps even understandable. I just found myself running down a long road toward a destination that I could only dimly perceive, hoping for an answer to a question I could barely articulate. I ran because I had to and because I needed to see the landscape out there past the point of everything I could imagine.

When I committed in mid-October 1998 to trying next year's Badwater, I wasn't really a runner, though. And I almost immediately lost my ability to even *be* a reporter in researching the race. I was overwhelmed, so frightened and insecure by what I'd embarked upon that I couldn't even pretend to be an objective observer. There were real Badwater runners out there, and how could I even talk to them? What if they asked about my running experience? I couldn't lie, but I couldn't bear to think of telling them the awful, embarrassing truth, either. *Hi, I'm about to run my first marathon, and I'm in Badwater next year.* It was ridiculous. Marathons were things these people did before lunch.

At the top of the list of people I knew I should call but couldn't was Ulrich. The name by that time had already become monstrous in my fevered imagination, symbolic of everything I was afraid of. *What would Ulrich do?* The answer was easy—everything I couldn't. And as I began my research I felt that he was capable of emerging at any moment to remind me of my inferiority. Drifting through the Internet one afternoon, for example, cruising the ultramarathon sites, I came across a list called "Runs You Don't Want to Try." Two of the top three involved Badwater, and the number one position, as perhaps I should have expected, was held by the very Zelig of my Badwater torments. Ulrich's run-you-don't-want-to-try came in 1994, when he'd mapped out an alternative Badwater route that went south to north through Death Valley. It was the same distance as the regular Badwater race, which goes east to west, but with even more time spent in the frying-pan valley bottom— since going north eliminated the climb into the higher elevations of the Sierra Nevada where the temperatures were lower.

The smart thing, I suppose, would have been to slay the demon by simply calling Ulrich, introducing myself and getting it over with. The call you're scared to make is the one you should do first. That's the hard-boiled maxim of the newsroom. Come on, what are you, a sissy? What's the worst he could do, or be?

But somehow I just couldn't do it. The line I was walking between objective reporter and terrified participant was too fluid, too nebulous. The reporter wanted to get Ulrich on the blower and nail him on what this damn Badwater thing was about. "All right, Mr. Fancy Pants Endurance Guy, give me the skinny on this desert business—you people all nuts or what?" That would been the method of the veteran journalist I thought I was supposed to be. Pin 'em down, get the straight poop.

The participant was more like a delicate shrinking violet, and he had the last word. I was afraid of being laughed at. I was afraid of being patronized. I was afraid of anything that would shake my confidence. I was afraid of anything that would make me overconfident. The only thing I wasn't afraid of was being afraid. Fear, in those immediate weeks of October into November, became a dear friend and trusted ally. Fear got me up and running and training and pushing as hard as my body would allow. I sometimes felt that fear was in fact just about all I had.

Fifteen months after Gary's death and four months after meeting Lisa Smith, I ran the New York City Marathon. I'd considered myself pretty well prepared beforehand, and through the first 15 miles I felt good and strong. At 17 miles, however, as I was heading up First Avenue in Manhattan—a long gradual ascent into the Bronx—my energy began to falter. With every mile after that things got worse—my knees throbbed, my thighs ached. I'd slowed down to 12-minute miles by the time I turned the corner heading back down toward Central Park and the finish line. I desperately gobbled energy gel packs and electrolyte drinks and anything else I could to try and reboot my struggling body.

But my resolve remained unshaken. I knew I'd make it, even if I had to drag myself the final miles. It felt inevitable, a certainty of nature, and partly, I think Badwater was responsible. *This is only a marathon.* The thought ripped through my head during that long stretch up First Avenue.

It's only 26 miles. I can do this. And if I can't . . . It was a thought I didn't allow myself to complete. Dropping out and going home was no longer an option for me. I was committed to a far longer road than the paltry climb up First Avenue, however hard it seemed.

And I had Gary with me, too, I think. Before the race, his wife, Kathleen, had sent me a box full of his old running shorts, telling me to do with them whatever I wanted. They had a lot of miles on them—and a lot of machine washings. The waistbands had long since given up their last gasp of elasticity; there were holes and frayed edges and signs of so many morning runs that I could almost feel Gary in their fatigue. I couldn't wear any of them. But I cut a six-inch square from one red pair and pinned it to my shirt. The red square became my coat of arms, my little banner of memory. No one else knew what it meant, or what weight it carried. But I looked down at it from time to time, especially during those miles into the Bronx when I was grasping at anything I could. My square became a kind of compass. It pointed the way home, marking the trail that I should follow.

I didn't break my four-hour fantasy. Not even close. It took me 4 hours and 27 minutes to reach the end, where they hung a medal around my neck and cheered.

Return with Honor

In December 1998, about a month after the New York City Marathon, my mother died. Her death was sudden, but not particularly unexpected—her physical and mental and emotional health had been deteriorating for so long that no one in the family was really shocked. She'd faded from the world and from the family long before. When I'd called to tell her about the marathon and about Badwater, I wasn't even sure she'd really heard me, or understood, or even much cared. But her death brought the family together for the second time in a little more than a year, and once again, as we had after Gary's death, we stayed at my sister Pat's house outside Salt Lake City.

This was a more complicated grieving. With Gary, we'd sometimes simply had to hold one another and shake and let the tears come. With Mom, we felt the loss, but we'd all seen how bitterly unhappy and removed she'd become from life's joys. She'd left the party years earlier, retreating into a small circle of self-pity from which, in her last years, she never reemerged. Perhaps, said those of us who believed in such things, she's happier now. That possibility made it easier.

But one jarring thought was clear: The family had lost its center. Dad had been dead for 20 years, and the kids and grandkids and cousins were spread out all across the country. Mom, as distant as she'd become, had still been the axle that connected the wheels—the center of the family and the reason for gathering back in Utah—and now we'd have to find those reasons ourselves. We'd have to make them up and take the initiative to hold the clan together or we all feared we'd just drift away.

That realization pulled my thoughts over and over, even during the funeral itself, to the question of Badwater. Our family needed new glue to bind us, and I would need a crew to be with me in Death Valley. There was a connection and an obvious opportunity. As we went through Mom's things and talked about the family, a Johnson team at Badwater came to seem more and more appropriate to me—an answer to everything we'd been talking about since Gary died. But it also sounded like a potential recipe for disaster. When the talk turned to the race, I usually said something vague and general about needing to put together a group to help me do it. But I pointedly and specifically didn't ask any of them. How could I? How could I ask anyone to do something like that?

If running a marathon, not to mention an ultramarathon, is an act of base and selfish egoism, then the idea of assembling a sycophantic band of worshipers to tag along and supply one's every need was surely pathological.

But it was also a hard-and-fast Badwater requirement. One of the race's starkest singularities is that it takes place in what is almost a vacuum—a desert that for mile after mile constitutes one of America's emptiest places. The ab-

sence of aid stations and volunteers is just the beginning—
over the 135-mile distance, there are only a couple of places
to even buy anything like food or gas or water. Every runner
therefore has to decide or guess in advance what he or she
will need, haul it out to Death Valley and then somehow in-
duce a group of friends, family—or, some might say, vic-
tims—to go along for the ride. The crew generally leapfrogs
the runner, driving up ahead a mile or two, where they wait
to perform pit-stop-style functions like filling water bottles
and spraying water on frying heads and making sure their
runner is coherent and conscious.

Getting my family involved also presented an emotional
risk. Beyond the physical ordeal it would represent, I feared
that it might not bring us together at all and in fact could
do exactly the opposite. Close confinement, harsh conditions, little sleep, tempers frayed by exhaustion—there were
a thousand things that could make it the worst experience
of our lives.

I also knew, because I'd heard it from some other spouses
and parents who'd crewed a relative in Death Valley, that it
could be painful even to watch a loved one go through Badwater. Fran and I had already decided by then that she probably shouldn't be there with me for that very reason.
Watching me would be hard for her, and I couldn't bear the
thought of that. Seeing her in pain during the race would
sap my will to go on because I'd know that by stopping and
giving up, the vicious cycle would end. And neither of us
wanted even the remotest possibility that on some level I'd
then be able to blame her for my failure.

The nature of my family also complicated the decision.
It's not that we were exactly distant. But there were spaces
between us of varying sizes and depths—some narrow, others that were rather like the Grand Canyon. It was partly a
matter of geography—we were spread apart in four states on

different sides of the country—and partly a matter of some huge differences in personality and age. Gary had been almost sixteen when I was born. Pat was twelve, Wayne was nine and Wendy was three. And the three oldest had all moved out of our house before their twentieth birthdays, which meant that as the youngest child I had no memory of Gary at home at all, and not much more of Pat. Sometimes they'd almost seemed more like aunts and uncles than siblings. I'd been very close to Wendy when we were younger, but even we'd stopped calling very much or writing in recent years.

And as for Wayne and I, we might as well have been from different planets, we seemed to have so little in common.

Wayne and I had shared a room when he was in high school and I'd just started kindergarten, which was probably in itself a formula for strained relations. I was pesky, obnoxious and whiny and Wayne had a chip on his shoulder big enough to fill the room itself. We were Oscar and Felix— the family bookends, extreme in our differences. I remember crying to Mom and Dad night after night about needing the lights turned off so I could go to sleep, no matter what Wayne wanted. And I went through an even more neurotic phase about that same time that must have driven him crazy. I couldn't go to sleep until I'd called out "Good night, Mom," and "Good night, Dad," like John-Boy Walton. And I'd shout until I was hoarse, over and over and over until my parents would respond with "Good night, Kirk." I would have hated me, too.

Mostly back then I thought of Wayne as mean. I remember one winter building a snow fort in our backyard. I'd crawled in underneath a big mound of snow, trying to dig out a tunnel. Wayne came up behind me, grabbed my legs and shoved me deep into the pile, so tightly wedged I couldn't move my arms or legs. I was immediately panicked and screaming, claustrophobic and terrified in the dark, tight little space. I don't know how long I was in there. Perhaps Wayne pulled me back immediately and the whole thing was over in five seconds. Or maybe he left me to wiggle my way out—I really have no idea. I only remember the terror, not the release, so it's hard to definitively say one way or the other—little brother as sissy who couldn't take a joke or big brother as tormentor—only that the memory had never faded even after 35 years.

Other times, being Wayne's little brother just meant ordinary humiliation. One summer day, for example, he asked me out of the blue if I wanted to see a spectrum. I immediately said yes, all excited, even though I probably didn't have the remotest idea what a spectrum was. Wayne said great and told me to go find an empty paper towel tube and a glass of water. Fantastic, I thought, as I scrambled to go find what he'd said. A spectrum. Wow. This'll be great.

When I came back, we went out onto the front lawn and Wayne told me to lie down on my back and hold the tube up so I could look through it. He said he'd hold the glass of water just right so the sunlight would filter through it, creating a beautiful rainbow effect that I could view from down below. It was a dazzlingly sunny day, brilliant and blue. Perfect for a spectrum, I thought. I was ready.

You might already have a good idea what was going to happen next, but I didn't: Without the slightest of pauses or pretexts about finding the proper angle of refraction, Wayne simply poured the glass of water down the tube into my face.

Okay, I was gullible. No question about it. I was dumb for not suspecting some kind of trick. If I tried something like that with my own kids, I'm sure they'd see in a minute what I was up to. But I never forgot my disappointment. I'd really had my heart set on that spectrum, whatever the heck it was.

It's not that Wayne and I were antagonists in any particular way. There was no real animosity, I think, no long-buried issues or secrets, smoldering over the decades. We were just very different. We'd go months and months without talking, sometimes as long as a year or more, which made it hard to pick up where we'd left off even if we'd both been trying hard, which we weren't. We cared about each other in our own ways, but we really didn't know each other's lives. He'd never been to visit me in nearly 20 years on the East Coast, and I'd been to his house exactly once.

I'd also felt from my very youngest days that I was different within my family, and it took me a long time not to think of those differences as flaws. My dad had built our house from scratch, without a plan or any help from anyone except my mom. Wayne and Gary both built their own homes, too. They'd simply taught themselves what they needed to know—plumbing, wiring, framing, Sheetrocking, shingling—then went ahead and did it, just like that. They hunted, at least in their younger days, and stocked their freezers with the product of their own labors. Wayne took a whole car apart and put it back together when he was in high school. Gary built a self-heating electric driveway for his house one year so that he wouldn't have to shovel snow anymore, just by reading a book about it.

I couldn't do any of those things, and had no interest in even trying. I couldn't fix things. I couldn't build things. I had little interest in cars and was so inept mechanically that just putting in a new light fixture had on one occasion resulted in our calling an electrician to repair the damage. For a long time I felt I was half a person, born without the "Johnson genes," as Fran has called them. I'd wanted to be a writer from the time I was in high school, and was the first among my siblings or any of my cousins on my mother's side to graduate from college. When I was twenty-one, I'd moved

2,000 miles away to New York City—the place least like Utah in the world, as far as everyone in my family was concerned, including me—and never even thought of moving back.

But now on the morning after Mom's funeral, Wayne and I were sitting at Pat's kitchen table drinking coffee and I'd never heard him talk so much, or ask so many questions about anything. He wanted to know all about Badwater and Death Valley and the other runners and the crew system and the history of the race.

"This sounds just amazing," he said. "I'd love to be there."

So I told him everything I'd learned and heard about the geography and the heat and the race records and the hallucinations that the runners experience. And I realized as it went on, and his questions kept coming, that it was probably the best and longest conversation we'd ever had about anything in our whole lives. I felt like he was volunteering to be there, reaching out to me in the spirit of family cohesion we'd all been talking about.

And I couldn't reach back. What would happen to us, trapped together in the middle of Death Valley through an ordeal like Badwater? I feared it could blow our already fairly distant, tenuous relationship into fragments that could never be reassembled. I feared losing another brother, even if what we had together now was considerably less than perfect.

So I remained noncommittal. I couldn't be sure he was really serious in his interest, but I knew if I asked he'd feel pressured to say yes. Were the vows we'd been making to stay close influencing his judgment? Would he wake up in a month and think, whoa, what kind of stupid idea was that?

And I wasn't sure what I wanted, either. Did I fear screwing up the family? Or was it something else?

Finally I just had to run away. I made an excuse that I had some Christmas shopping to do, but really I was just scared.

I didn't know what I was doing, either in getting myself ready to run the race or in getting anyone else involved in it with me. I was falling down the rabbit hole and I didn't know where or how I'd come out.

I kept thinking of the little brass plaque that Gary had attached to the door leading into his garage not long before his death. RETURN WITH HONOR, it said. He'd positioned it right at eye level, a little message to himself about the world and his ideals that he could read every time he left the house. I still didn't fully understand what it meant—or meant to Gary—and yet now I felt that the message was somehow more applicable than ever. But what was the honorable course to take?

I returned home from Mom's funeral feeling very alone, having been chased 2,000 miles back and forth across the country by questions I couldn't answer. I'd lost my mother, and our family was at risk of losing its way. I hadn't been able to decide whether dragging my family to Death Valley would be perfect, or perfectly stupid. I hadn't been able to fully communicate my need to do Badwater to anyone, including my wife. I'd been isolated by my decision to take on the race, and I saw that the months ahead would only take me further down the road I was on, with no end in sight. I could only hope that there would be a way back, but even if there wasn't, I saw then that I'd probably keep going anyway, and that scared me, too.

A Lost Piece of the World

I spent an entire night, early that spring, as a volunteer aid station worker at a 100-mile trail run in Virginia called Massanutten, which loops through the Blue Ridge Mountains near the town of Front Royal in the George Washington National Forest.

I was posted at the 88-mile point on the course, at a place called Powell's Fort, which had been the site of some kind of military outpost during the Revolutionary War, but which was now simply an isolated spot in the middle of nowhere on a mountaintop at the end of a long steep dirt road.

I was there as a spy. My plan: Infiltrate an ultramarathon, suck out every detail and nugget of wisdom, every hoary old superstition or tradition, every vignette and anecdote of the ultramarathoner's creed I could, in the hope that some of it might rub off and help me when my time came. But I was also on the trail of something more subtle than that. I was trying to understand endurance. I wanted to dissect it, to lift its outer layers and peer down into the beating heart beneath.

The never-say-die genre in literature and life has always sparked my imagination. As a kid, I couldn't identify very well with the intense and manly tales of bravery that most boys devoured. But I could imagine endurance. That only meant not giving up, hanging tough, slogging through and gutting it out. Endurance heroes didn't need to be brave, hard-charging charismatic leaders; they only had to be tough and strong somewhere deep down inside, and even a wimp could picture those traits in himself. It made me a sucker for any story of iron will, no matter how it turned out. If the result was a triumph, well, that was fine, but a doomed failure was often even better.

I could put myself inside all the great stories: Henry Stanley crossing Africa; the ancient Israelites wandering 40 years in the wilderness; Davy Crockett and his men at the Alamo; Balboa slogging through the rain forests of Central America and seeing, for the first time, the Pacific Ocean; Scott of the Antarctic, frozen inside his tent, scribbling his last; Magellan, circumnavigating the world; Robinson Crusoe, fighting the elements and the specter of madness in his desert island fastness.

My favorite movie when I was twelve years old was *The Flight of the Phoenix*, which starred Jimmy Stewart as a pilot whose plane crashes in the middle of the Sahara Desert. He and the other passengers ration out their water, fend off desert tribesmen and stare death in the eye as their lips get all cracked and ugly. And yet, working together, they're somehow eventually able to build a workable plane out of the shattered parts of the original and fly it out. Pretty implausible, overall. But I couldn't get enough of it—how the tide of hope ebbed and flowed, and how, in the end, it was what kept them alive. All the passengers realized, even as

they were building their plane, that it might not and probably would not work, but that the doing of it was the thing.
That idea kept them going, putting one foot in front of the
other in a place that was screaming at them to lie down and
die already. I read the book on which the movie was based
over and over, and every time—though secretly, because I
was twelve and insecure about things like expressing emotions—I cried when it finally worked, as it always did, and
they miraculously survived.

But with Badwater less than four months away, I was now
much more than just a student or a voyeur of human determination. I'd become an acolyte, a worshiper at the altar. I'd
come to see endurance as the trait above all others that
marked greatness in the species—a sign of grace, a telltale
indicator of the elect. What is endurance? Who has it?
Where do they get it?

I'd also become a packrat for every trick of the ultramarathoning trade that I could beg, borrow or steal. If there was
an ace up the sleeve, a technique of hydration, a food that
worked well at 90 miles or a better pair of socks, I wanted to
know about it. So I examined the shoes and the mud-gaiters
of the Massanutten runners as they passed, and how they
carried their water and how much they ate, but mostly I
studied their eyes. In the buggy glare of the Powell's Fort
lamps and flashlights, then later as the stragglers came
through the station after sunrise, I tried to see inside them.
What were their secrets? What was the slow burn that had
brought them to such an unfathomably remote place as
this—88 miles into a 100-mile race? I became a miner for
the traits of endurance, a prospector for the gold that had
come to seem the most prized thing I knew.

One of the people I met that night had been, at one
time, a minor legend of the ultramarathon circuit. He'd
won a few 100-mile races in the 1980s, but then, for rea-

sons he wouldn't elaborate on, he'd stopped running, and now he just came back year after year to help at Massanutten as an aid station volunteer. He was in his early forties and so gaunt that he was almost skeletal. One end of his belt flopped out no matter what he did to stop it, as though his waist was just too inconsequential for a belt to bother with.

But it was the way he spoke that really got to me. His name was Bob. That's all he wanted known, or maybe that's all there was. Bob struck me as a boiled-down human being—what you'd have left, essentially, if you threw a regular person into a machine that would distill the essence. Like his fatless body and the absence of a last name, Bob's language had been minimized. He'd dispensed with certain articles of speech entirely, as though adverbs and pronouns were profligate expenditures that must be saved for some grueling push across the linguistic finish line.

"Frogs," Bob said. "Lot of frogs, these woods."

It was just before dark, and we were walking up along a dirt road on a part of the Massanutten course, tying phosphorescent glow-sticks onto the branches so that the runners who would be coming through later wouldn't miss the trail.

"I've heard that frogs are disappearing, getting rarer," I said.

"Don't know," Bob said. "Doesn't seem like." He paused. "Drive my truck to the ponds here—back up and put the stereo speakers facing the water, turn it up loud and play Bach's Toccata and Fugue."

Around us, the night was getting thicker and deeper, amplifying the power of Bob's voice. "They change their singing as it goes on," he continued. "Like a chorus."

I was a bit skeptical of this, but I also didn't want to tease him. Bob was a little scary, especially there in the darkness.

He was entirely unpredictable to me. "Do you think the frogs like Bach in particular?" I asked, trying not to sound like I was making fun.

He didn't hesitate for an instant. "All living things respond to quality," he said.

I knew as soon as he said it that I'd never hear frogs again in the same way.

About a third of the Massanutten field had dropped out by the time they got to Powell's Fort, so the runners I met were essentially the survivors—if they'd made it this far through the course's steep and rocky trails, they were almost certainly going all the way.

And as I sat there waiting for them in the dark with my lamp and my bottles of water and bowls of boiled potatoes and electrolyte refills and oranges and salt, watching for the next set of flashlights to come bobbing down the trail out of the trees, I really felt I was inside the beast somehow. The secrets of endurance were out there somewhere in that darkness with the whippoorwills. The people who were going through this long night had called forth a spirit, a living presence, and all I needed to do was hold out my hand— like the breeze, it was there to be touched but never held.

Some runners—mostly the leaders, the front-of-the-pack racers—were sealed boxes, quiet and efficient, barely even moving their eyes. They reminded me of reptiles—completely motionless, eerily calm, every surface stilled, making no movement beyond the minimal amount necessary for their continued forward motion. They scared me silly in their intensity.

Later arrivals—the middle-of-the-pack runners and stragglers—trudged in full of needs and wants, craving attention to their hunger or thirst or suffering. I loved them to death because I could so easily see myself in their position. They'd devour anything put before them—conversation, sympathy, food, drink. They seemed like they were trying to suck in whatever physical, emotional or psychic support they could get for the miles they still had left.

One man showed up at dawn saying he'd been running all night stark naked, and had finally pulled on some shorts when he'd heard noises on the trail behind him as he approached the station. Another man, who at age seventy was the oldest runner in the field that day, arrived looking like a question mark, bent sideways, shuffling over the rocks and roots that covered the path. I wasn't sure whether the race had done this to him or if he'd looked like that at the start. He leaned against a post, while his wife and daughter, who'd driven up a few minutes earlier to await his arrival, hovered around, offering him whatever they thought he might need. Their job was made more difficult by the fact he never so much as opened his mouth to speak. He was like an ancient oracle that had to be interpreted to the world—a leathery, clinch-jawed old god of the forest. The two women held out bowls and bottles and ointments like supplicants and he either took them or he didn't and who knew why. Then he took off again, just as bent as when he'd arrived, but still moving.

The last person to come through that morning was a woman in her early thirties who'd been on the course for nearly 31 hours. And though I never learned her name or what became of her after she moved past Powell's Fort, I'll never forget her. She was both larger than life and smaller at the same time. She'd been reduced, after so many hours and miles, to a pure essence of will that was both terrifying and inspiring at the same time. She groaned and looked confused and exhausted, and was afraid to sit down, she said, because she might not be able to get up. And I believe she was probably right—she seemed barely able to stand, like a willow that bends with every breeze. But she didn't stop and she didn't sit, and she made it out of our station before the time cutoff that would have kicked her out of the race, and then she moved on down the trail. I watched her leave, walking slowly, every step by that point a struggle. If I'm ever in a fight, I'd take her on my team before the guy who won the race.

I'd been looking for endurance in the library, too, that spring. I started with *Running and Being* by Dr. George Sheehan, which was given to me as a going-away gift by a friend at the *Times*. References by Sheehan in turn led me to Robert Bly's book *Iron John*, about the struggles and strengths of the male identity, and to William James's *Varieties of Religious Experience*, where I searched for insights about states of ecstasy and aberration, and the points where the spiritual and the physical might cross paths. Somehow that connected me to Shivas Irons, the mystic golf pro of Burningbush in the Scottish Highlands, who tried to teach author Michael Murphy about the power of sports to transcend physical reality in *Golf in the Kingdom*, and from there to *Zen in the Art of Archery*, about Eugen Herrigel's search for enlightenment in Japan in the 1950s through the study of the bow and arrow under a forbidding Zen master.

I don't know exactly what I was looking for in all this. Inspiration was certainly part of it, I suppose—the same vicarious thrill that had electrified me as a kid in reading about the lives of the great explorers. I wanted to find the inner state of endurance—the mental and emotional formula that creates it and the psychological portrait that defines it. I wanted to steal the intellectual recipe, just as I'd stolen ideas at Massanutten about the best socks. And though I rarely admitted it to myself, my search was also informed by a hidden, almost secret assumption—that real, true endurance was more than the sum of its mechanical or psychological parts. There was a spiritual element as well, I believed, or at the very least a thread that couldn't be quantified by the confines of the scientific method.

The training of my body, I'd already come to see, would be the easy part of preparing for Badwater. The far more daunting territory that I'd have to master was off the map, in the interplay of the mind and the heart and maybe the soul or spirit—those places beyond the modern world where I believed the real fuel for endurance was to be found.

So I tried to understand Poon Lim. He was a Chinese sailor who survived for four and a half months alone on an open raft in the Atlantic Ocean in World War II after the British merchant ship on which he'd been serving was torpedoed and sunk by a German U-boat. Poon told the disbelieving fishermen off the coast of Brazil, where he was rescued, that he'd survived by drinking rainwater and eating the fish and seagulls he'd managed to catch. But even he couldn't say, when it was all over, how he'd sustained the will to go on—what fire had burned inside him that made it possible to face another day and another fight for life, week after week.

And I tried to imagine myself into the lives of the Chiricahua Apache Indians of the American Southwest, who'd defined and embraced endurance as an element of the life well lived. Young men of the tribe, as they approached their coming of age, would be required to run up and down a mountain before dawn, or continuously for two days and two nights without food or sleep, or for miles carrying water in their mouths that they would discipline themselves not to swallow.

I'd also discovered a website on the Internet where I could buy books about super-endurance, and they turned out to be just what I'd expected—grubby little tracts, mostly self-published, often even self-typed, with smudgy gray pictures. They'd arrive in my mailbox hand-wrapped in brown paper, looking like old-fashioned pornography. But that was part of their charm, too. I loved getting another crude little tome in the mail; it bolstered my belief that I was on the right path. I was stumbling toward what I imagined as a kind of Shangri-la, a lost piece of the world that now only existed in the darkest groves of the forest, guarded by the endurance priests and priestesses who were mailing me their little books. By the very fact that the ultramarathoning world was so small and obscure, I told myself, there was hope that it could contain a larger, undiscovered truth.

Mostly, though, my small and obscure booklets contained small, obscure information. I learned about hair and fingernails, for example. During extreme exertion and fatigue, or so I read, the body floods itself with endorphins that reduce pain and promote healing. The external evidence of that regenerative process is that a body produces more hair and cuticle cells running a hundred miles than it does sitting in front of a television screen. Why this fact was remotely valuable for me or anyone else to know, I had no idea.

Then I read a book that had absolutely nothing to do with ultramarathons or sports or endurance at all—*Walden* by Henry David Thoreau—and I felt I was finally getting close to what I sought. I'd read portions of *Walden* in college, but back then I'd dismissed him as a fussy, pretend frontiersman who'd thought he was roughing it living out in the woods in the 1850s within walking distance of a town in New England. He wouldn't have lasted a week, I thought, in the genuinely wild and unsettled West of his day. I'd considered him a coward and a fake.

Now I realized with almost every page how much I'd missed the point. Thoreau, as prissy and preachy as he might well have been, was not trying to find the frontier life outside Concord, Massachusetts, but rather a whole alter-native existence. Simplify your lives, he told his readers. Toss aside the baggage that you cannot carry and reject what the commercial culture tells you is important. Find the rhythm that makes sense for you and follow it.

Thoreau, sitting by his little pond 150 years ago, had de-fined the very universe I was trying to explore. The ultra-marathon was not merely a strange little cult, I saw, but a full-fledged counterculture, a living descendant of Tho-reau's critique. It was not just different from the conven-tional running world, but deliberately removed from that world, separate and apart.

Where mainstream America worships speed, the ultra-marathon is all about distance. Where the big urban marathon is premised on sunny middle-class optimism, physical fitness and personal growth, the ultramarathon is about limits and the virtues of stoicism. Where marathons are built around community and crowds and cheers, ultra-marathons are all about being alone. Even Thoreau's most famous line about marching to the beat of a different drum-mer has found its place in the super-distance vocabulary. Forget everyone else, ultramarathoners invariably say, and "run your own race." It's just you against the course, you against yourself, you against everything that tells you to give up. Reject the world and look within. Every living thing re-sponds to quality.

Of course, I was looking for the hallmarks of endurance most of all within myself.

I still couldn't think of myself as an athlete. It was too easy to remember those Friday nights in high school after the big game when the athletes and their cheerleader dates would stroll into the Italian restaurant a mile from my school where I worked rolling pizzas. I was outside their universe, hidden in the kitchen behind the pizza counter, stoking a pathetic anger that said I was somehow superior by my very exclusion. I couldn't entirely disavow the place from which I'd come; it was too much a part of me. From those long-ago Friday nights I'd learned to despise arrogance above all else.

But now, with this year, I'd finally leaped over that counter and seen a part of what my hated high school jocks had possessed. Through missteps and happenstance and grief I was beginning for the first time to understand and discover my own body. I was living someone else's life in training for Badwater—not the rarefied life of the mind I once considered the highest form, but a sweaty, stinky, joyously physical one that left me aching at the end of the day. How far I'd run, whether my workout would include hills or not, or cross-training on the bike or with weights at the gym, became the main items on my daily desk planner. And every milestone of distance I pushed through was also a new landmark on the mental journey, until I sometimes wasn't sure whether my body was setting the pace or my mind was, because everything was so intertwined.

The very landscape of my emotions was being altered. I often found that after a long, hard workout, I could break down in tears over nothing—a sappy piece of music, a news story on the radio, or sometimes even more vaguely just by how the world looked and felt and smelled. I came home sometimes wanting to hug my wife and my kids for reasons I couldn't put my finger on except that I'd realized how much I loved them.

I'd become a runner like some people find God—suddenly, upon turning a corner, without preparation or warning—and that made it all new. I learned the rhythms that can emerge suddenly in the mind after 50,000 footfalls down a road. I learned how to breathe—really breathe—for the first time: soul-sucking, life-dependent breathing that rises like a curling wave from the toenails up—the breathing of a body in a journey of deep physical fatigue. And I learned to love fatigue itself for what it could teach me about what was real and what was not.

I'd always thought that feeling tired was the signal your body made when it was time for you to stop. The real adventure began when I found that I could ignore that signal and simply keep going. A whole world opened that had never been explored because I'd never known of its existence.

But I was still terrified. The more I thought about the interior spaces that Badwater would take me to, the more I began to fear that I just wasn't up to it. Badwater was too big, too hard, too frightening. I was too inexperienced. I was still, somewhere inside, everything I'd ever been—the fat boy, the anti-athlete, the sissy—and I couldn't reinvent that past now. Those old chunks of my identity were like zombies—buried but far from dead. I still couldn't climb the damn tree.

But I began to think I could perhaps build a kind of alter ego who could go where I couldn't—an interior athlete, an ultramarathoner of the mind. I found a certain refuge in the idea that I could be the architect and engineer of a Badwater runner. It protected me from the idea that I would really have to face Badwater. It would, instead, be my "other," my running self, the fearless part of me who could be invested with everything I could learn, every trick I could glean from all the ultrarunners I planned to interview, every book I could read, and every ounce of training that could be crammed into the meager time available to me.

My Badwater runner would be lean in all the ways of the mind and body. He'd be small. He wouldn't need speech or brains, which would only get in the way of his mission. He'd be as primitive as I could make him, savagely determined, one-dimensional and capable of only a single thought—finishing Badwater—but incapable of pursuing that goal with anything less than complete dedication. Doing Badwater, I'd decided, meant tossing over the side all the mental and emotional ballast that was too heavy to carry. Freed from the entanglements of civilization, my runner would be a singularity, a minimalist—Henry David Thoreau in a jockstrap.

In April, I ran my first 50-mile race. It was called the Long Island Endurance Run, held in the wealthy New York City suburbs on the north shore of Long Island. About 30 of us ran all day in and around Teddy Roosevelt's old town of Oyster Bay, past mansions and gated estates and woods, and it took me just over 10 hours to finish, at an average pace of about 12 minutes a mile.

Only five months earlier, my first marathon in New York City had just about killed me—I'd felt broken down and used up by the end and had been unable to climb or descend stairs for days afterward without pain. But now, after a distance nearly twice that far, I'd simply jumped in the car and driven home, going faster than I should have so that I could catch my son Anthony playing trombone in a middle-school production of *Guys and Dolls*. In some ways, I was arcing across the sky, a self-made meteor—I'd already achieved the impossible, or what would have seemed like the impossible in any other year of my life. The intense, accelerated schedule of training that I'd embarked upon was building me a new body, right before my eyes.

But for all my purpose and determination and the new vistas that sometimes seemed to open at every step, I still often felt lost. The whole notion of what was too far had been shattered. I'd seen too much and read too much and experienced too much about what the mind and body can do to say with any certainty that there even *were* limits. *Ordinary* and *extraordinary* no longer had meaning because I was no longer sure where one ended and the other began.

Before that year, running 50 miles would have been the most astonishing physical feat I could ever imagine doing. Now it was just 50 miles. And I suppose that's the bittersweet payoff of pursuing any goal that is, on its face, beyond reason. It pushes you to places you didn't think you could reach by reducing them to mere stations on the road. Badwater, looming over everything, overshadowing everything, had made my little achievement possible, while at the same time robbing it of any meaning. There was only the question of what would come next and how much time was left on the clock in which to go further and train harder. I'd finished my first ultramarathon, but that only made me a guy who'd run 50 miles in 65-degree weather. Big deal.

I'd signed up by then for the Bethel Hill Moonlight Boogie 50-mile run in June in North Carolina, thinking that an all-night race would be good practice for Badwater's around-the-clock rhythm. But again, the Boogie was only 50 miles—it wouldn't take me, I thought, any closer to the frontier of endurance than I'd reached at Oyster Bay, two hours from my house—and my training time was quickly running out.

Paul pointed out the painful truth when we were talking about my Long Island experience the next morning over breakfast. Wow, Dad, he said, calculating in his head. The total mileage of all the races you've run in your whole life— a couple of marathons, one 50-miler and a few shorter events—has finally passed the 100-mile point! He was excited for me, trying to be supportive.

I saw the glass as half empty. My whole cumulative running experience only added up to about four-fifths of Badwater's distance. In Death Valley, I'd run the equivalent of every race I'd ever completed—under conditions far beyond anything I'd ever remotely faced—and I'd still have a marathon to go. Badwater was just three months away.

Great, I said. Thanks a lot, son.

Western Wind

I told myself that after I'd run my first 50-mile race I'd finally be able to call Marshall Ulrich. I'd have at least that little chevron on my sleeve. I wouldn't be just a guy who'd run a marathon and then somehow found himself suffering delusions of grandeur. I'd be the real deal then, I thought, or at least close enough.

But it didn't work. About as soon as I'd done the Long Island Endurance Run, the phrase "only a single fifty-miler" began to stick in my throat when I'd rehearse what I might say to Mr. Badwater or all the other runners I'd been too cowardly to call. Sitting there looking at the phone, I practiced my best mumbling and fudging techniques. "Well, if you count training runs, I've done, you know, quite a few ultras [cough, clear throat, quickly change subject]." Then I tried out this one. "By the time of the race I'll have done, of course, a bunch of fifties, at least [pause, cough, feel guilty about lying, change subject]."

Every possible fake conversation scenario I came up with

still left me feeling like I was barely legitimate in Badwater company. My 50-mile threshold, as huge an accomplishment as it was, seemed just too minimal to count. But I also gradually began to see as I agonized over how to reach out to these people that on some level I was probably capitalizing on my own fears and using them.

My sense of inadequacy was pushing me to train harder, and the hurdles I was setting up that were supposed to make me a real-enough Badwater runner—my first 50, or my first back-to-back 26-mile training runs two days in a row, which I'd also done by then—were complete frauds. I knew I'd never reach the point of saying I was "real," no matter how hard I trained. But trying to get there—trying to claw my way to a hypothetical shelf from which I could speak to Ulrich as a semi-peer—had now become part of my fuel. On some level, I probably didn't even *want* to become a legitimate Badwater runner, whatever that meant, because then I'd lose the scratchy edge of anxiety and doubt that was yanking me out of bed every day to push myself farther and harder and longer.

Whether such a cycle of false-front, self-fueling, never-to-be-fulfilled goal-setting was a sign of excellent mental health or not—well, I just didn't want to go there. If it was pushing me to train harder, then it was good. That's all I needed to know.

But it wasn't all a ridiculous mind game, either. My original plan that spring, to try and meet as many of the Badwater group as I could, and short of that, to talk to all of them on the phone, had blown up in my face with one of the first calls I made. I'd phoned a guy who I'd heard was running Badwater for the first time, figuring perhaps we'd have something in common. He'd probably be scared, too. So when he answered I'd introduced myself and told him I was in the race, and he immediately asked what I'd run be-

fore. I swallowed hard, paused, and told him the truth—
only a single marathon up to that point.

Perhaps, in fairness, I called this guy on a bad day, or
maybe he wasn't the diplomatic type, or maybe he just
didn't like reporters pretending to be ultramarathoners, but
he let out a long low whistle that slid up my spine like an
icicle. I quickly jumped in to tell him that I'd done lots of
marathons in training, of course, which was stretching the
truth just a bit. But it was too late. My worst fears had become real.

"And you're really going to try Badwater?" he said, openly
incredulous and just a shade this side of mocking.

It was the kind of exchange that made me want to
disconnect my phone. I had plenty enough confidence-
eroding anxiety without strangers giving me more. So Plan
A—call everyone—pretty quickly became a file in a folder
on the desk and not much more. When I'd think of calling
somebody, my instinctive response was to go for a run instead.

What happened was that my clever little training device
of cultivated insecurity had come back to bite me. It had all
been well and good for me to tell myself that I was a fake
and phony—when I was the only one doing it. Having
someone else point out my staggering lack of experience,
however, was too much. Maybe, it occurred to me, I'd had
my delusions mixed up. Self-induced terror wasn't a training trick at all and I really was just as much of a fraud as that
long low whistle had suggested.

My cowardice and confusion left me stranded in the middle of another contradiction. I was searching for the roots of
endurance, but too scared to reach out to the one group of
people in the world who'd be most likely to have the answers I sought—the Badwater runners I'd be with in July. I
knew that Lisa Smith was in the race for the fourth time

(and, no, I hadn't been able to call her yet, either), and Ulrich, of course. The other runners were mostly a mystery—just names on a list. So I began to circle the field, in a way, to sketch out the boundaries and learn as much as I could without terrifying myself silly.

I called Matt Frederick, the race director and marketing manager at Hi-Tec, and he gave me a rundown on what he thought were some of the more compelling stories that year. There was a schoolteacher from California who'd survived breast cancer and was running Badwater for the first time. Eric Clifton was trying the race for the third time. A set of twins from Austria who ran races all over the world had entered. There was a chauffeur from London, a police-dog trainer from Northern Ireland, a businessman from Hong Kong and an optometrist from New Mexico. About half of the runners were first-timers to Badwater, Matt said, and half were veterans. Forty runners had been admitted this year, he said, and 18 more were on a waiting list in case a spot opened up.

As Matt went down the list, Dan Jensen's story had immediately leaped out at me. Dan was a Vietnam vet, Matt said, who'd lost a leg in the war, and was now a commercial photographer living in Sioux Falls, South Dakota. He was one of two amputees in the race that year, Matt said. The other was a former British soldier named Chris Moon who'd lost an arm and a leg to a land mine. That's all Matt knew. Both were Badwater first-timers.

And that's really all I knew when I first called Dan and introduced myself. I was thinking like a journalist at that point. Dan was a good story. A guy with one leg running Badwater was an incredible thing to even imagine, and I just had to meet him. I also tried to call Chris Moon, but he was out of the country. (Only later did I learn that Moon was crossing the entire length of Cambodia on foot that spring to raise money for the disabled.)

But there was a weak and sorry side to my call as well. Dan, I figured in my pathetic way, was a "safe" runner to contact. He would probably struggle at Badwater, too—perhaps even as much as I would. He'd be less likely, I thought, to mock me or suggest I had no business attempting the race. If he'd reached the point of saying he could face Death Valley, maybe I could become stronger by meeting him and learning about his strength, and maybe I could share with him what little I had of my own.

I felt I could probably identify with Dan—that was a big part of it. He was a one-legged runner and I was a half-assed runner, and maybe between those two points we'd have something in common. So I took a deep breath and dialed.

Dan was immediately friendly and enthusiastic and thankfully easy on the questions about my racing background when he called me back several days later. I told him I was planning a loop out through the Upper Midwest to visit a couple of other Badwater participants, which was a bit of a stretch, since he was the only person within a thousand miles I'd called up to that point. He said he might have some photography work to do, but otherwise his schedule was open and he looked forward to meeting me.

So then I looked at the map. Frederick at Hi-Tec had mentioned a guy named Mick Justin who lived on a lake somewhere up in the north woods of Minnesota and worked as an accountant. Something about that combination had intrigued me: an ultramarathoning CPA. The inherent wildness of Badwater seemed so antithetical to the world of dry debits and credits. And on some level, I think I also imagined that Justin was a "safe" call. Being from Minnesota, and being an accountant, he'd probably be nice, I figured, or at least not overly threatening or mocking.

Mick said he'd be happy to see me, too. He was running a race just about every weekend, he said, but anytime during the week would be just fine. So I packed my running shoes and booked a flight.

Showing up at the home of a person you've never met is one of journalism's oddest things. I'd flown to Minneapolis, rented a car and driven 250 miles across the prairie to Sioux Falls, and now I was about to ring the doorbell and step into someone's life, right into his most private personal space. And my ambiguous double identity made it all the stranger. I was a runner and I was a writer, and in a somewhat creepy way, I had to acknowledge, I was also a bit of a voyeur—I'd been drawn to Dan's story, after all, specifically because he had a handicap. It was a combination that left me feeling acutely self-conscious and not entirely pleased with who I was.

In any case I didn't want to show up empty-handed, so I stopped and got some bagels and cream cheese at a place in Sioux Falls, found the house on a nice tree-lined street, parked the car and took a deep breath. Before I could even open the door, Dan bounded down the front steps to greet me at the curb.

My first impression of him was how incredibly thin he was. He immediately reminded me of Massanutten Bob, the pared-down former runner I'd met in Virginia. Dan's body seemed utterly without fat—an impression accentuated by his close-cropped hair, which he said he'd cut himself and was a little embarrassed about. His daughters thought it made him look like a mental patient, he said. The second thing I noticed was his smile. It was huge and loose and just a little lopsided, and it appeared suddenly, transforming his lean face with warmth, as though a switch had been turned.

As soon as I shook Dan's hand, I felt the question of my

double identity being answered. I wanted to be there as a runner. I wanted to paint myself into the picture. So I left my notebook and tape recorder in the car, grabbed the bagels and followed Dan into the house, where he introduced me to his wife, Robin, and we all sat down together at the dining room table.

I felt intensely awkward, having invited myself into their lives with my conflicted agenda. Sitting there, I thought of Gary's little garage door plaque. Why had I come, really? And would I return with honor? I smeared a bagel with cream cheese, noticing as I did that Dan ate his plain. We talked about general things. Dan said he'd grown up in Sioux Falls, just a few blocks away from the house he lived in now. Robin was from Texas and still had a bit of the Lone Star twang in her voice. I told them a little about my family and what it was like at the *Times* and the town we lived in, in northern New Jersey. Then the conversation petered out. Dan had insisted when we'd spoken on the phone that I spend the night at his house, and now I was regretting that I'd said yes. A whole day and a night there was beginning to sound like a long time.

So when he asked if I was interested in going for a run, I jumped at it. I was anxious and edgy after my long drive and I hoped that running would open up our conversation a little more. And I was curious, too—probably thinking like a cold-blooded journalist again—to see how Dan ran with his prosthetic leg. That had been more or less the impetus of my visit, after all, though I'd been afraid to ask anything about it, or about his experience in the war, during our little chat at the table.

But as we began to get our gear together there in his living room, my professional curiosity as a journalist quickly gave way to personal awe. Dan's right leg ended just below the knee, and I watched out of the corner of my eye as he slipped his stump into the saddlelike enclosure of the prosthesis and attached the straps. He was utterly nonchalant and matter-of-fact about it all, however, and that relaxed me. He was what he was.

Dan asked if I felt like some hill work, and I said fine, so we drove to a ski resort just outside of town called Great Bear, parked on a dirt road, stretched for a few minutes and took off. By the time we'd turned up the trail toward the first big hill, I'd forgotten he even had a disability. His stride wasn't exactly the classic runner's poetry of motion—the prosthesis required a slight twisting of the body and an additional lifting of his right side and hip to keep his forward momentum going—but he was as strong or stronger than I was, and faster when he pulled out on the flat. And he had a rhythm that held it all together. He ran like he was supposed to run this way, not like he'd accommodated himself to some lesser form.

Almost immediately, we also began to talk in a way that somehow hadn't been possible back at the house.

Dan only began running at age forty, he told me, when a prosthetic running foot was finally perfected. And when he described that first day with the new foot, how he'd run down the block—really flown down the block, he said, so freed was he from the leaden gait of the old leg—I really felt it myself. He'd immediately found that with the proper equipment he could do things he'd never imagined. Running had taken him, over and over, he said, to a place where all he wanted to do was give up, where it seemed there was no more left to give and no ability to go on. The attraction of the ultramarathon, he said, and the other endurance events he'd done, like the Ironman in Hawaii, was that you had to specifically reject that place of limitation, or find a way around it. He'd completed the Ironman for the first time in 1997, taking first place in the "Physically Challenged" division with a time of 12 hours and 24 minutes for the three events—open-ocean swim, bike ride and marathon. He struggled most on the 112-mile biking portion, he said, from cramps in his good leg, but then recovered and ran a 26-mile marathon in 4:23, faster than I'd done my first marathon—and I'd been younger, well rested and equipped with two real legs.

The feeling of having nothing left, Dan said, is simply one side of your brain—the rational part, or maybe the smarter part—analyzing a situation and saying that enough is enough. The joy and the power come from not listening, from pushing on to that desolate plateau where reason can't follow. Time stops. There's no past and no future, only a crystallized, clarified and overwhelmingly powerful present tense that swallows everything.

"You're just here now," he said.

Dan told me, as we ran, that losing the lower part of his right leg to a land mine in Vietnam in 1971 was ultimately a lucky experience—it saved him, he said, by taking him home and out of the war after only six months. Because of his injury, he was able to avoid what he believes were Vietnam's real wounds—the debilitating emotional and psychological scars that were suffered by soldiers who actually had to kill people, if only to avoid being killed themselves. Dan shot his gun, certainly, and he went out on ambushes in the jungle waiting for the enemy to come. But when they did come, he showed me how he pulled the trigger, with his head down and his rifle up, shooting blindly in the direction he was told to shoot, shredding the leaves with his bullets and he knew not what else.

Dan and I ran together for two and a half hours that day, side by side, and by the end I felt I was beginning to understand present-tense endurance. It was about running down a slope and getting dirt in your shoes and giggling like a five-year-old. It was about being a child, because only a child has the strength to reject those grown-up, rational voices of fatigue that holler out from your brain telling you to stop this nonsense and come in now because it's time for supper. Kids just don't listen, and that was their secret.

And for the first time since I leaped into distance running after Gary's death, I also felt real joy—a pure, mind-blowing, directionless physical innocence that flowed through me with every step and every breath. Dan exuded joy from his pores. He floated on it as he ran. He was a grateful runner, and that was an immense source of power.

I drove north from Sioux Falls the next morning toward the town of Nisswa, Minnesota, my head buzzing from the strongest coffee I'd ever tasted, a concoction that Dan called his "Morning Blast"—an extra-large dark roast with a shot of espresso. Around me, the Upper Midwest prairie land rolled on and on, endless and empty, and though I'd never been to this part of the country, it felt familiar to me somehow. I knew the taste of the wind that hit me in the face whenever I stopped to buy gas or to stretch my legs. It was a western wind—or at least a wind of the wide-open spaces—the kind you just know has gone a long, long way to reach where you're standing. It was thick and musty with the smells of soil and grassland and rain that it had picked up on its long journey. And it took me back to my childhood as much as running with Dan had.

My mother was descended from Mormon pioneers who'd scratched their way across land like this, trying to get to Utah in the 1850s. They were so poor that they couldn't afford horses or wagons, and so driven and desperate that they went anyway, pulling all their belongings with handcarts. But they'd left too late in the year to make it all the way across the Great Plains in safety and in November 1856, in western Wyoming, they faced their crisis. They ran out of food, just as the first storms of an early winter were setting in, and were reduced to chewing shoe leather. My great-great-great-grandfather died of starvation along with seven other men on a single night and was buried in a mass grave near present-day Green River. His son John Oborn, a teenager at the time, survived. The rescue party that had been summoned out from Salt Lake got there in time, and John went on to become the patriarch of a huge and extended polygamous clan south of Salt Lake, from which my mother was descended.

I'd been carrying the Oborn family saga around in my head ever since I'd begun hearing about it from my mother and my grandmother when I was very little. But something in the air that day on the prairie, combined with the mood of joy and loss and strength I'd picked from Dan, suddenly brought it home to me in a new way. My grandmother—a granddaughter of John Oborn and old enough to remember him—had always taught me that the core of the Mormon pioneer story was what she called its "connections." Physical struggle was part of the process of spiritual growth, and endurance was a demonstration of faith. That's how our family had come to be where it was, she'd said. That's how they'd survived crossing the plains.

I thought I'd forgotten Grandma's lessons, but that day they all came back. The child who'd cried—or wanted to—every time he'd heard the great hymn "Come, Come Ye Saints" was still inside me somewhere, and he'd been awakened. I could close my eyes and feel the rush of emotion I'd experienced in hearing the Mormon Tabernacle Choir climb its way, measure by measure, to the hymn's climactic last line about surviving to the end of the trail or not. The sopranos fly up and over the top, just like angels: "And if we die before our journey's end," they cry, "all is well, all is well."

About a year before Gary died, he and I began talking about getting together to do a big walk across these plains in memory of old John Oborn. I'd had the idea of a book about the two of us retracing all or part of our family's Mormon trail. I'd write about the old threads of our history—faith, endurance, desperation, poverty, the dreams of building God's kingdom in the West—but also, and especially, about the conversation between the two of us that I imagined we'd have along the way.

Gary was the only good Mormon among the five siblings—he never drank alcohol or coffee and never smoked. He alone had stayed true to our roots. What I proposed was a kind of two-month ramble through history and family—oldest and youngest, hashing over what it all meant and where our different roads had taken us. He'd loved the idea, both as a physical adventure and as a spiritual journey to try and explore who we were.

Much of the attraction of the project for me was that I'd get to spend a really long time alone with Gary. I wanted to hear why the old religion still worked for him, and over a long walk, he'd have all the time he might need, in his slow-talking way, to explain it. I also wanted to understand the relationship between the things I so admired in him and the faith that he seemed to draw such strength from. Was he a good man and a strong man because he had religion in his life, or was it the other way around?

But I'd let the idea molder and grow stale until it withered. I lost interest. A deluge of news articles and film coverage had been released after the Mormons had staged a one-hundred-fiftieth-anniversary reenactment of their initial 1847 pioneer trek. The subject, which had seemed so fresh and new when Gary and I first talked about it, now felt tired and clichéd. It'd been done.

About a month before he died, he called me and said he thought we should keep the conversation going. Even if nothing came of the idea of our journey together, talking about it was good, he said, because it was bringing us closer together.

"Great," I said. "Sure."

But I was humoring him. I wasn't really listening. I'd written the idea off. Gary had called me as a brother and I'd listened as a writer. It was the last time I ever heard his voice.

I met Mick Justin that night. And in many ways, he was the perfect antidote for the vague sense of melancholy I'd felt during the drive north, precisely because he was everything I hoped he'd be: a practical, modest, down-to-earth accountant from Minnesota who also happened to be an ultramarathoner. He was thin, though not as emaciated as Dan, and bearded—a quiet man with a shy smile that often seemed to be hiding behind the hair that covered his face.

Like Dan, Mick was a Vietnam veteran—a former paratrooper. And again like Dan, he'd only started running as he approached middle age, in Mick's case as a way of controlling his weight.

"It was either that or hang out in the bars," he said with a tight-lipped little laugh.

At first, he'd barely been able to run 100 yards, puffing along in some old tennis shoes he found in his garage. But gradually he pushed that to 200 yards, and then a mile. Sitting in the restaurant where he took me to eat, he described the day he ran, for the first time, the full seven miles around the lake where he lives. The astonishing power and joy of the accomplishment changed his life, he said. It made him realize that he could do so much more than he'd ever thought possible. It's what had started him on the road to Badwater. If he could run seven whole miles, he thought, what else might be out there that had seemed unthinkable?

Mick was humble about having finished Badwater three times. He described his huge discomfort and surprise when the local newspaper in Pequot Lakes, where he works, had somehow gotten wind several years earlier that he'd done some wild thing out in Death Valley. They'd written a big embarrassing spread about him, he said, and everybody in town had kept telling him how incredible he was until he just couldn't stand it.

A big part of the problem was that the newspaper story had portrayed him as some kind of conquering hero, when the main lesson that Mick said he'd come away with was exactly the opposite. Badwater, he said, was about accommodation, not triumph.

"You have to take what it gives you," he said. "In Death Valley, you can't be macho and survive."

The real question of Badwater, Mick said as he tucked into his plate of ribs, is how a person faces the moment of his own imminent failure. Finishing the race is about finding a way past those times that look and smell and taste like defeat.

"Are you going to be able to go on when everything says you shouldn't? When all the voices say stop? That's the test," he said.

I tried to eat, but the more Mick went on, the more macho it all started to sound, despite his protests to the contrary. Finding a path of accommodation, which was how a soft-spoken guy like Mick would characterize it, required an inner steel that I wasn't at all sure I had.

"It'll happen more than once that you feel like you can't go on and that you've reached the end of the road," he said.

"At that point, you pause and rest for a while, and gradually the picture changes and you think, well, maybe I can go another mile. Then you go another mile and things look different again and you keep going."

He looked at me over the table for a minute, as though sensing a question I hadn't asked.

"You can finish Badwater," he said. "You just have to want it badly enough."

I got up the next morning and ran around Mick's lake—he was nursing a sore foot from a race the previous weekend and wanted to stay off it—then packed up and drove back down to Minneapolis to fly home. My head was filled with phrases and images I'd absorbed over the past few days, but the more I thought about it, the more it seemed I hadn't really learned anything.

Dan liked to confront the voices that told him to stop so that he could willfully ignore them. Mick's strategy was to wait them out. But it was all just talk. Having never in my life faced a crisis of imminent physical failure, when all the voices told me to stop, their strategies were only theory for me. I could fantasize all I wanted that I might be able to stand up as they did and face down my fears, but I really had no idea. I didn't know what I was made of, deep down in the places that I knew Badwater would expose, and I saw that now more clearly than ever.

And yet I also felt I'd glimpsed a little more of the machinery of how it might work, or rather, how it might begin—with something as small and simple as running around a lake or sprinting down the block on a new leg. Everything, even Badwater, was a matter of facing the world one step at a time. I felt grounded by that somehow and brought back to earth. And it made me realize I could no longer put off the task of assembling a crew that I'd dreaded

and avoided for so long. Mick, especially, had been so organized that it shamed me. He already even knew where he
planned to get the blocks of ice that he'd haul down into
Death Valley in July in the event that ice was unavailable
there, as had been the case several years earlier. Practical,
concrete steps—that was my new formula.

So I called my sister Pat in Salt Lake. She was a marathoner herself and the obvious first choice as my anchor.
She knew running and its demands, and she knew the
desert country even if she'd never set foot in Death Valley.
She agreed instantly, though I couldn't quite shake the edge
of doubt about the whole thing that I sensed in her voice.
Then I called Wendy, but she wasn't able to get time off
from work in July.

That left Wayne. And again I delayed for days and days.
Wayne had certainly made clear his interest back in December. And he'd taken an early retirement by then from
his job, so I knew he had the time. There were a hundred
good reasons why it all made sense, and yet I kept putting it
off. Finally I broke down. I picked up the phone, going over
and over in my head what I planned to say and how I'd say
it. My breathing was shallow, my heart pounding much
more than I would have imagined. There seemed to be so
much at stake and so many things that could go wrong.

After we'd talked about our families for a minute, I got
right to it. I reminded him of our conversation at Mom's funeral and the interest he'd expressed back then. I told him
I couldn't ask—it was too great an imposition to even suggest—but that if he was really still interested, I'd be honored if he could join Pat and me. There was no perceptible
pause at the other end.

"It sounds great," he said with what sounded like real enthusiasm. "I'd love to do it."

"You're sure?" I said. "I mean, I really don't want you to

feel obligated or anything. This could be a hard, awful experience—"

"No, really, it sounds wonderful," he said.

I wasn't sure I believed him. *Wonderful* was too positive a word for what we'd face in Death Valley. *Powerful, overwhelming, frightening*—all those things I fully expected. *Wonderful* was over the top, the word of someone who was trying to convince himself that he wasn't walking out onto a ledge. But I let it pass. Things were in motion.

A Bunch of Crazies

One night in late May, just before the Memorial Day weekend, I walked into the Badwater Saloon in Stovepipe Wells, California, elevation sea level, to have a beer. What I really wanted was conversation—the beer was just pretext. I'd come to Death Valley several days earlier for what was called "a training weekend," of running in the desert and acclimating to the heat, and I felt I'd been swallowed alive. Death Valley was more than I'd imagined—emptier, bigger, deeper and wilder. It had reduced me to the merest of specks in disturbingly short order.

I don't know what I expected from a bartender—sympathy, I suppose, or maybe a pat on the back for being out there willing to try something so tough. But that wasn't at all what I got. When I told her why I'd come to California, she immediately launched into her favorite Badwater story.

It seems that her boss, the manager of Stovepipe Wells Village—a motel, general store, gas station and campground about 80 miles from the nearest real town—had been outside his office the previous year during the race when one of the "crazies" had staggered up and passed out on the ground, right there in the parking lot.

"He has kind of a sick sense of humor, this guy," the bartender said of her boss. "So he reached down and grabbed him by the shirt and said, 'You having fun yet?'"

I nodded and smiled and tried to swallow the beer that seemed suddenly stuck in my throat.

But by then her story didn't come as a complete shock, either. I'd also heard of other local residents who had less than positive attitudes about Badwater. And I was beginning to understand their point of view. People like the bartender and the motel manager who lived year-round in Death Valley respected the place as only a desert dweller can. They'd learned not to challenge its harsh climate, but to accommodate themselves to it and live within its rules.

Badwater makes new rules. Badwater says that Death Valley's envelope—what it allows and what kind of physical activity is possible—can be pushed and expanded. To a local, I'm sure that sounds like heresy, like the talk of outsiders and, who knows, maybe even New Yorkers, for God's sake. It sounds crazy—or worse, disrespectful—like the greenhorns who go to Alaska and think they can survive in the bush because they've read a book about it. Alaskans hate those people, too.

The runners of Badwater, with their collective Lisa Smith–style upbeat optimism and sunny self-assertion, are completely antithetical to Death Valley's basic premise. They declare life and possibility. They wage war, in a real way, against the idea of Death Valley and the collection of things that it has come to represent, especially and particularly death itself. They buzz and twitter with life in a place where living things, in their endless balancing act of heat and hydration, are by nature quiet, nocturnal and low-key. They intrude on the landscape, or at least they appear to. Mick Justin's quiet game of internal accommodation was all in his head—a soft-spoken accountant's way of facing down his demons. To the world, he was just another macho crazy out there challenging Death Valley.

Perhaps the Stovepipe Wells manager and the bartender perceived some rebuke of their lives in the Badwater race. Perhaps they believed that the runners who blow into the valley every July with their sleek bodies and their can-do attitudes are arrogant and superior—everything, in short, that my teenage pizza-cook self had smoldered over on those long-ago Friday nights after the game.

In any case, I had no defense or rebuttal to make on Badwater's behalf because I wasn't so sure about it myself. Did Badwater really respect the land, or was Death Valley just a stage set for some grand opera of struggle and redemption? Did the race simply use Death Valley's attributes—the heat, the mountains, the wind—as particulars of an arduous running course and no more? I didn't want to believe that, despite the warnings and rumblings from quarters like the Badwater Saloon. I wanted to believe that the locals were wrong. Badwater comes and takes a different measure of the place—that's all. I needed this to be true, even as I'd begun to wonder whether it was.

The original idea of the Badwater race, beginning back in the late 1970s, had simply been to explore and exploit one of the great quirks of American topology. The lowest point in the Western Hemisphere, Badwater, is only about 150 miles from the highest point in the lower 48 states, Mount Whitney—or about 135 miles from Whitney's trailhead, which eventually became the Badwater finish line. Lowest to highest—that was it. The first pioneers of the race, who'd simply started doing Death Valley on their own with no structure or rules or formal finish line, had had no more of a goal than that.

But by and by, lowest to highest came to be seen as *not hard enough*.

The first overlay of added difficulty came in the late 1980s, when it was decreed by a group of runners who'd already done the crossing that in order to count from that point on, all Badwater-to-Whitney runs must be done in the peak summer month of July or August. In 1997, it was determined that the traditional nighttime start at Badwater, which got the runners through the worst of Death Valley's heat under cover of darkness (Ulrich's record of 26 hours was with a 6 P.M. start), was also too easy. That year the starting time was switched to 6 A.M., which guaranteed that every participant would receive his or her full measure of the valley's solar energy at its midafternoon apogee.

And so Badwater became idealized and isolated—a set piece that with each year, and each little modification, came to mean more and more than just a long race in a hot place. From being just another ultramarathon, it became a cultivated, isolated, radically more difficult ultramarathon. From a simple race, it evolved into a kind of overheated melodrama—outsized and exaggerated, full of grand passions and artifice, dreams and pathos, all the while drifting ever closer to the line of masochism.

I hadn't been able to wait or sit still when I'd arrived in Las Vegas. My bags took forever to come down the luggage carousel at the airport. The wait at the car-rental counter was an agony. I didn't have enough patience to even look at a map. Death Valley was calling out to me, two hours north, and I had to get on the road.

So I stopped at a convenience store off the highway, bought four gallons of bottled water, a loaf of bread, some peanut butter and jam, threw everything in my little rented Mitsubishi and stepped on it. And as the weird desert suburbia of the Las Vegas fringe flew past—shopping centers and housing tracts all hard alongside gleefully tasteless casinos with revolving cowboys and Indian chiefs on their roofs—I rolled down the windows and tried to suck it all in.

I felt like every turn of the car wheels was propelling me toward the center of the world and that the future was hitting me in the face with every new blast of desert air. Death Valley, dead ahead. I turned off the air conditioner, the better to build up my heat tolerance, chugged water and Gatorade, sweated and felt as though Hunter S. Thompson could roar by in a convertible at any moment, shouting obscenities and shooting guns in the air. I was on a strange trip, too.

It was partly the effect of coming home to the desert. Though I'd never been to Death Valley, I knew the feel of the sun and the hard, brittle, crumbly texture of the land in places where rain is a startling event. Dry air and earth formed the core of a chemistry that had always suggested to me the notion of being *out there*. The desert was the place you went to escape from the rest of the world: It meant fishing trips to the eastern Utah scrub country around Flaming Gorge Reservoir with my parents and uncles, and later the spontaneous drives out into Nevada with college friends to search for that unmarked place in the road where the rules stopped being enforced.

I'd reserved the cheapest possible room at Stovepipe Wells. It was part of my regimen, another plank in my alter ego's harsh education. I'd envisioned my Badwater runner as an ascetic, a being of sinew and will who had no need or desire for luxury, and Stovepipe Wells did not disappoint. My key opened into a tiny white cinder-block-walled box of a room that was almost monastic in its simplicity—no telephone, no television, no frills of any kind. One wall in the bathroom was peppered with tiny dried tomato seeds from some old food accident that no one had ever bothered to clean up. The air conditioner wheezed and rattled. The one window looked out onto the parking lot. It was absolutely perfect. I lay down on the bed and tried to think minimalist thoughts, soaking up the barren, pristinely empty ambience of it all. Then I went out, checked the thermometer by the swimming pool and called home on the outdoor pay phone.

It was 110 degrees in the shade. I'd arrived.

Before Memorial Day, Death Valley had been image and smoke, shapeless but in other ways perfectly idealized. I'd created it in my head out of imagination and memory. I'd studied the parameters of heat and endurance. I'd read a dozen books on Death Valley history and geography and stolen every piece of ultramarathon lore I could get my hands on.

But I didn't know the smell of Death Valley sagebrush, and how it suddenly fills the air as you climb above sea level to the higher slopes where it can grow. I didn't know the peculiar feel of desert dust and the chalky emollient of dried sweat and dirt that even a short walk can leave on the skin. And I didn't know the Death Valley sky.

On my first night at Stovepipe I sat for an hour on the retaining wall outside my room as a sandstorm blew through the little settlement. There were probably patterns in that chaotic stew of heat and dust and clouds, but the forces were so complex and so huge that I knew I could sit out there every evening for the rest of my life and never remotely figure them out. The visibility fell to perhaps 100 yards or so and after that it became simply a gray-white sheet—a curtain of blowing sand that seemed to stand between me and everything else in the universe. And then there was only the feel of it—the hot wind and the sudden blasts of grit and dust that pelted my face and left my hair and eyebrows frosted and thick.

I'd seen, just in that first day, dust devils meandering across the salt pan of the valley floor, looking like giant fingers doodling with the earth. I'd watched thunderheads form over the valley, with rain streaks coming down that never reached the ground because the precipitation they held would evaporate in midfall. And I learned why Death Valley is so hot. At the Visitor Center in Furnace Creek, rangers are so sick of the question that they've set up a whole display wall in the museum to answer it. Death Valley, the museum's wall of heat told me, is essentially a giant solar collector. The depressed valley floor, created by a vast lake bed that has been sinking and drying into the earth since the end of the last Ice Age, concentrates and focuses the sun's energy every day. And the high mountains that surround the valley then keep the heat from escaping.

The result is a daily cycle that ratchets the temperature up like a car's jack: Warm air rises from the valley floor and starts to cool, but then picks up heat all over again radiating sideways from the mountains. Heavier, cooler air from the upper atmosphere, meanwhile, settles down from above, like a wool blanket, or a lid on a pot. The air in Death Valley, cleansed by the high Sierra Nevada to the west, is also about the cleanest you'll breathe in America these days. And while that might sound nice, fewer impurities means less filtering out of the sun's radiation. Plant life also tends to moderate the temperature, and the valley's barren and caustic salt-pan bottom—alien to even the hardiest of desert twigs—thus provides the final insult.

But I was also beginning to see that heat would only be part of the story at Badwater. An equally powerful force was the complete and profound dryness of the air. At 115 degrees and 3 percent humidity—average midday conditions in July—a person can lose as much as two gallons of liquid a day *sitting completely immobile in the shade*. Even moderate hiking in the full sun will double that loss. I'd gone running my first morning in the valley in temperatures not much past 105 and immediately understood why Badwater requires a support crew: If you carried all the water you'd need even for a few miles, you'd stagger under a load that would burn you up faster than you could drink.

Even sweating was a different experience. You don't bead up and get wet with perspiration in Death Valley. Rather you look down, say, at your arm, and realize that you already have sweated—perhaps heavily—and you didn't know it because the sweat was evaporating the very instant it appeared. The only evidence you have is a white residue of salt. Richard Benyo, the former executive editor of *Runner's World* magazine and one of the founding fathers of the Badwater race in the 1970s, has likened it to a sponge drying out. Your body tissues are hydrated and fine, then suddenly, if you haven't been drinking enough, they're dry before you know it or can even react.

I'd read a lot, maybe too much, about what can happen after that. The body feels the first sensation of thirst after the loss of about a quart of liquid. A gallon produces fatigue and apathy. Further water deficits start attacking various body systems, like balance and speech, and eventually reason.

Richard E. Lingenfelter, in his history of the region, *Death Valley and the Amargosa: A Land of Illusion*, writes that beyond a certain threshold of dehydration, the typical Death Valley spiral is fairly standard. You basically lose your mind.

"You are likely to discard your hat, clothes, and shoes, which only hastens your dehydration and suffering," he writes. "Bloody cracks will appear in your skin and you'll soon be dead."

Now, sitting there in the Badwater Saloon with the bartender, I felt like the man who knew too much. I wanted the bartender to tell me I was brave, and I wanted to tell the bartender that I was sane. Look at me, I wanted to say. I'm going to run this race and I'm not one of the crazies, right? *Right?*

Dr. Ben Jones, known to most people as Badwater Ben, or the "Mayor of Badwater," as he was dubbed in a ceremony by a group of runners in the early 1990s, is a desert man in his mid-sixties, lanky and creased and full of odd pauses in his speech that emerge suddenly as punch lines to some dry-humored joke that often takes half a beat to understand. He moved to Lone Pine, a town on the valley's edge—the 122-mile marker on the Badwater course—in the early 1960s just out of medical school, at a time when there wasn't an internist in any direction for 200 miles. And even then he was marching to a different drummer. He bought an antique Model A Ford to make house calls. He fell in love with the desert. And gradually over the years of treating the peculiar illnesses and injuries of heat and dehydration, he became an expert in the specialty of desert medicine, though he concedes he had to more or less make it up as he went along because there was no one to teach him.

By the 1970s, as the ultramarathon movement was gathering steam and the first few wild souls like Richard Benyo began doing the Badwater-to-Whitney run on their own, Jones was already perhaps the world's foremost expert in the kinds of questions hardly anyone had even thought to ask: What does a place like Death Valley demand from the body and the mind and what does it give in return?

The medical equation he developed in response came to be known in ultramarathon circles as Ben's Rule of Three. Badwater tends to attack three systems of the human body: the skin, the stomach and the bladder. Skin burns and blisters. Stomachs stop accepting food or liquid. Bladders go into sulky withdrawal.

"If a person can keep a grip on his systems," Jones says with a smile, "Badwater can be done."

His wife, Denise, who works as a hairstylist at a salon in Lone Pine, has become the race's foremost expert on foot care—how to prevent blisters in the desert and how to treat them and keep going when it seems they'll stop you. Ben has completed Badwater three times. Denise has done it twice and was preparing, when I met her, for a third time that July.

Like Death Valley itself, the Joneses are a mixture of impulses—some lofty and inspirational, some darkly comic and macabre. From his den, Ben coordinates a Badwater nerve center of e-mail and website communications, and his dispatches, in keeping with the ultramarathon culture, are hopeful and brutal in equal measure. He writes of a 50-mile trail run that he and Denise did in the Sierra Nevada and how his hands got so cold he couldn't feel them, but how swell it was to see old friends. Stories of a triumph—a person completing his first Leadville, Colorado, 100-miler, for example—appear side by side with tales of who had to drop out with gastroenteritis, complete with all the disgusting details.

Ben can say with a smile how Badwater is a race that

changes lives, then the next minute tell you a story about a guy who had to be carried out of Death Valley on a stretcher in 1998 because he'd blistered so badly he could no longer walk. Ben also claims to be the only man who has ever risen from a coffin to finish Badwater. When he did the race in 1992, he brought along an ice-filled portable body bag he'd borrowed from his hospital morgue, and would periodically climb into it to cool off. It was, without doubt, the perfect Death Valley prop.

I'd gone to meet Ben and Denise at their home in Lone Pine two days before the clinic, which was to start that Saturday at Badwater. I really didn't have a lot to ask them. I think I mainly just wanted to see them. I wanted to *feel* what Badwater was about, and everything I'd heard told me that they were the place to start. Ben had helped invent the race. He'd given it shape, presided over it when no one cared and ministered over and over to its injured. Denise was its reigning queen.

We were sitting in their kitchen chatting about nothing in particular when the phone rang. Ben picked it up, paced around the house for a few minutes, speaking quietly. I heard my name mentioned. Then he handed the phone to me.

"It's Marshall Ulrich," Jones said. "He wants to talk to you."

I swallowed. *The day had come.* In the throes of my Badwater neurosis, I'd avoided this moment and yet I'd known it was inevitable—a threshold I'd have to cross on my way to Badwater. Now I felt a kind of relief as I put the phone to my ear, even though I had no idea even as I did so what I would say, or how I'd say it. Was I a reporter or a runner? I ended up, I think, being neither.

"Hey, how are you?" I said jauntily and falsely, as though I were a member of the old gang, just another Badwater pal.

"Great," he said.

Ulrich wasted no time. Without so much as clearing his throat or introducing the subject, he began telling me about his rickshaw plan, almost as though I'd asked about it. And by and by, with the breeze blowing off the desert through Ben's open windows and Ben sitting across the table watching me, I began to understand what Ulrich was talking about—and that probably should have frightened me right then and there. He sounded nice and he sounded normal, not unlike Lisa Smith in his calm and straightforward confidence, and he was talking about dragging a handcart across Death Valley.

"I like to come up with things that people think can't be done, and then find a way to do them," he said matter-of-factly, but entirely without arrogance, as though he were discussing some innocuous little hobby he did in his basement.

I'd already understood the basic facts of the run, which he intended to undertake over the July Fourth weekend, which was also the occasion of his forty-ninth birthday. He'd go from the Badwater bottom to the Whitney summit all alone, taking only what he could transport in the cart he'd built. He'd calculated how much water he'd need (21.5 gallons) and food (8 pounds) and extra clothing (6 pounds). Then he'd installed a solar-powered motor that would pump water from the cart through a rubber hose that would extend up to his mouth so that he wouldn't ever have to stop to drink. The contraption weighed 290 pounds. This he would pull down the road.

What I only understood for the first time that afternoon was why he wanted to do it.

"I've tried to create the purest expression of self-reliance that I can," he said. He'd devised other restrictions for himself as well, all in the interest of that same concept: *purity*.

That was the driving force for Ulrich, clearly. But I saw as he went on that purity was also full of subtleties and contradictions. The pure place, it seemed, was that point where the maximum applied force of individual human will and self-reliance could confront the desert in the most natural way possible—all, of course, within the context of a totally contrived, artificial and on some level even ridiculous event like pulling a handcart down the highway. Ulrich stressed, for example, that he would allow himself to take no shelter under any man-made object through the whole course of the crossing—which in treeless Death Valley basically meant that he'd get no relief from the elements at all. Taking assistance from anyone along the way would similarly disqualify the run as a "pure" solo under the Ulrich Rules.

Actually, he told me, he'd tried a pure crossing once before and failed. His water-hose system hadn't worked. He'd had to suck through the hose so hard to get water from the cart that he'd gotten sick from the sucking, he said. The solar-powered motor was intended to solve that problem.

I wished him luck, but as I handed the phone back to Ben, my mind was reeling with what I'd heard. I felt like I'd just been introduced to a new foreign language that was alien—and yet not entirely alien, either. I couldn't fully grasp the nature of "pure" endurance, and yet I felt it was the same general breed of beast that I was chasing myself. That's just how I'd fallen into Badwater's spell in the first place.

Maybe, I began to think as I drove back toward Stovepipe Wells that day, Ulrich's legendary powers don't come from trying to go farther and longer at all, but from something else—a problem to be solved, a theoretical point to be proven. Perhaps endurance, for him, was just a by-product.

Maybe the answer to my question—*What would Ulrich do?*—was as simple as that. Go suck on a hose.

But it also occurred to me that just as I'd been seduced into Badwater's outer orbit, maybe I'd now been given a glimpse into the universe beyond that, an inner circle where Badwater's impulses were rarefied down to the ideal. Maybe there was further still to fall.

However much I'd come to feel like a desert rat in the days leading up to Ben's clinic, I realized on the morning it began that I'd been living under an illusion. I stood out like the utter rookie I was when I walked out of my room at Stovepipe to join the group assembling around Ben's beat-up old Dodge van. I was dressed, as I'd thought pretty much everybody else would be, in the white head-to-toe desert suit that I'd assumed was the appropriate attire. The outfit, which had been on the list of recommended items sent to me in my Hi-Tec race packet several months earlier, looked like a cross between hospital scrubs and pajamas—long sleeves, long pants and a big white hat with a floppy neck drape. The general idea, as I understood it, was to create a sort of mobile shade system, much as the Bedouins of the Sahara do in covering themselves head to toe. The fabric breathes, but the solar glare bounces off. It'd made perfect sense to me when I'd ordered it from the catalog of a sun-protection products company that Ben had suggested. And even though I looked utterly ridiculous when I'd examined myself in the bathroom mirror, standing there next to my wall of dried tomato seeds, I figured I'd fit right in when the group assembled.

I was wrong. The other runners, who were all far more experienced than I—or savvy enough, at least, not to pay attention to every little list they're sent in a race packet—were mostly dressed in shorts and white mesh shirts. I might as well have worn a sign around my neck that shouted out my hollow running credentials. I was the good little list follower from back East who'd bought what he'd been told to buy, and there I was, looking ready for night-night, or surgery, or making semiconductors in a clean room, perhaps, but certainly not for running.

The white suit provided yet another plank in my structure of insecurity. I was ready to try this thing and I'd shown up in an outfit that said, hey, here's the reporter from New York in his fancy desert running clothes. He thinks that's what you wear out here, ha, ha, and he's going to try and run Badwater! Everybody come look!

Ben, who had volunteered to be the one-man support crew for three of us in the clinic that day, even introduced me at one point as the "Media Guy." I think he meant no harm in it, but I was devastated. However much I'd convinced myself that I was somehow coming home to the West and to the desert, and that my training had made me a semi-legitimate ultramarathoner, I'd now been exposed as the New York phony, the endurance voyeur who didn't belong. I'd locked the reporter half of my identity firmly in my room that morning, wanting only to be a runner, nothing more, and Ben had opened the door. So now, for reasons that went beyond proving to myself what I could do, I had to overcome the horrifying if inadvertent put-down of Media Guy. My fashion choice was simply a reflection of an identity I couldn't escape.

But I'd gone into the clinic that week loaded with psychic burdens anyway. Certainly I needed the training, and the exposure to the heat and the distance. But even more than that I needed the mental inoculation of being there. If I could say, when Memorial Day was over, that I'd been able to complete 30 percent or 40 percent of the Badwater course over a weekend, it might function like a vaccine—a little bit of the virus and perhaps I'd have an immunity, and an ability to control my terror when the real race came.

About a dozen runners had come for the weekend, and they were all assembled at the Badwater sign, milling around and joking when I pulled up with Ben just before 8 A.M. The sun had already come up over the Black Mountains to our right. But before us, somewhere in the distance, was Furnace Creek, which would be our first real rest break, 17 miles away.

It was there I first met the twins—also known as the Twin Team—Angelika Castaneda and Barbara Warren. They were originally from Austria by way of Mexico, where Barbara had had a first career as a movie star and Angelika had launched a line of fashion boutiques. They were fifty-six years old, perfectly sculpted, intensely athletic and so identical that people could never keep them straight.

"But they don't mind," Ben had told me on the drive down from Stovepipe, as he described all the runners who were expected for the weekend. "Each will answer to the other's name. It's okay."

The twins apparently did just about everything together, especially outrageous endurance events, which they then drew upon for the motivational seminars they gave to corporations and sales groups. This was to be their fourth time at Badwater, and they were preparing, even as they trained that weekend, for an around-the-world endurance event, just for women, that was to be held in conjunction with the turn of the millennium. Racers would have to travel on their own power, on bikes or on foot, across every continent and try to do the whole thing in 2,000 hours. Barbara and Angelika had done triple Ironman triathlons together, run twice the length of the Grand Canyon together—from South Rim to North Rim and back—and had been the second and third women across the finish line in a seven-day race in the Sahara Desert in 1990.

The twins scared the bejesus out of me. Maybe it's the fact that there were *two of them*. That far more than doubled their intensity, I thought. They were beautiful and identical in their French Foreign Legion–style hats, sunglasses and shiny, sunscreen-coated faces, and I knew that either one of them could break me like a matchstick.

And they also had different ideas, perhaps owing to their foreign background or their close relationship with a twin, about personal space. When they said hello, they came up right into my face, mere inches away. This, to me, was the most frightening of all. I felt ready to run down the road if only from that.

I also met Louise Cooper-Lovelace, a Los Angeles elementary school teacher and breast-cancer survivor who'd still been on chemotherapy only that spring. Louise was an experienced adventure racer in her mid-forties who'd done ultramarathons all over the world, but never Badwater. She was cheerful but nervous, and surrounded by a small, intensely dedicated army of women who'd pledged themselves to helping her.

"I'm here for Louise," one of them said to me simply when I introduced myself, as though helping Louise were so all-consuming as to erase one's own identity entirely.

And I met Bob Ankeney, who'd run Badwater for the first time the previous year and was coming back. Ankeney was a juvenile-probation officer from Placerville, California—a big, relaxed, bearded, slow-talking guy who reminded me a lot of the actor Bruce Dern. Ankeney struck me as a former hippie who'd found a return to inner space through the ultramarathon. Sprawled in the back of Ben's van during the drive down to Badwater for the start, he told me the cryptic conclusion he'd come to the previous year, when he'd struggled through terrible blisters that had almost knocked him out of the race.

"Death Valley doesn't allow mistakes," he said simply. "You make one mistake and it will cost you—big time."

The only thing I could think of as I looked at him was the crusty old foreign correspondent who'd told me much the same thing, more or less, 17 years ago in the *New York Times* cafeteria: Don't screw up. I still hadn't figured out what that meant.

Heat training, or heat acclimatization, was the primary reason most of the runners had assembled that morning. It's one of Badwater's unstated rules. You do it—you subject your body to incredible heat strain in hopes of building up your tolerance—because the only thing worse would be not doing it. Then you'd have to face Death Valley in July without the myriad tiny adaptations to temperature and stress that heat exposure can supposedly bring. If you heat train, so the wise heads of Badwater told me, your body is braced, in a way. It gets better at regulating internal temperature. Your heart learns not to panic and beat too fast. Doing it doesn't guarantee you'll finish or finish well. Not doing it makes it far more likely that you'll get squashed like a bug on a windshield when Death Valley has you in its grip.

One Badwater runner was going to Borneo for his heat training that summer, to run a race in the steaming tropical jungle. Major Curt Maples, a United States Marine Corps battalion commander in southern California, was suiting up every afternoon in a flak jacket and ski parka. Maria DeJesus, a young Englishwoman from the Jersey Islands, lived in a place that was always delightfully cool—sadly for her. So she was training in a sauna, and running up hills dragging a tire behind her attached with a rope.

Carlos Banderas, a chemical-plant worker from West Covina, California, ran on a treadmill in his garage with the vent hose from his clothes dryer propped up so that it could blast him in the chest. Robin Smit, an ophthalmologist from Fresno, bought a rubber wet suit and had planned to run in it until his wife told him she'd divorce him if he did.

I mostly just overdressed. But even that could be strange enough. On one steamy spring day, for example, not long before the clinic, I was out running in our neighborhood in my standard heat-retention attire—black winter running pants, T-shirt and heavy dark green sweatshirt. I was drenched with sweat and panting when I jogged by a man out watering his shrubs. He froze and stared at me as I went by, then shouted down the street, "Hey, you're wearing too many clothes!"

His voice had an edge of annoyance to it, I'd thought, as though what I was doing were a personal affront: The weather was warm and I wasn't behaving properly. Or perhaps he simply figured me for an idiot. I was the runner as mental incompetent, the paradigm of the dumb jock, too stupid even to realize my own discomfort. I imagine he expected me to stop and thank him and then strip down right there in the street, while slapping my forehead like Homer Simpson.

One certainty of Badwater, however, was that there was always someone training harder. I'd felt like I was running long until I heard about Banderas, who—in addition to his clothes-dryer treadmill work—was running a 26-mile marathon *every day* before work that spring. And I'd thought I was heat training until I met Stephen Simmons. Simmons, a thirty-three-year-old landscaper and former army paratrooper from Bluefield, West Virginia, was an experienced 100-mile-runner but a first-timer at Badwater. I'd called him earlier in the year and we'd chatted occasionally over the months about our progress and our anxieties as the race approached. Simmons was terrified of Badwater's brutal heat, and his method of preparing for it was, as a result, just as brutal.

This is one of the heat-training exercises he described to me: First, he said, he put on a T-shirt, a sweatshirt and a thick, insulated Navy pea jacket and sweatpants. Then he topped that off with a thick nonbreathable dark green raincoat and finished the ensemble with gloves and a cold-weather hat. Thus encased, he took off down the road. The temperature that afternoon in West Virginia was in the nineties, with high humidity.

The moment came, an hour or so later, when Simmons could no longer bear it. He had to sit down in the weeds on the shoulder—overwhelmed, smothered and choked by his thick wet layers of clothes. His heart was racing, his head throbbing.

"I felt as if I was suffocating," he said. "I could only sit still a matter of seconds and the panic would set in and I'd have to move—lean back, sit up, put my legs out, pull them back up to my chest. Nothing I could do would relieve the monotony."

All it would have taken, of course, was to tear off some of his sweat-soaked clothing. What a sweet relief it would be. But Simmons couldn't do it, and that's what separated him from most of the rest of humanity. Like me, he was on a road from which he felt he couldn't turn back.

"It would have been like reaching the surface and taking a big breath of air," he said. "I needed to do it. But I wouldn't accept it."

I chugged into Stovepipe Wells—42 miles from Badwater—after about 10 and a half hours on the first day of Ben's clinic. I called Fran to say I'd survived and then immediately climbed into my bed for the next hour, shivering in some kind of heat-induced fever of dehydration.

I'd made it, though—that was the important thing, I kept telling myself as I piled every blanket I had on top of me, even though it was surely close to 100 degrees in the room already. I'd kept going as the afternoon temperature spiked close to 115 degrees near Furnace Creek, and through the sandstorm that descended just outside Stovepipe. Some of the other runners, like Bob Ankeney, who had nothing to prove that day, had climbed in with Ben to ride the last few miles after the storm hit. But as the greenest of rookies, I couldn't do that. So I squinted against the wind and felt the sand-tears rolling down my face and the dust going down into my lungs and I told myself I was tough and brave. And whether it was Media Guy who kept me going or my Badwater alter ego, it didn't really matter.

The next morning we heard that Louise Cooper-Lovelace, who'd blown by me at one point, utterly undeterred by illness, had fallen into dehydration, too—compounded, apparently, by her still-compromised immune system. She'd made it into Stovepipe, but a park ranger had taken one look at her during the night and ordered her airlifted to a hospital in Las Vegas, where she'd been rehydrated intravenously.

The news cast a shadow on the clinic runners as we prepared to continue on the Badwater course heading out of Stovepipe. There was a seriousness and gravity in the air that hadn't been there when we'd left Badwater together the previous morning. Everyone wondered how the incident might affect Louise's confidence when—and if—she was able to return in July. When the Twin Team stopped to say good-bye, about eight miles out of Stovepipe, it almost felt like a prayer group assembling there by the roadside.

The twins, Angelika and Barbara, had charged by me earlier that morning, running up the steep slope toward Towne Pass with steady puffing strides that would have exhausted me in minutes, then had turned around and come back down to join us slow plodders briefly before going home. They talked about their own experiences the previous day and what they'd seen of Louise's troubles, and everyone said something about her courage and the meaning they drew from it. Doing Badwater in perfect health made all the rest of us seem pretty ordinary, someone said.

Then the twins loomed in on me. They wanted to know about my pajama suit, and there they were, side by side, inches from my face. One began fingering the fabric of the shirt.

"What did you think of this?" one of them asked.

"Were you happy with it?" the other said.

"Will you use it in the race?" the first said.

I had to fight my shallow breathing. It was like being faced with two goddesses—they emanated power. Finally, I swallowed and stammered that yes, I had liked it, I felt it had shielded me from the sun and kept me from losing moisture during the sandstorm as well.

Then, in the next moment, I learned why Ben had said everyone loves them so much. Satisfied with their inquiry about the suit, one stepped up to embrace me, then the other.

"You did great yesterday," one of them said of my slogging little shuffle into Stovepipe Wells.

The other glanced around at the group. "You all did great," she said. "I love walking around just knowing that you people are out here, trying this," she said. "That's why we're all here—to see what is possible."

The hug by the twins sparked something in the group. We all hugged one another as though we'd known each other for years. Some people got teary, and we all said we'd see each other in July, and then the twins jumped in the van and were gone.

When I got home, I rattled on for days and days to Fran about the wonders of Death Valley. But it was an edited version. I didn't tell her about Louise.

The Paradoxical Heart

One day early in my training for Badwater, Fran and I were at the grocery store and she caught me staring at a shelf of vitamins and supplements as though I had a clue what I was looking at. I was, in all honesty, staring blankly, wondering whether there was something I *should* know, some hole in my knowledge. Would zinc help me? B12? Folates? Antioxidants?

"Don't get weird," she'd said simply, giving me a light kiss on the cheek and a brief but candid look of concern.

I pondered that phrase, and that look, for months as I pounded the streets in my early morning 10-mile warm-up runs. No, this isn't weird, I'd said. And I thought of it again the first time I ran 30 miles two days in a row all alone through the hills of northern New Jersey. And yet again when I began jogging in place in the sauna at our local YMCA to build up my heat tolerance. Strange as well as extreme, I concluded, but still and all, more or less reasonable under the circumstances. I'd *had* to do all these things—the road to which I'd committed myself allowed nothing less.

But now, in the final weeks before the race, I was no longer sure of anything. Weird and normal, possible and impossible—everything had melded together like an overcooked stew.

The Memorial Day clinic in Death Valley had affected me far more than I'd anticipated, and sometimes I wasn't sure whether I was better off or not for having gone there. I'd been able to keep up with at least a few of the others at the clinic, and I'd seen what I could do in conditions that Ben had said were fairly harsh for late May—110-degree-plus temperatures, high winds, blowing sand—and all that had bolstered my confidence. But I'd also glimpsed, in my own struggle getting into Stovepipe Wells and in Cooper-Lovelace's fight against her weakened body, how hard and how far Death Valley could push, even in May. I'd returned with a greater sense of myself, but at the same time a lot more awareness of how small and powerless that made me. A friend said I had a harder set of my jaw when I came home, like someone, she said, who'd been to war.

Then, shortly after that, I'd gone to North Carolina for my last big training run, the 50-mile Moonlight Boogie, where 43 miles—*forty-three miles!*—had almost broken me. The Boogie left me further than ever from being able to say I knew where the margins of my endurance were to be found, and whether I'd be able to confront my own failure and keep going. And now the clock had run out—I was as prepared as I would ever be.

But I was also beginning to see how much the months of training had already changed me. I'd thought that preparing for Badwater would simply be a means to an end; now I saw that it had become its own destination. I'd arrived, even before Badwater ever began, at a place where all my old assumptions seemed open to question and where the rhythms and definitions I'd once clung to about the good life well lived no longer seemed so certain.

Up until that year I'd generally agreed with the modern view of the world that faster is better. It's the basic premise of the twentieth century: Fast is young and futuristic. Slow is stodgy and archaic.

In my journey to Badwater, I had to throw all that out the window. Speed was suddenly of secondary importance—distance had become the prime variable of every equation. I no longer cared whether I was running eight-minute miles or 12-minute miles, or even walking, so long as I was putting one foot in front of the other and covering the distance I'd assigned myself for that day. Clocks became dispensable, stopwatches and timed quarter miles at the track useless and pointless. The whole hectic world around me had to be set aside.

I had to learn how to run, I sometimes felt, like a medieval man, before the pace of life got so fast and the dictatorship of the clock was imposed on our lives. Certainly there would be a race clock at Badwater, with a 60-hour cutoff that would require consciousness of the time, but it was a clock where seconds and even minutes wouldn't matter and where instead the passage of whole days would be the matters of consequence.

In getting to Badwater, I had to embrace the rhythm of the ultramarathon at its paradoxical heart: From slowing down comes going farther. By moving less in any half hour, you move more in any 12 hours. By throwing out the timed quarter mile, the 40-mile run comes within reach.

I'd also begun driving slower. People would ride up on my tail and honk and give me the finger sometimes when I drove in what I thought of as my "Badwater style," and I'd gaze back at them blankly like a cow, especially if I was just returning from a very long run. They probably thought of me as an old man behind the wheel—that's certainly the eye-rolling, elbow-in-the-ribs attitude my boys took when I'd drive them somewhere.

"Twenty-five miles an hour is plenty fast enough for anybody," I'd say whenever the boys complained.

I felt, in accepting and embracing a slower running pace, that my pulse and my heart rate and even my thoughts had slowed as well. I felt like a tree when the impatient suburban moms in their sport utility vehicles would zoom by me with cell phones plastered to their ears, multitasking their way through some blitzkrieg on life.

Following Badwater logic out to its full range of implications, however, is a mighty scary business. If slowing down equals going farther, then by coming to a complete stop you should reach some infinity of constant motion, right? To me, that sounded like Zen, which teaches that all illumination comes through stillness—of the mind as well as the body—and that a lack of motion is not a measure of idleness, but rather of strength and discipline. I'd worked hard to try and incorporate that vision into my running after reading and rereading *Zen in the Art of Archery*. Never aim for the target, the archery master tells our narrator again and again. Think only of the perfect release of the arrow, and then stop even thinking of that. When you have perfected the release without conscious thought you will have achieved the archer's place of perfect calm. And with perfect calm will eventually come perfect accuracy.

But it made me wonder, sometimes, at the trajectory I'd put myself on. What happens if you simplify your life too much? Can you still function? Will I eventually drive my car so slowly that I never leave the driveway?

Perhaps when they come to administer my Thorazine because I've stopped getting up out of my chair, I'll respond that I have finally become the perfect ultramarathoner. I'll have found the plateau of endless forward motion through complete motionlessness.

Don't get me wrong: This is no criticism of people who fantasize about shaving down their time to qualify for the Boston Marathon, or engineers who dream of shortening the wait at the New Jersey Turnpike tollbooths. All I'm saying is that turning down the road to Badwater made speed irrelevant to me. My goal was to try and finish, however I could do it. Not only did I no longer need to run the seven-and-a-half to eight-minute miles I'd once prided myself on, but I had to consciously try and reject that rhythm. I had to push myself to go slow so that I could go long. And that reversal of thinking rippled through me like a river that had overrun its banks, cutting whole new channels to the sea.

Where Badwater had once seemed like the remotest edge of the fringe, an outpost on the far frontier of normal, I was now beginning to see it as natural and perfectly suited to the human animal. I imagined that if I could bring one of my ancestors into the present, say from half a million years ago, he'd look at ESPN with no comprehension whatsoever. He'd see football, with its padded suits and steroids, or basketball, with its seven-foot behemoths and slam dunks, for the bizarre spectacles they truly are. An event like Badwater, however—essentially crossing a desert on foot and climbing a mountain at the end, all the while carefully husbanding one's limited energy and resources in order to cover the distance—would make perfect sense. I see, my ancient grandfather might say, a survival game.

I began to build a whole Badwater society in my head. It would respect old people because they'd been down the long road and paid their dues. It would embrace solid-state circuitry over the transistor on the basis of durability and a Volvo over a BMW for the same reason. I wasn't so sure about vinyl records versus compact discs, though. Old-fashioned records probably do sound warmer and more natural, but they wear out. CDs possess the trait that is the singular idol of Badwater worship: They endure.

The plain fact of the matter is that Badwater, or more specifically, Death Valley, imposes its own slower pace. In most footraces of whatever distance, weather conditions are generally treated as things that get in the way of going fast. If marathon day in New York dawns warm and muggy, people cluck their tongues and shake their heads sadly and say, what a shame, no records will be broken today. Good conditions for a race mean that people will be able to run as hard as they can to get great speedy times.

In Death Valley, all those definitions and parameters are thrown out, because the simple truth is that Death Valley *has* no good conditions. It has impossible conditions. It has conditions that will kill you. And so it becomes almost a race turned inside out—where going too fast can be lethal, Badwater's mandate is moderation and management. The way to run Badwater, I'd been told, is to go as fast as you can without going so fast that you get sick or die.

Back at the clinic in May, it was a message that Ben had emphasized over and over: If you see a runner ahead of you in the race and you feel like you want to speed up and pass him, don't do it. Fight the racer's impulse. Most of the people who've failed to finish Badwater, including Eric Clifton in both of his previous attempts, Ben said, were thwarted by their desire to go faster than Death Valley permits.

"See those white dots up there?" Ben had said at one point when he'd pulled beside me on the road on the first morning of the clinic. He nodded his head toward the front and the faster runners like the twins I could see up ahead.

"Let 'em go—you'll never see them again. But that's all right. Out here it's just you against the course."

One of the experts on heat and exercise I'd contacted earlier that spring, Dr. David E. Martin, who'd been an adviser to the Atlanta Olympics in 1996 on heat-stress issues, had put it even more bluntly: "If you run across Death Valley, you croak," he told me. "That's it."

Dr. Martin had incorporated Ben's basic notions about white dots and pacing into hard science. He sent me a line-graph system he'd designed for Olympic officials to use in calculating the stress levels for athletic events in the humid subtropical summer of the Deep South.

One line measured the heat produced by the human body through exertion. The other variable was the environment in which that exertion takes place. At a certain point, the two lines cross and the body becomes unable to cool itself and an event becomes too dangerous. An athlete who can't cool down begins to cook from within. Death Valley in July was off Dr. Martin's chart entirely. Running a flat-out marathon pace in 115 degrees, he told me, would take an athlete into the deadly outer frontier beyond possibility of cooling in just a few minutes.

And so, to avoid croaking, you go slower. Badwater's 60-hour cutoff is more than twice as long as some 100-mile races, which typically allow runners a maximum of only 24 to 36 hours to go the distance. At 60 hours for 135 miles, all you have to do—on paper, at least—is average 2.25 miles per hour around the clock for two and a half days. That's 26 minutes and 40 seconds a mile—not even a moderately fast walk. When I'd first punched those numbers into my calculator, I'd been encouraged. But then, in looking deeper into the race records, and at other 100-mile-or-more events with long cutoff times, I saw that optimism was not the correct response.

Longer and slower does not mean easier in the world of the ultramarathon, and usually it means exactly the opposite. The Hardrock 100-miler in western Colorado, for example, which is usually ranked among the toughest trail races in the world because of its steep mountainous terrain, allows a full 48 hours for runners to cover the distance. With a minimum average required pace of just under 30 minutes a mile, Hardrock is thus both slower and shorter than Badwater.

Mick Justin, talking about Badwater over his plate of ribs in Minnesota that spring, had told me he believed that Badwater's slow pace was one of the hardest things for newcomers and nonultramarathoners to comprehend: If you can somehow average 12-minute miles—barely a slow jog in the real world—you'll break the Badwater course record of 28 hours. And only people who'd done the race, he said, could understand why the 12-minute-mile threshold had never remotely been crossed.

"In Death Valley, going forward is going fast," he said.

It was also about this time that Pat and I began discussing what we called, "The Line." We both knew the possibility was strong that I wouldn't finish Badwater, and that meant the likelihood of a decision—a moment when I'd have to come to terms with my surrender and find a way to say the words that would end it: This far and no farther. The trick, we agreed, would be recognizing The Line when it emerged before us. How could I distinguish a wise decision to withdraw from a cowardly one? What would be the difference between exhaustion and pain and despair, which I fully expected to encounter, and outright peril? How would we know?

Pat's main argument was that I might not know I'd crossed The Line, that I'd be too caught up and compelled, or too delirious and delusional, to rationally make such a call and that it would therefore be up to her and Wayne.

"You don't want to do anything that would permanently injure you and leave you unable to run," she said.

I agreed in principle. My main position was that the *apparent end*—the point where things seemed pushed to the wall, where hope and faith and energy had all but expired—would occur long before the *real end*. The crucible of any ultramarathon, I now knew, was to be found beyond those moments that seemed devoid of hope and light. The end would be an illusion, at least most of the time. And Pat accepted that idea in principle, too. So we were left with a disembodied debating point—the issue had been framed, more or less, but it would only become real when and if it had to be acted upon. The Line would thus be a fiction and a mirage until that moment when it was not, and the heart of the matter would be in understanding the distinction.

I knew it was the worst kind of spot to put her and Wayne in: Be protective, but not overprotective; keep me going forward, but prepare to restrain me; don't listen when I say I think I'm at the end of my rope, but take action when I really am.

It had been on Pat's advice that I'd stopped running in early July, more than 10 days before the race. In traditional 26-mile marathon training, tapering off in the final week is the standard advice—five days of rest before a race, most marathon experts say, allows the body to heal and build up energy reserves without losing any edge of muscle tone or endurance. Pat argued that facing five marathons at Badwater should also mean more downtime beforehand.

"Better to be too rested than not rested enough," she said.

I didn't argue, partly because I was quietly panicked over the state of my knees. I'd come home from the Boogie in mid-June feeling almost as bad, physically, as I had after my first marathon seven months earlier. Fifty miles of hills only a month before Badwater might have been too much, too late. I desperately hoped that a few extra days of rest might heal me.

Paring down my exertions also felt like a small concession to Pat that I might later be able to use against her. I didn't want her to be able to say, at some angry, tortured moment during the race, that I'd never taken her advice. When the question of The Line arose, I wanted to win whatever argument we might have. Conceding something now, before Badwater, seemed like a small chit I might have on my side of the table for later in the game.

But I couldn't just stop all physical activity, either. My body had been tuned for months to what was almost a fever pitch—burning 3,000 to 5,000 calories a day just in exercise. I was a stoked coal furnace that couldn't stop cold. So I walked for hours, sometimes 10 miles a day or more, and I baked myself in the sauna at the YMCA, and I pushed my weight training harder than ever.

Mostly, though, I worried. I was haunted, in those final weeks, by the thought that I'd been unable, in my six months of crash-course training, to synthesize within myself the single most important thing of all for a Badwater runner to have: experience. Many ultramarathoners had told me over the previous months that the key to survival in a super-distance race is to see the being inside you—the inner runner—as you never have before. Know thyself, they all said, speaking like oracles. In running 100 miles or more, the body, the mind and maybe even the soul get depleted in ways that are—like the distance itself—beyond the realm of everyday experience. To make it to the end of five marathons, I'd have to learn how to sense my body from within—what it needed at any one time and what was adequate. I had to know what it felt like to need salt, or sugar, or liquids, or carbohydrates, and then react to those needs before they became critical. Partly, I was told, it was a matter of instinct. You learn by experience what the particular internal sensations are of, say, a low-salt condition, for example. It's not something that you can think through and self-diagnose. It just is and you know it. But how would I know it?

As race day grew closer and closer, I still hadn't remotely figured that out, and the hard-won experience that develops honed instincts—the multiple 100-mile races that were the learning curve by which most people got to Badwater—would simply not be possible in my case. I knew I needed instincts, but I wasn't at all sure I had them, and I had no clue how to get them.

I kept thinking of the story that Carlos Castaneda tells in one of his books about how Don Juan, the mysterious Indian teacher, tells the author one night to find his perfect rock, the one that would give him peace and rest in the desert. Search until you find it and you'll know it when you do, Juan says. So Castaneda searches all night in the area where he's been told to look. He grows discouraged and disillusioned and disgusted with the stupid futility of the task he's been given. Finally, near dawn, he slumps down in exhaustion by the nearest boulder and falls asleep.

Juan wakes him later that morning. "Congratulations," he says. "You found it."

Castaneda is, of course, skeptical. It was just the nearest rock, he says. But no coincidence, Juan replies. When your nonreasoning mind took over, near the point of exhaustion, only then could the right rock and the proper choice emerge. By looking for it with your conscious mind, it could never be found.

That was exactly how most veteran ultramarathoners had

said it had to be—feel it from within. Know it, don't think it. Toss out reason and find truth.

But I would have no Don Juan at my side, ready to tell me that I'd learned my required lessons. There would only be me, trying to gaze into the strange places I was taking myself. And what frightened me even more was the realization that there truly *were* no universal answers. The more tales I heard of what worked or what didn't for individual runners—the combinations of foods and goos and drinks and foot wraps and socks and shoes—the more I was driven to the conclusion that every person is utterly unique in the world. The important thing was not what you ate or drank—as I'd thought back at Massanutten—but rather having the self-knowledge to choose. Every ultramarathon runner might have a piece of hard-won truth gleaned from his or her experiences; I'd have to find my own.

And that left me grasping wildly for truth wherever I thought I saw it. It turned me into a hyperactive ninny of a consumer, despite Fran's prescient warning about the dangers of runaway weirdness. Upon my return home after Memorial Day, I began to assemble a "foot box" of all the things Denise Jones the Badwater Foot Queen had told me I would or might need. I bought Betadyne, a red-colored hospital disinfectant for treating wounds and blisters. I bought roll after roll of hospital tape for covering up the skin to prevent blisters, and tincture of benzoin, a mysteriously sticky substance that smelled like vanilla and would bind tape to my skin like iron. I bought burn pads that were good for treating blisters, and special pointy scissors for lancing blisters. I bought a pair of unwearable size-12 running shoes—a full size larger than normal—because I'd been told to expect swelling during the race. With every passing day I felt more susceptible to the powers of suggestion—and just about anybody's suggestion would do. I told myself I was preparing for all contingencies, when in truth I was merely grasping at straws.

If I couldn't trust that I'd have the right instincts during the race—or have them at all—then I figured I should at least have a lot of choices to draw from in the spirit of trial and error. If I didn't really know who I was at that point— deep down inside the way a real ultramarathoner should— then I might need just about anything, and that made me the ultimate sucker. I wandered into a GNC store in our town one day in early July and the clerk reeled me in like a fish. Potassium tablets, he said. That's the stuff. They help the cells hold in water. Bike racers use them.

Great, I said.

Better get some salt pills, too, for where you're going, he told me with a knowing nod, athlete to athlete.

You bet. Load me up.

I sent away by mail for an electrolyte powder that I'd seen used at Massanutten. It tasted like hell—salty and sweet at the same time. But I figured I'd need salty and sweet in Death Valley, so I bought enough cans to make 12 gallons. Some runners had told me that when they push toward 100 miles in a race they like to drink multivitamin beverages like Boost and Ensure that are advertised on television to pep up old people. So I bought cans and cans of that, too, though I had no idea what the stuff even tasted like. I called our local Avon lady and bought four huge tubes of some- thing called Silicone Glove Hand Cream because in one of the ultramarathon books that piled up by the side of our bed some guy had said he'd used it on his feet once on a long run to prevent blisters. One guy, one time, in one book.

It was rather like being in the grip of a craving that could never be satisfied: What if I wanted this? What if I needed that? I couldn't say no to anything because I had no idea what I was really doing.

I'd become a divided being. On one side sat my simplified alter ego, my Badwater runner, who was as free from the baggage of day-to-day life as I could make him. On the other was the ultimate consumer, eager to become a storage closet for anything he might need. Badwater Boy might sniff that he required almost nothing. A pair of shoes and let me at 'em—that was his creed. Consumer Boy was like a fussy overprotective mother figure, worried over everything, fretting about taking all the precautions and don't forget your rubbers. When in doubt, and Consumer Boy always was, the answer was the same: Get it, buy it, bring it.

Mick Justin had told me over our dinner in Minnesota that tomato juice had tasted good to him in Death Valley the previous year. Tomato juice! The very idea of it made me queasy. It sounded thick and gaggy and horrifying in the heat. So of course I'd immediately decided to bring lots and lots of it.

I realized there was nothing to do but juggle. I had to keep all the balls in the air because I would, or might, at some point in the race, need one of them. I had to bring every possible thing that might by some wild stretch of imagination make a difference because it might be the one thing I'd need most of all. I wanted every mental trick, every psychological crutch and every nuance of self-delusion I could pack. Like my foot box of unguents and creams, I might not use them all, but by God, I'd better have them just in case.

I feared, sometimes in those last days at home, that my little thought experiment really had gone too far. I'd embraced the fantasy life—dropping out of the rat race to become, for this year, an athlete. But now I'd gone past the point of dropping out. The floor had given way entirely and I was in free fall. I found myself thinking about the race more and more, and found it harder and harder to disengage. One night in my last week at home, I dreamed about Badwater all night, or so it seemed. In my fever, I ran and couldn't stop. Every time it seemed I'd reached a place of rest I'd be told I had 10 more miles to go. I woke up exhausted.

Other nights my head rattled with lists. What had I forgotten? Did I have enough socks? Were the shoes I planned to wear broken in enough? What would be my strategy during the race? Did I really trust Silicone Glove Hand Cream, whatever the heck it even was, or should I go back to good old Vaseline, or nothing at all? Were my brother and sister really still into this thing or was I dragging them out into the desert on some selfish, idiotic quest that had no meaning? What would happen if race day came and I was still so filled with doubts and dreads as this? How could I face the world and the starting line and all the real runners who would be there?

I began to cultivate, in those dark hours after midnight, a secret fantasy: I wouldn't do Badwater at all. I imagined what it would be like to wake up on July 15 at the Furnace Creek Ranch Motel and refuse to come out of my room, and then I embroidered the scenario with full, nightmarish detail. I pictured how I'd look curled up in my bed, frozen into immobility, looking at my watch as the hours rolled past through the morning and the race progressed and how I'd ignore the insistent, concerned knocks on the door from my family. I'd abandon myself to paralysis, surrender to my terrors and let them take me. I'd fall to the bottom and complete the trajectory I'd begun.

The physical risk of competing in Badwater, I decided, was nothing compared to the mental and emotional peril of preparing for it. All the sacrifices that the race demanded as the price of admission—the winnowing down of life's baggage, the relentless focus, the long hours of training—were also the things that could ruin you if carried too far. Perhaps it was another one of Badwater's innumerable paradoxes: Attempt to reach beyond yourself and you risk arriving at your destination having lost the sense of who you are.

Staring at the ceiling on one of those sleepless nights, I recalled a hike I'd done in Death Valley over the Memorial Day weekend to the 11,000-foot summit of Telescope Peak, the highest mountain in the park.

The hike had taken about four hours from the trailhead to the top, and all through that time I was alone, feeling like the last person on the planet. I'd seen only one other hiker on the way, and when I got to the summit the signs of civilization were almost entirely gone, like everything had sloughed away. And something about that depressed the hell out of me. What if all this searching and sweating had put me on the wrong trail? Was Badwater the cause of the loneliness I felt? And if it was, might it ultimately leave me isolated—as alone, perhaps, as Gary had been on his last morning? Was I being boiled down into nothing more than the sum of my obsession?

I went back to Stovepipe after coming down the mountain and immediately called Fran from the motel pay phone. I sat outside on the little bench and told her about the hike, and that I loved her. I said I'd stopped and picked a flower by the side of the road on the way down and pressed it into a book for her, but it had already become an obliterated mess and I'd try to find another.

After that, "Telescope Peak" became a sort of incantation for me, right up there with my little sing-song nonsense about what Ulrich would or wouldn't do. But where my Ulrich mantra was intended to keep me going, "Telescope Peak" was all about where I might end up and what it might cost me to get there. All I needed to do was say those words and think about the hike and I'd feel like a compass needle was swinging into view and the proper alignment of my navigational array would come in line. It always made me want to go give my wife and my sometimes mystified boys a hug for no reason whatsoever that they could see or understand.

One of the final tasks I had before the race was to try and toughen the skin of my feet. This was Consumer Boy's glory moment. I'd bought a book several months earlier called, *Fixing Your Feet* that detailed half a dozen ways to reduce one's chances of blistering, most of which required a small chemistry set to create. Feet fixing gave me something to focus my energies on as I tapered down my training, and it was also a great excuse to loiter at the drugstore, where I could pester my pharmacist for oddball stuff that wasn't on the shelves.

Skin toughening is a delicate balancing act: You want the soles of your feet to be thick and blister-resistant. That's good tough. But definitely not callused—that's bad. If they're callused, my foot Bible said, then you're liable to blister underneath the calluses, which is a very nasty business indeed because then you or someone else will have to dig through the calluses with a knife or scissors to reach the blister. The book even kindly included a disgusting illustration showing how awful and painful an experience that could be.

I finally settled on two plans. The first was called the "Betadine-tea soak." I'd dip my feet every day, many times, in a mixture of tea bags, water and Betadine, the disinfectant I'd bought for my foot box. I had no idea whether it would work, but I somehow liked the idea of putting my feet in tea bags. It seemed so civilized and proper, and yet so wonderfully crude at the same time.

I also invented a skin toughener myself that I liked even

more: I called it the "playing Frisbee barefoot in the back-yard with my sons" method. I'd discovered backyard Frisbee by accident, but in those last few weeks it became a ritual. Almost every afternoon at about four or five, I'd holler to the boys and we'd gather.

Our yard is deeper than it is wide, but it's big enough for a pretty good three-corner Frisbee toss. So we'd stake out our regular spots—me by the deck, Anthony typically in the left rear corner by the compost pile, Paul near the vegetable garden.

Anthony always wanted ones he could barely catch—long soaring throws that required him to race across the yard and leap at the last second. Paul preferred perfect throws that would allow him to make nonchalant piece-of-cake catches full of finesse and style from where he stood.

Backyard Frisbee came at a time when all three of us had become altered beings. The boys were pushing thirteen, full of the joy of movement, acutely conscious of their changing bodies, intoxicated by the end of childhood. And I'd pushed myself to a new place, too, through my training. I some-times stood at a mirror and felt I'd become little more than a giant set of thighs with a life-support system attached at the top. We were all three of us a kind of biology experi-ment unfolding together there in the yard.

I also saw how my sons had *not* changed, and how the traits I'd seen in them since they were babies were evolving as they both sprinted toward manhood. Paul had always been the subtle one, the child who rejoiced in games of in-tense concentration and fine motor skill. It seemed a nat-ural progression from the little boy bent over his Legos to the young man making a catch with an arm raised up like a flamenco dancer, or with a twisting shrug that declared some inimitable Paul style of its own. Anthony had also stayed true to form. His running catches were just what I would have expected from the child who was always the one with the broader statement to make, the one who wanted things a little faster and more dramatic.

Frisbee hour made me realize more than ever what I had and what I risked at Badwater, and it made me start thinking differently about The Line. How far and how hard would I really push the envelope? What was the defining point of my courage, and what did I really value? How close would I go to the edge if it meant somehow risking what I had right here at home?

Perhaps, it occurred to me one afternoon in the backyard as the sun was low in the sky and hot against the back of my neck, I wasn't quite as obsessed as I'd thought. I'd throw a high hard one to Anthony and laugh out loud at Paul as he'd catch one with his eyes wide open in surprise and hands extended out like a demented French mime and I'd think for that minute that nothing else on earth mattered.

Other times the question seemed more complex. On one of my last days at home, we all went to our town swimming pool. And to my surprise, Anthony and Paul—who'd been increasingly conscious that summer of appearances, wanting not to be treated like little boys in public—asked me to horse around with them in the water the way I had when they were small. Maybe they were feeling some sense of risk or loss, too, if only from growing up. So I tossed them, and whirled them, and dragged them around by their ankles in the water, and they stood on my back while I lay on the pool bottom thrashing wildly and pretending to drown, and it was all just like the old days. But then in the middle of some kind of roughhousing maneuver I jammed my right big toe into the cement. Pain came shooting up from my foot.

This is it—this is how the whole thing ends, I thought, as

I held my foot and cursed. I break a toe the week before the race and it's all over.

The pain subsided; the toe wasn't broken. But somehow my spirit was. I had to get out of the pool. I had to stop. I had to walk away from the sons I loved who were still ready to play with me.

On July Fourth weekend, just a few days before I was to fly to Salt Lake, Ulrich did it—the solo run with the hand-cart. He averaged two miles an hour and made it from the bottom of Badwater to the summit of Mount Whitney in 77 hours and 44 minutes. Everything was simplified and boiled down, Ulrich wrote, in an account of the crossing that was posted on Ben Jones's Badwater website. There was nothing in the universe but him, the cart and the road. He'd been reduced, he said, to the level of a beast.

But he didn't lose his sense of humor. When tourists would stop to ask him what the hell was going on, he'd tell them he was just trying to get home. He'd lost everything but these few possessions there in the cart on a bad run of cards down in Las Vegas.

And what would be easier to believe? The truth, perhaps?

PART TWO

"Not till we are lost, in other words not till we have lost the world, do we begin to find ourselves."

—HENRY DAVID THOREAU,
Walden

Held Together by Hope

When Pat and I pulled into the parking lot of the Best Western motel in Lone Pine, California, Wayne immediately climbed out of his truck with a book in his hand and a pair of glasses perched on the end of his nose. I didn't associate him with either of those things: I hadn't known he needed glasses to read, and I hadn't thought of him as much of a reader. The angry teenager I remembered sharing a room with had been more likely to want to throw a book than read one.

But glasses and a book suited him, and I realized it was me who was out of touch. My image of Wayne was 35 years behind the times, frozen in a long-gone past. He and Pat hugged for a long time. He and I hugged briefly and awkwardly. It was a strange start.

The idea of meeting at Lone Pine, the 122-mile point in the race, had been a courtesy to Wayne. Lone Pine was a shorter drive for him, coming down from Washington, and would be a shorter drive home as well, since the finish line was just 13 miles up from the motel at the Whitney trail-head. Meeting there would also allow Pat and Wayne to see the whole Badwater course in daylight as we drove back toward Furnace Creek where our rooms were reserved. But beginning our journey together on the far side of Death Valley also meant about 200 miles of extra driving for me and Pat that day, and by the time we hit Lone Pine, I felt like the inside of a sore throat—irritable, fragile and frayed. The road out of Death Valley toward the Sierra Nevada had seemed endless. Sections that were imaginable when I'd been there in May stretched on forever, to the furthest horizon of reason and hope. One hundred and thirty-five miles was a long way even in a car. And now, after picking up Wayne, we faced the prospect of doing it all over again, going back in the other direction.

Wayne, in keeping with the spirit of our venture, had brought along just about anything that he'd thought we might have some possible if vague and uncertain use for. And now, as he opened the back of his truck and we all stood there looking at his boxes and bags, the question was how much of it to transfer into the van, which already seemed stuffed to capacity.

Our central problem was that we were all completely clueless. None of us had any experience with an adventure race of any kind. None of us had ever been 100 miles into Death Valley on foot. We didn't know anything at all, really, and the result, like my consumer frenzy in the weeks before the race, was that we weren't capable of saying with any remote shred of certainty, "No, we definitely won't need that." We might. We just might. That was the spirit that moved us.

So we tossed in just about everything Wayne had brought: the dried fruit and the stove and the chairs and the four big coolers. The list went on and on.

"We can organize it later," Pat said.

Our van, like our team, seemed held together in those fragile first moments by its own wish fulfillment, its own dream of being or becoming a real vehicle for the pursuit of Badwater. Anyone else would have said, as we threw in ever more food and equipment, that it was just a mess. The beautiful, brand-new, baby-blue 15-passenger Ford that we'd picked up in Salt Lake already looked halfway to trashed.

At the rental lot, the van's cargo hold had looked huge and ample, especially with all the seats removed but for the two front buckets and the bench right behind that. Pat and I had peered into it for a while and imagined lining up all our supplies on the sides of the van's shell, leaving an aisle down the middle that would be left open and clear. Everything would be carefully and cleverly organized on either side, like a little rolling supermarket. And for rest breaks, we said, the aisle could even become a bed! Perfect!

An aisle system was probably ridiculous when we thought of it. Our six big ice chests dominated everything, and they alone would have destroyed the dream of anything neat and tidy—not to mention clever—because, as we realized only after it was too late, the chests couldn't be stacked. Or, more to the point, they couldn't be stacked if you had any intention of ever opening them to get anything out. The ice coolers were our 800-pound gorillas, sprawled everywhere. We also had a big plastic bin of food about four feet long by three feet across, four five-gallon water cans, four blankets and pillows, a folding cot, a stepstool for getting in and out of the van, a cheap portable toilet, a propane lamp, a large suitcase full of running shoes, my foot box, another box of first-aid supplies and sunscreen, a case of my salty-sweet electrolyte mix, 10 gallons of Gatorade and bag after bag of extra clothes.

By the time we added Wayne's stuff, we looked like Ma

and Pa Kettle, or the Joads on their way to California, as though everything we owned had been piled in there. Pillows and blankets were stacked and pressed up against one side window, while the cot and the toilet and all the clothing bags were pressed up against the other in a loopy, amateurish mess. But in its own way, our mess was somehow comforting, too. It was hard for me to imagine at that point needing something we didn't already have, even as the hope of finding any particular item became more and more remote.

Think we might have some use for that monster 10-battery industrial-strength flashlight? [Glances, shrugs.] Well, throw it in. Another water can? You can't have too much water, right? More food? How can you say no to more food? Half a case of Valencia oranges might be exactly the thing we need.

One of the most ridiculous items that floated around the van was a huge portable stereo of Pat's that I'd insisted on bringing. I'd recorded about 10 hours of what I called my Badwater Tapes—a greatest-hits list of songs chosen for their adrenaline levels, or their emotional connections. Every selection had meaning of one sort or another. I'd envisioned coming up to the van when we were out on the road and using the music like a jump-start for my psyche, a visceral audio jolt that would elevate me out of myself. Somewhere out there, I believed, a little Ramones or Lucinda Williams might be just the thing I'd need. In the spirit of taking no chances, I'd even recorded a bit of opera.

As we added Wayne's things, though, the boom box emerged as the crowning touch of absurdity—it sat on top of everything, unstowable in its bulkiness, a teetering symbol of our top-heavy unpreparedness. And as we left Lone Pine heading back down toward Death Valley, our accumulation fell into a further jumble with the first good bump in the road. I looked back. Our pile was going to eat us up before we even started.

But it struck me that our little venture was also taking us home, in a way.

My family grew up in a house in Midvale, Utah, that could charitably be described as small, though tiny—if not downright claustrophobic—would probably be more accurate. There were five children, and for a few years when I was little, an uncle who moved in as well after a messy divorce—eight people, all told, in a house with three small bedrooms and one bath. The house, on a stretch of Greenwood Avenue that had once been part of my grandfather's strawberry farm, had no basement, no attic, no dining room and, perhaps more to the point, no place for anyone to really escape the group except by going outside.

Greenwood Avenue hadn't seemed all that small at the time. It was home, that was all. But I think its pressures—the absence of privacy or any space to call one's own—did shape us. We'd all moved out just about as soon as it was legally possible. We'd fled our confinement, I'd come to believe. And now I'd created something that in its own cramped and chaotic way was taking us back.

On one level, what began unfolding in the Best Western motel parking lot was thus sublimely perfect, an organic and natural extension of everything we'd vowed to each other after Gary's death, and then again after Mom's. Badwater was bringing us together. That we were reuniting in a symbolic little tin box of a home only completed the picture.

But I was still very nervous about whether the distended, stretched-out family that we'd become over the years would be strong enough for the stresses we'd face. And the awkwardness in Lone Pine had done nothing to make me feel any better. Pat and Wayne and I—plus a fourth person we hadn't even met yet who'd be riding with us for part of the way while shooting film for a documentary about the race—would be literally on top of each other in the coming days. We were a crew, at least on paper, and we were family by blood, but I didn't feel like either designation had really been tested. We were a declaration of purpose with little substance to back it up. Nothing had meshed.

All of this went through my head as I sat there in the front passenger seat on the drive back into the valley, with Wayne at the wheel and Pat in back—but I said nothing. Things were too tentative and tender. Only general subjects seemed safe. I didn't say I was glad we were all together, because I wasn't really sure yet that I *was*. And I didn't give voice to my fears that we'd end up hating one another by the end because I was afraid that saying so might somehow make it come true.

I got my first real massage the next day, on the morning before the race. In my old life, as I now thought of everything before Badwater, I'd considered massages to be an unnecessary indulgence—a luxury of pampered movie stars and overfed society matrons. And I'd lumped them as well with the overpaid-athlete culture, which I still on some level deeply mistrusted despite my year as a sportswriter. But now, in trying to become a Badwater runner, I finally surrendered. Getting a massage was one of the last dying gasps, I think, of the angry teenager behind the pizza counter who'd still been somewhere inside me. Now he'd thrown in the towel, too. To do Badwater, I finally had to get over high school.

Lisa Smith's sister, Julie Gross, a professional massage therapist from Seattle and a member of Lisa's crew, had sent around an e-mail notice to all the runners a few weeks earlier, saying she had time slots available in the days before the race. Somehow that made it all click for me. Lisa, without ever intending to, had propelled me down the road to Badwater. My own family was now on that road with me, and getting a massage from Lisa's sister connected everything back to family again. I felt a sense of completion in it somewhere, the closing of a circle. So I drove the van alone the 24 miles back to Stovepipe Wells, where Julie was staying, leaving Wayne and Pat at Furnace Creek.

I realized with a start as I approached Julie's room that I was entering the domain of a *real crew* for the first time. People were bustling in and out, looking busy and important. Inside, it felt like a military supply depot, with mysterious and powerful-looking athletic items stacked against the walls—cases of bottled water, giant dispensers of Gatorade and boxes of things I couldn't even identify. Everything seemed crisply organized and planned—and, what was especially startling, neat and tidy, too. I was in the presence of the big leagues now, the real deal. There was even a logo on the window: THE DREAM CHASER TEAM, it said. I was in the heart of the Lisa Smith experience.

I saw with a flush how amateurish our own little effort was by comparison. Our stuffed jumble of a van seemed suddenly ludicrous, our searches to find anything in the mess, completely pathetic. These Dream Chaser people knew what they were up against. You could feel it in how they moved—like soldiers, with purpose and alacrity. Pat and Wayne and I were just the Johnsons from Midvale, as we always were and always would be, bumping down the road with our fold-up toilet in the window.

Everything about us had been captured for me that morning when I was getting ready to drive to Stovepipe and I'd stopped in at Pat's room. I'd found her there trying to dry out our energy bars. The whole supply, everything we'd brought from Salt Lake, had become completely soaked with water. At Stovepipe, Lisa's crew was planning an assault and conquest; back at Team Johnson, we were trying to dry out our food. They were the Dream Chasers. We were the Soggy Carbs.

My brilliant insight into energy bars had been this: I probably wouldn't want to eat a whole one at any one time—just bites every now and then. But in Death Valley, bites of a bar would melt, right? My solution had been to cut up about $50 worth of Clif Bars and Balance Bars into thirds, throw them in a freezer bag and then put the bag in the cooler, where I could grab a piece whenever I wanted. And they'd be nice and firm and crunchy, too. Back at Pat's house, it had seemed incredibly smart. But now, looking around her motel room, *smart* was about the last word that came to mind.

Pat said she'd opened up one of the coolers that morning to check the ice supply and discovered a clumpy, congealed brown lump, floating in a bag half filled with water. She'd broken up the lump and was spreading the chunks out on towels when I walked in, and if I hadn't already known what this strange sodden material was, it would have been easy to think the worst. The nubs resembled nothing so much as little brown dog turds, and even if they weren't, they didn't look like anything that you'd ever, ever want to eat.

"They taste all right, though," Pat said, looking up. "Little mushy, that's all."

The gobs, as they dried, tended to crumble, so she'd had to bolster their integrity, in a way, by squeezing them. Unfortunately, that made them even more bizarre to look at, since it destroyed whatever vague energy bar shape they might once have had. And the crumbling couldn't ever quite be reversed anyway, as though the water had destroyed their will to be energy bars at all. Like our team, they were held together by hope.

"It sure seemed like a good idea," I said.

Our food had become waterlogged in Death Valley, one of the driest spots on the planet, and Pat was abusing good Furnace Creek towels for the silly purpose of nub repair. One more piece of our plan seemed ready to fall apart at the seams. I felt like a fool.

But now, standing there at Dream Chaser headquarters, I began to see our partially ruined food supply in a new light. Mushy brown nubs might be emblematic of our crew, but so was the ability to laugh about it. Our carbs might flag, but not our spirits—that was what it showed me. Let Lisa have her efficient, sleek and polished Dream Chaser machine. We were what we were, and that was all right. I wished we had a giant banner with a little turd on it to wave above our van as a coat of arms—a symbol of our goofy, stumbling re-sourcefulness.

A lot of good old Johnson family character was declared by our nubs, I decided. They reflected a streak in all of us that was unsophisticated and rough-cut—a proudly unpol-ished spirit that found its purest form in some of my uncles and cousins who lived the deep rural life in the mountains of eastern Utah. I'd always imagined our family was the way it was because of the old Mormon pioneer blood that flowed through our veins, and I now saw, standing there in Julie's room, how much that legacy still shaped me. Whatever else might happen over the whole course of the rest of my life, I was and always would be on some level a hick. Gary had been one, too, however articulate and well read he'd be-come.

Gary was in his forties when he first began to get seriously interested in running and biking. A natural ability he'd never tapped quickly turned him into a real athlete. But his inner hick, as I've come to think of the secret heart beating within the Johnson family, remained to be convinced. For three years in a row, he rode 150 miles on his bike in a two-day race in Utah for multiple sclerosis, but insisted on doing it—in the middle of the summer in Utah desert and mountain country—in the straight-legged Levi Strauss jeans that were and always had been his uniform in life. Gary thought that shorts—let alone spandex bicyclist shorts—were pretentious and unnecessary, if not downright prissy. The ride was the thing, not the fancy look. Only later, and gradually and grudgingly, did he come to accept that padded pants were not so bad after 100 miles in the saddle. But he had to be dragged to that place by his own pragmatism. He resisted.

Julie the masseuse had just been finishing up with a guy named Brian Manley, a high school cross-country running coach who lives near Denver, when I walked in. Manley, a first-timer at Badwater, had the classic gaunt runner's look I'd seen everywhere since we'd arrived in the valley. He was talking nonstop about how nervous and scared he was.

"I've only done a single hundred-miler," he said sheepishly, glancing around the room with a shrug, as though someone might laugh.

I held my tongue, waiting for him to leave so I could get my massage. The charitable thing, I knew, would have been to say, "Hey, pal, there's somebody right here who's got even less experience than you. The farthest I've ever run in my life is fifty miles." That might have bolstered his confidence, and it probably wouldn't have done mine any harm. But I couldn't bring myself to do it—not there, especially, in the lair of the Dream Chasers. What if they *did* laugh? Or roll their eyes, or let out long low whistles as that one cruel runner had done to me on the phone? I couldn't take the chance.

So I let Manley leave the room thinking he was probably the least prepared and qualified runner in the field, while I was more conscious than ever that I was the one who held that pallid distinction. And he'd been brave enough to be honest. It was not my proudest moment.

Much of the day before the race moved in slow motion, or at least in a kind of altered flow. I was acutely conscious of every moment, as though the minutes and seconds were passing slowly enough to examine, like grains of sand through a glass. The central event of the day was the pre-race meeting in Stovepipe Wells. It was held in the motel "auditorium," a 30-by-60-foot room that Stovepipe proudly advertises as the biggest indoor meeting space for 100 miles in any direction. Of course, in Death Valley, that's not saying much.

The auditorium was utterly jammed when we walked in. And what was even more striking and startling was that this was a Badwater room—a space completely dominated by the culture and people of the race. I hadn't reckoned on the effect of that. Badwater is the obscurest of the obscure, a cult within a cult. And yet, for this one window of time and place, it dominated everything.

The meeting reminded me of one of those elements of particle physics that flicker into existence for eight-tenths of a nanosecond or so and then disappear forever into the void. But the added proviso in this case was that during its flicker of life, the particle would also completely dominate and consume the universe. For this one hour, within these four walls in the middle of nowhere, Badwater was the world. Its values and mores and history defined culture and society.

Everywhere there were trappings of Badwater identity. A water bottle was one. Every runner and crew member seemed to be attached at the wrist to a plastic squeeze bottle from which he or she would sip more or less constantly. Total absence of body fat was another. You could have scraped down the room with a scalpel and not come up with more than a stick of butter's worth. There was also a subtle but pervasive energy that was harder to describe—a strobe-light mixture of confidence and strung-out nervousness that made the place feel jangly and electric and unpredictable.

Wayne and Pat and I slipped in like the interlopers we were, and found ourselves stuffed up near the back by the doors. We were barely in the room at all, and that somehow seemed appropriate. We were at Badwater by our finger-nails, and in the prerace meeting by the same margin.

Angelika (or was it Barbara?) of the Twin Team immedi-ately walked up and embraced me. That helped. And Bob Ankeney, the Bruce Dern probation officer I'd met in May at the clinic, also ambled over. I saw Dan and Robin Jensen and their teenage daughters, Thea and Josie Lee, seated to one side of the room. Lisa Smith stood on the other side with Louise Cooper-Lovelace, the schoolteacher who'd re-turned despite her experience with dehydration over Memorial Day.

At last I was in Badwater's inner sanctum. And yet, even now I was not. I'd been an unqualified fraud when I'd started down the road to this ultramarathon, and then over the months I'd paid a price in sweat and dedication, enough so that I believed I'd earned the right to at least stand here. But all these people still utterly intimidated me. I remained the man without a country. I was not like them, really, and I was aware of that fact all over again. I felt suddenly, acutely responsible for Pat and Wayne, too, and whatever discomfort they might be feeling as well, thrust for the first time into the middle of such deep strangeness. I'd seen Wayne, especially, retreating farther and farther to the back of the room as the last of the runners filtered in. But there was nothing to do about it. We were all three of us in over our heads.

The meeting itself, conducted by Ben Jones, seemed to have two primary functions. The first was to celebrate Badwater's existence and hand out the race packets and bib numbers that the runners would wear on the course. Lisa Smith and Gabriel Flores, the current women's and men's record holders, came up to have their pictures taken with Ben, who spoke briefly but eloquently about the unique spirit of the race and the love he felt for everyone in the room. I walked to the front when my name was called and got my race bib number, 18.

The other purpose was to have people come in and yell at us.

The park rangers yelled first. It was clear from everything about them as they walked up to the front—their stiff postures, their fake smiles, their jokey joviality, their hands resting casually on the butts of their guns—that they hated us all pretty thoroughly. And while maybe *yelling* is a slight exaggeration, their hostility-disguised-as-advice certainly made it seem like yelling.

The rangers were primarily concerned, it seemed, with peeing and pooping. They granted that there weren't rest rooms out there in the desert, and so of course contingencies must be made. But we should at least try, they insisted, to respect the ordinary tourists who might be tooling down the highway in their cars, unprepared for the sight of people squatting openly by the roadside.

They didn't exactly say it in so many words, but the point was clear enough: They wanted Badwater people to try and masquerade as normal visitors to the park. Don't be weird and disgusting, they seemed to be saying. In other words, don't be who you are. But the weird and disgusting people of Badwater were barely listening by then. Contempt had bred contempt. The conversation level in the room had risen perceptibly as the tone of the rangers' voices became evident, and I felt proud—or at least part of the group—to be paying them no more attention than they deserved.

"Try to be discreet," one of the rangers said with an edge in his voice that clearly communicated a lack of faith that his message would be taken to heart, almost as though he were holding his nose already from the thought of us all out there defiling his desert.

The state police then yelled at us not to get run over and killed. They told us that we should pull our vehicles all the way off the road onto the shoulder when we stopped, and obey every little shred of law on the books—especially littering. And they promised, or warned, that they'd be out there along with the park rangers, ready to "assist" us at any time, should the need arise.

I kept thinking of the bartender I'd met six weeks ago, and her story about her boss and the "crazies." It was hard, standing there in the meeting, not to feel like part of an alien invading force that wasn't welcomed or even respected for what we were about to do. I felt sad about that—both for the runners and for the authority figures who despised us—even as I blended in by adopting a posture of smug obliviousness. The officers were the ones drawing the line in the sand, I felt, not us.

The meeting, in turn, was followed by a "foot clinic," hosted by Denise Jones. The clinic had the feel of a cable TV talk show—something that might be seen on the Foot Network, if there were such a thing, or perhaps the Blister Channel. She sat in the front of the Stovepipe auditorium with a volunteer, Adam Bookspan, a classically trained trumpet player and frighteningly intense race-walker from Florida (no, I hadn't been able to call him, either), and took questions from the audience as she worked. She taped Adam's feet and then punctured and drained the hypothetical blisters that developed anyway despite her best efforts.

The clinic made me see that even though my overdiligence in following whatever guidelines and advice I'd received had at times turned me into a dork—I still winced at the memory of Memorial Day and Media Guy—being a good student also had its merits. Our foot box, if nothing else, was well stocked. Every time Denise mentioned some obscure tincture of whatever or bizarre-sounding blister-relief goo, Pat would glance over at me with an anxious look and I'd be able to give her a self-assured little nod and a thumbs up that said, no problem, it's all in there. I might not be the best-prepared athlete in the field, but I'd done my homework.

Robin Jensen, who'd positioned herself up near the front with a legal pad on which she scribbled notes, punctured my smug little reverie with the first of what became a series of questions that Denise—for all her expertise in Badwater skin trauma—couldn't answer.

"How do I protect Dan's stump?" Robin asked in her hard Texas twang. "Would tape work for that? He's also had some redness and swelling recently—do you have any suggestions for treating that, or preventing it from getting any worse?"

There was long silence in the room after Robin finished her question, as though everyone had stopped to take a breath. We'd all been joking and laughing as Denise had squeezed Adam's pretend blisters and he'd grimaced in his mock torment. Now we were in the presence of real issues. Robin had made it serious. Denise looked around the room for help, for suggestions from anyone who'd ever dealt with anything even remotely similar to what Robin was talking about. But no one could offer anything, so with a nod and a helpless shrug of sympathy for Robin's concerns as a crew leader, Denise continued on with her demonstration.

I couldn't recover my previous mood. I just watched Robin after that, raising her hand again and again.

The foot clinic was intended for us Badwater rookies, of course. The veterans who'd learned the tricks all by themselves—people like Lisa and Ulrich and the twins—had already left to attend what was called a "smoothie reception" in the Badwater Saloon, hosted by the film company that was in Death Valley to make a documentary about the race. The runners got free yogurt drinks and in return the cameras got to record their supposedly candid prerace chitchat.

And it was there, after so many months of tortured and silly ambivalence, that I finally came face-to-face with the invisible man of my heroic, nightmarish fantasies, Ulrich himself. I'd seen him at the prerace meeting, when he'd been brought up to the front, accompanied by wild applause and cheers, to receive a little plaque in recognition of his solo run, and now I knew that it was time to put aside all the childish things that had stood in the way of this moment. I stepped up and introduced myself.

He was a compact man in a baseball cap—only about five feet eight or nine inches tall, I'd guess—and boyish-looking at age forty-nine, with a smooth, unlined face that also seemed oddly familiar. His smile was easy and quick but not what I'd call relaxed. He immediately cut to the chase, just as he had in our one telephone conversation in May in Ben's kitchen.

"So," he said with a businesslike manner, as though setting out the agenda for a board meeting, "what are your goals?" He stared into my eyes with an intensity that gave me a glimpse of why he'd been able to propel a rickshaw across Death Valley only two weeks earlier and now was back to run Badwater the old-fashioned way.

"My goals?" I repeated the words to give myself a little more time to panic. My goals had seemed pretty solid and respectable until that moment—first, to avoid dying, and second, to somehow reach the finish line within the time allowed. But telling that to Marshall Ulrich felt inadequate and wimpy. What's finishing Badwater to him? It's nothing, like saying my goal was to clip my fingernails or avoid undercooked pork or something. In his presence, I felt completely insubstantial. I cleared my throat.

"Well, my first goal is to finish, and then after that to try and get as close as I can to a buckle, I guess," I said, taking a big sip of smoothie. *A buckle?* Where had *that* come from? Thinking there was a chance of my finishing the race in under 48 hours was like saying that I might also try and spit across the English Channel next week. It was utter nonsense. I'd met The Man and I'd proven myself not merely insubstantial, but downright unworthy. The truth, if I'd had the courage to articulate it, was that I hoped to scrape and scratch and claw my way to the end, somehow or other, using every shred of determination that was in me. Ulrich just nodded.

"Sounds great," he said.

And I think he was sincere, too, not just humoring me or laughing quietly to himself. He seemed mainly to want to know that I *had* a goal, because he was clearly and instantly satisfied with my answer. Acquiring the target was the thing that mattered to him, it appeared, not the specifics. And maybe he saw through my nonsense as well: My goal, whatever its dimensions, was daunting enough that I'd lie about it. That probably meant it was in the right proportions—big enough to hang over me like a cloud that could make me stupid with fear. Anything less wouldn't be worthy of Badwater.

Only after I walked away to refill my smoothie did it strike me where I'd seen his face before. He was the Badwater Runner himself—his image was on the race-packet material that had been sent to me and on the Badwater 1999 T-shirts that had been distributed that afternoon at the meeting. In the photograph, he's shown running down a road that stretches out behind him all the way to the horizon through an impossibly empty-looking red-brown landscape that might as well be Mars. And he was smiling. No wonder he'd haunted me.

As we drove back toward Furnace Creek, the wind started picking up and the horizon grew dark and ominous. Though the sky had been only slightly overcast when we'd left Stovepipe, the clouds now descended like a blanket, heavy with threat and humidity. By the time we were nearing park headquarters, blowing sand and occasional splatters of rain were slapping onto the windows and the metal roof like a syncopated drum solo.

Rain.

Death Valley does get rain, typically about two inches a year—most of it during the winter months in a handful of gully busters that erode the hillsides and flood the roads. But precipitation in July was extremely rare, and I sat in the backseat of the van feeling like those raindrops were going to beat their tattoo right through the roof into my brain. The prerace activities at Stovepipe had left me feeling small and defenseless; now I could add weather to my list of things that went bump in the night.

"Boy, this should cool things down," Wayne said from behind the wheel.

"It'll be great for the race," Pat added.

I wasn't so sure. As we pulled into the motel complex, the sky was greenish black, and sand was blowing horizontally through the thick and sticky air. Running in conditions like this was unimaginable. It was hard enough just breathing. Thunder rumbled off in the distance.

And then it broke. Lightning, wind and pouring rain—everything that was not supposed to happen in Death Valley in July arrived all at once just as we got to our rooms. There was an awning outside—meant for shade from the burning sun, of course—but now we sat in chairs with our water bottles and watched it pour down in front of us. The rain made little rivulets that skittered down the dirt road past the motel bungalows, and in my mind they became raging rivers and torrents.

I pictured myself retreating into the van as a storm like this descended tomorrow or the next day somewhere out in the desolate wastes. I saw us all huddled inside as the water began to rise and the inevitable flash flood swept down across the road. We'd sit there in silence as the sand was washed away under the wheels. Everything would be doomed.

Pat and Wayne chatted happily next to me, but I was beyond speech. I'd tried, in the months before this night, to achieve a state of calm and fatalistic acceptance about the forces of the wild that I might confront in Death Valley. But I'd always thought of that in terms of baking heat and the desiccation of the bone-dry desert. Nature had now decided otherwise. Nature was in control here, not me, not Ben Jones, not the Dream Chasers, not Ulrich. That was the message of the storm.

Then even darker thoughts descended. Rain like this, in a place like Death Valley, has to go somewhere. Back in May I'd seen a section of road near Stovepipe Wells that had been closed for more than six months because of a flash flood during the previous winter. Now, with every minute and every new stream bubbling past our rooms, I began to imagine the worst: The race itself would be in jeopardy. My fantasies began leaping toward what I'd do then and how it would feel to have prepared with all the obsessiveness that was in me for something that wouldn't and couldn't happen. I'd explode. I'd simply pop from the pressure.

141

Then it got worse. The power went out. The yellow awning lights that had come on in the gloom silently expired. The restaurant and the store across the parking lot winked into darkness. Furnace Creek was isolated and alone in the desert. And still the rain came down.

Dan and Robin Jensen and their girls, along with an old buddy of his from Vietnam who would round out their crew, arrived in the middle of the storm looking confused and disoriented and wet. I could think of nothing to say except, "Welcome to the neighborhood," and after that we just stood there under the awning of their room—directly across from ours—watching this least likely of events unfold in all its astonishing power. The lack of electricity meant that there might be no ice in the morning for our coolers. The water pouring down meant there might be no roads. And no roads meant no race. Disaster scenarios flickered around our little circle like lightning.

In that awkward, fearful frame of mind I went into the room to sit on the bed in the dark to call Fran. It was about 10 P.M. back home, our bedtime. She'd be lying there, probably reading a book, waiting for my call, and I sat holding the phone a long time before I dialed. I wanted this to be a great last conversation before the race. I'd imagined and yearned for some mutual stirring of our souls that might crackle across the wires, some last-minute inspiration, a reaffirmation of the bonds of love that still held strong and true. But I was feeling so besieged, so close to the edge of screaming, that I pretty much knew before I dialed that it wouldn't be what either of us really needed and wanted.

I wouldn't be able to make her see where I was, the cloud I was under, how this sudden turn of the weather terrified me only 12 hours from the start. The spaces that had grown up in our marriage over the past year suddenly seemed yawning and deep, too broad to find a way across in one conversation. I couldn't communicate to her from this place.

"How are you, baby?" she said.

"Pretty overwhelmed," I said. "You're not going to believe it—it's raining like hell here. I don't know what that's going to mean for the race."

"What does it mean for the book?"

"Fuck the book," I snapped. "The book doesn't matter. I can't think about that."

There was a silence on the other end of the line.

"I'm sorry . . . I'm just . . ." I sighed, resigned to a breakdown of communication that I probably couldn't repair, not now, anyway. I wasn't a reporter anymore. I'd fallen all the way to one side of my little balancing act by then, and it was a sign of how little I'd been able to communicate that she'd even ask. I was too far inside Badwater to even imagine at that point writing about it. I'd willed myself to become a Badwater runner, and that identity had squeezed out everything else. "This isn't about a book anymore," I said. "That's the last thing in the world I want to think about, or that I *can* think about."

I told her I was sorry again, but my hair-trigger anger and anxiety had set a tone from which I couldn't recover. I was in a hole I'd dug myself.

"I love you," Fran said finally.

"I love you, too," I said. I sighed again, wanting to say something more, but not knowing what.

"Call as soon as you can—I've got the whole network on hold out here, ready for news," she said. "Or have Pat call me, anytime—day or night."

"Okay, I promise."

Then she wished me luck and we said good night and I replaced the receiver and lay back on the pillow, feeling very alone in what I'd done, and in what I hadn't. I was in a tunnel and the only exit was through the starting line at Badwater at 6 A.M. I had no other way out, and no other way home that I could see. I had to go forward to find my way back to my wife and my old life. The wall of rain spattering outside the motel room window seemed like just one more barrier blocking the road.

The storm finally ended just before dark with a full-arc rainbow that stretched from horizon to horizon south of park headquarters. People came out of their rooms and stepped around the puddles and snapped pictures and spoke in quiet tones of wonder about the strangeness of everything that had happened. All that remained by then were echoes—the moisture rising out of the wet ground, the lightning flickering occasionally in the distance, the smells of sand and sage. The world still felt off balance, and yet somehow cleansed and healed, too. Though I hadn't been able to enjoy the storm while it lasted, the clarity that was left in its wake now filled me with a peacefulness I wouldn't have imagined possible. As we walked over to the Furnace Creek restaurant for our last meal together before the race, I felt that the deep stillness of the landscape had also climbed inside Pat and Wayne. We were all quiet, as though the storm had had the final word and we could add nothing more.

I hadn't shared a room with Wayne or seen him in his underwear since I was eight, and yet it was as though the clock had stopped somehow when we said good night to Pat and closed our door several hours later, after filling up our ice chests and gas tanks and water containers. We'd even somehow ended up—or maybe, on some level, chosen—the same beds we'd had back at home: Wayne on the left, me on the right, just as though 35 years had never passed.

Around us, the tiny space was jammed with stacked coolers and boxes and bags piled every which way, a mountain of preparation that had accreted around this one night. Everything in the room, I felt—the collected evidence of our being on the threshold of Badwater—had a story of how and why it had come to be there. And even though I knew on a conscious level that I should have already been asleep, trying to eke out every moment of rest I could before the race, I resisted closing my eyes. Going to sleep would mean losing forever this moment of anticipation and wonder and memory.

Denise Jones had also strongly recommended at her afternoon foot clinic that the runners tape their feet the night before the race. The morning of the start, she said, is so hectic and frantic that the job can get rushed and botched, leaving wrinkles in the tape or dirt on the skin that can make blistering even worse. The tape would be just as secure in the morning anyway, she'd said. You could even take a shower and not worry.

So we climbed into our beds at about nine, and I began. First I cleaned every surface with alcohol. Then I daubed my toes and heels and the balls of my feet with sticky benzoin, and then I began wrapping. Done efficiently, pretaping should probably take no more than half an hour, but I was both inefficient and neurotic about it. If the tape seemed bunched or wrinkled on a toe, I redid the toe. If a loose end flapped and couldn't be secured, I tore it off and started again. I felt a huge pressure to get this one thing right. But I was also enjoying the moment—Wayne and I there together talking in our beds on the eve of our adventure.

I asked him how long we'd shared a room at home. I couldn't quite piece together the chronology of who'd bunked with whom over those years. Wayne couldn't quite remember, either, but my question triggered another memory, I guess. It was a story I'd never heard, about the day he'd come home from school in seventh grade and found, with-out any ceremony or explanation from our parents, that he'd been kicked out of the room he shared with Gary. All Wayne's stuff was piled in the living room, where he was told he'd now sleep because Uncle Doug, my dad's youngest brother, would be moving in.

Wayne slept in the living room for the next two or three years, all through junior high, without any real place to call his own—no sanctuary, no escape at all from our claustro-phobic little house.

"Pat was dating then," he said. "And she'd have boyfriends over to watch television, so I couldn't go to bed until they left. A lot of nights I fell asleep at the kitchen table."

He was still angry about it after all those years.

"I'd never do that to my kids," he said with a dark edge in his voice that seemed familiar to me from my childhood.

"Did Mom and Dad ever apologize?" I asked.

"Nope. They just said, 'This is the way it is.'"

I suddenly felt I understood my brother—not to mention my parents—in a way I never did or could have when we were at home. I'd been about three at the time of Wayne's eviction, too little to know what was going on. I later did my time in the living room, too, but for me it had been a step up, not down. When Doug left, everybody got a rota-tion: Wayne moved back in with Gary, and I graduated from my parents' room, where I'd still been sleeping in a crib, to what I thought of as a major grown-up luxury—an entire living room all to myself.

And I was still a little kid when I got the living room tour. Wayne had been right in the middle of one of the toughest times of growing up—junior high. I thought of the pictures of him from those years—always looking like a rebel, with a shank of slicked hair down across his forehead and a tough glint in his eye that suggested he was ready to punch out the photographer or anybody else who might get in his way. I'd never understood until now.

As I continued to tape and snip, Wayne turned to his book, the glasses once more perched on the end of his nose. He'd fallen asleep by the time I finished at about 10:30, and I sat looking at him for a minute, thinking how strange and unpredictable the world was that we'd be together again at such a time and place. Then I set our three alarm clocks to go off at 3:45 A.M., called the front desk to request a wake-up call just in case and turned off the light.

Losing the World

Dan Jensen and I met up outside our motel rooms in the predawn darkness as we packed the last few items into our vehicles for the ride to the starting line. I had a cup of coffee in my hand; Dan thought he'd better not drink any that morning, though I saw even in the dark how he glanced at my mug with the covetous eye of the caffeine-head I knew he was. I thought back on our first meeting and the afternoon of our run at Great Bear, and the morning I drove away buzzing from his espresso-laden Morning Blast. This was another of Dan's present-tense moments right here, I saw, in the Furnace Creek parking lot in the hours before Badwater. Nothing would ever again be as it was then, and I think we both knew it. Everything in our lives would unfold from this time on.

We were both nervous, tripping over our tongues in a chatter of prerace anxiety. We talked about the weird weather, and the possibility of more rain to come, and how scared we both were, and especially about Badwater details like foot tape. We were both wearing sandals, having apparently had the same impulse that morning—to spare ourselves until the last possible moment the confinement of putting on the shoes we'd be wearing more or less continually for the next two and a half days. Dan pointed the flashlight beam down onto his left foot and moaned. "We were up until eleven trying to do this—I've never taped my foot before. We didn't know what we were doing."

The tape was neat and spare like Dan himself, a minimalist zero-body-fat version of blister protection that covered only the toes and a bit of the ball of his foot.

"Looks good to me," I said.

He shifted the flashlight beam over onto me. The volume of tape I'd applied before bed made me look like I'd just wandered off the set of *The Mummy*—huge thick gobs were wound around every toe and pasted onto every other surface. I'd taped my feet before, but never more than I had that night. It was as though I couldn't stop—I covered any place that seemed remotely in danger of blistering, and then in some cases I'd applied an extra layer for good measure. I felt encased.

"Wow," Dan said. "Maybe I should have more on mine."

"I have no idea," I said. "Maybe I should have less."

We both shrugged and laughed and wished each other luck, then piled into our vehicles and left Furnace Creek behind. When we passed this way again, it would be on foot, 17 miles into the race.

I felt like screaming as we pulled out onto the road, as though all the things that defined me and bound me to the earth—the collected obsessions, regrets, tragedies and triumphs of my life—had come unhinged and were free-floating in space, no longer tethered by gravity. The dawn of Badwater was about consequences. All the decisions and actions of the past that had brought me to this moment were rushing toward me, blinding me and choking me, and I knew there was only one thing that could answer the situation: "Gimme Shelter," by the Rolling Stones.

And it wasn't just the song I needed. I knew exactly what part of "Gimme Shelter" I had to have—those incredible Charlie Watts drums, double-slapping on his tom-toms in a way that has given me chills since the very first time I heard it when I was twelve. I needed my Charlie Watts loud and pounding. I needed the beat to thrash up through my nervous system, burn out the wiring and blast open a space big enough to dump all the cascading terrors that I felt were about to take off the top of my skull. I needed shelter myself. So I put Badwater cassette number one, track number one, into Pat's boom box and cranked it.

Travis Gray, a twenty-six-year-old video production technician from Maryland, had joined us just as we were getting the van ready back at the rooms. He was working for the documentary film company and would hitch a ride with us for all or part of our journey. But he might as well have been invisible to me; I couldn't really see or understand anything about him. I felt that morning as though I were completely saturated—I could take in no new information or emotion. Travis's presence had washed off my consciousness in the same way that rain pours across a desert floor, because it can't be absorbed.

Wayne was at the wheel. Pat sat in front. I took the back passenger seat. And because we'd only budgeted room for three people in the van at any one time—since during the race I'd always be on foot—Travis got the introductory pile-of-junk position, riding in the back on top of our rubble of coolers and clothes.

But we were moving. That was all that mattered. We were in motion, heading for the cliff. As we neared the Bad-

Gary and I in the summer of 1996, a year before his death and the question it prompted: What makes us stop, and what makes us go?
(Credit: Fran Siciliano)

Lisa Smith was the sphinx of Badwater, an enigma of iron-willed endurance wrapped in a seemingly sunny middle-class countenance.
(Credit: Tony Di Zinno)

My sons Paul (left) and Anthony pose with me after the New York City Marathon in 1998. They were pushing 13, leaving childhood behind, and sometimes unable to figure out a father who'd been caught in the spell of a race that terrified him.
(Credit: Fran Siciliano)

In the real world, Marshall Ulrich is a small-business owner in a small town in Colorado. In the ultramarathon world he's a god, performer of some of Badwater's most unfathomable feats. I ran hundreds of miles while silently repeating the mantra, "What would Ulrich do?" (Credit: Ben Jones)

Ulrich with his rickshaw, July 4th weekend, 1999. He'd run Badwater seven times by then, and held the record for the fastest crossing ever recorded, but now he was doing what had never been done—a solo, self-supported crossing of Death Valley in July. (Credit: Ben Jones)

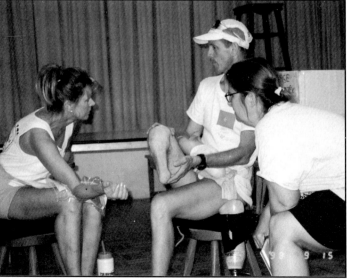

(L to R): Denise Jones, Dan Jensen, and Robin Jensen, at Denise's foot clinic the day before the race. Dan lost the lower part of his right leg to a land mine in Vietnam in 1971 and ceased running for nearly 20 years until a prosthetic running foot was perfected around the time of his 40th birthday (Credit: Josie Lee Jensen)

Rain is not supposed to happen in Death Valley in July, but when it does it relentlessly seeks the lowest ground, blasting away mountainsides and washing out roads. A quarter inch of rain—more than one-eighth of a year's average total—was recorded at the National Park ranger station at Furnace Creek the night before the race. (Credit: Wayne Johnson)

Team Johnson (L to R): Travis, Pat, me, and Wayne. The challenge of what lay ahead brought us together as a family, but I feared we'd be blown apart somewhere on the Death Valley course. (Courtesy of Pat Nosack)

By the time of the traditional prerace photo, with old, dead Lake Manly stretching out behind us and the temperature pushing 115, I'd lost all journalistic objectivity. I'd become, finally and unalterably, one of the "bunch of crazies." (Credit: Chris Kostman, AdventureCORPS)

Moments of genuinely unlimited potential, when the only thing that matters is what happens next, are extremely rare. Such a moment occurred at the starting line of Badwater. (Credit: Chris Kostman/ AdventureCORPS)

Ben and Denise Jones are the godparents of Badwater. He's a walking compendium of Death Valley trivia; she's the race's heart and reigning foot-queen. (Credit: Jane Byng)

The Twin Team—Barbara Warren and Angelika Castaneda. The twins have done it all. They speak four languages and have run twice around the grand Canyon. They've been actresses and entrepreneurs and set records together in triple ironman competitions. They are beautiful, unstoppable, and, in their competence, incredibly intimidating. (Credit: Jurgen Ankenbrand)

I'd been told that tape applied before the race could ward off blisters by creating a barrier against friction and heat. But as the race developed, I worried that I'd applied too much. (Credit: Pat Nosack)

Major Curt Maples, United States Marine Corps, and crew member (holding the flag). Maples saw Badwater as a test of whether a person had the "right stuff." In the way he dealt with his ordeal, he defined the word "honor." (Credit: Jurgen Ankenbrand)

Louise Cooper-Lovelace, near Stovepipe Wells, day one, after the storm. Louise, an elementary school teacher and breast cancer survivor, had been in chemotherapy only a few months before. (Credit: Nathan Bilow)

In the Badwater race, the vast landscape of Death Valley dominates everything. The earth is in control here, not the puny stick-figure humans who presume to trot across it—a reality that brings the participants closer together. (Credit: Nathan Bilow)

The field of Badwater participants stretches out immediately from the start and by the end of the first day, 50 miles or more can separate the lead runners from the stragglers. The implication is clear: After a very short time, you're racing against no one but yourself and the course. (Credit: Nathan Bilow)

Going into Badwater, I'd come to believe that the power of the Death Valley endurance experience could reveal something larger, something transcendant. Death Valley's visions and hallucinations are legendary, and it's at the end of the second day—36 hours into the race—that they typically begin.
(Credit: Nathan Bilow)

Rhyolite, Nevada—a ghost town on the eastern edge of Death Valley. Rhyolite lived and died in a single frenzied decade of gold fever around the turn of the century. Passing it mid-race was an eerie experience.
(Credit: Kirk Johnson)

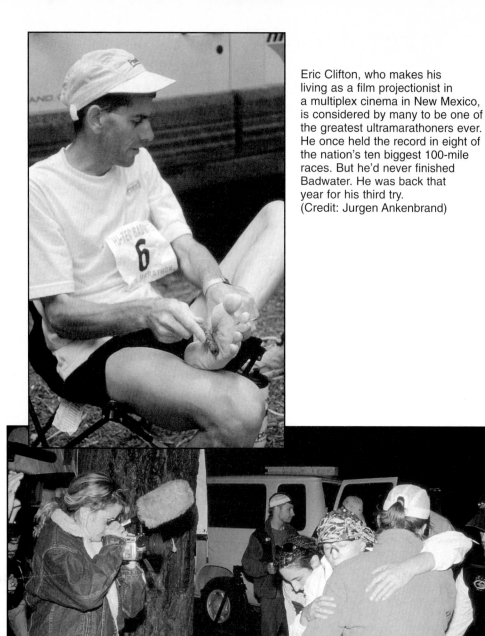

Eric Clifton, who makes his living as a film projectionist in a multiplex cinema in New Mexico, is considered by many to be one of the greatest ultramarathoners ever. He once held the record in eight of the nation's ten biggest 100-mile races. But he'd never finished Badwater. He was back that year for his third try.
(Credit: Jurgen Ankenbrand)

Angelika Castaneda of the Twin Team (in headscarf), shortly before 11 P.M., day two, Mount Whitney trailhead finish line. "We're all here," she said, "to see what is possible."
(Credit: Chris Kostman/AdventureCORPS)

water turnoff, I tried to block out my worries and simply feel the groove. I shivered as the music and the morning roared into me. Charlie would get me there, I felt, I just had to have faith.

Suddenly Wayne pulled up short. The turnoff to Badwater was blocked with barricades. A man in a Hi-Tec hat was standing there on the shoulder, gesturing. I turned down the music and we all leaned toward the passenger-side window.

"The road's washed out—we're going seventeen miles up 190 and start there," the Hi-Tec guy said. We all stared past him, blank and silent, looking down into the darkness at the road to Badwater we couldn't take, then to the left toward the unknown challenges of California State Highway 190, which forked toward the Nevada border. "This race is bigger than one washed-out road," the man explained, as though we'd asked him something. He paused again, waiting for us, I suppose, to yell or explode or at least speak to him. "Just go seventeen miles up," he said, waving us on. "You'll see the vehicles."

We all began talking at once as we pulled away, numb in our amazement.

A new starting line 17 miles up highway 190 toward Las Vegas would give the race the same final distance—135 miles—but it would change everything else. That road led up and out of Death Valley, toward the Great Basin plateau and the vast emptiness of Nevada. It wouldn't be as hot, and as I could see with every mile we drove, we'd also be running downhill most of the way to Furnace Creek.

It'll still be Badwater. That's what I said to myself and to the others in the van. Nature had spoken, nature had dictated its terms, and we'd simply have to adapt and accommodate ourselves—that's what the race is about, anyway. I kept saying it, and by the time we pulled up to the jam of vehicles and people milling about in the road, I'd almost gotten my head around to the point of believing it. What was I going to do, after all, go home?

But the elite runners were in revolt, and Ulrich, who was for many people the very embodiment of Badwater, was leading the fight. Eric Clifton and Gabriel Flores, both considered contenders to win, and Adam Bookspan, the race-walker, were at Ulrich's side arguing with the Hi-Tec team when I wandered up.

"This isn't Badwater," Ulrich said. "If we do this, it's just a hundred-and-thirty-five-mile road race."

Several runners said they would simply abort. They'd come to run Badwater-to-Whitney, they said, and that's what they'd do. They'd wait until the Badwater road opened, whenever that was, then head down and go it alone and whatever anybody else wanted to do was up to them.

Around us, dawn was breaking, and at 3,000 feet, it was cool—freakishly, weirdly, undesirably cool. And in my wishy-washy anxiousness, I found myself starting to agree with Ulrich. He was right: Starting here wouldn't be Badwater at all. This altered race would bypass most of the salt pan heat and in the process obliterate the original meaning and intent of the event—running from lowest to highest. I began to imagine jumping ship, too, and going down with Ulrich to start when we could at the place we were supposed to. He'd been a constant companion in my head as I trained, and maybe it would only make sense now to stand at his side once more.

Then in the next second I'd flop back the other way. I'd prepared for a race called Hi-Tec Badwater. If the form of that event now changed because of some freak occurrence, wasn't that part of the adventure? I'd gotten into this thing partly as a way of testing myself against the unpredictable, impossible forces of fate. Well, maybe this was just part of the test.

I stopped worrying—what would happen would happen. I'd go when and where the race led. I'd been reduced to pure impulse: I felt like a big, dumb, slobbering golden retriever bred to fetch, standing there in blank-minded anticipation wagging my tail, ready to take off and unable to think clearly about much else. Just throw the stick and I'd run.

Finally, at about 5:45, 15 minutes before the scheduled start, Ben Jones began huddling with the Hi-Tec officials, who all seemed to have phones to their ears. A couple of minutes later he yelled and everyone gathered around him in the middle of the highway.

"The park service says they think they can have the Badwater road open by eleven at the latest—so we can still do an A.M. start down there," Ben said. "That seems to be the consensus of what people want." There were cheers from the diehard group and ambivalent indecipherable murmurs from others.

Ben paused and looked around, waiting perhaps for someone to disagree or argue the point. "So I guess we'll all head down now to Furnace Creek, and we'll get you more specific information when we know it."

There were cheers again, if only of relief that some definitive decision had been arrived at. Ben just shrugged and smiled.

The Furnace Creek weather station had recorded a full quarter inch of rain in the previous night's storm, about as much as the valley typically receives during a whole month in the wettest part of the winter. And whether it was a result of all that water evaporating in the morning sun or the persistence of the weather pattern that had produced the storm in the first place, Death Valley had become down-right humid.

By the time we got back to park headquarters at about 7:30 A.M. and parked the van with the other Badwater vehicles lined up on the roadway, the moisture level of the air had reached 55 percent, about 10 times higher than normal. The storm had cooled things down some—it was still only in the nineties at the Furnace Creek weather station, well below the average for early morning in July. But the dampness, like a hot sponge pressed up against your face, had sharply escalated the power of that heat, and altered its effects as well.

Experiencing humidity in Death Valley in July is like seeing a real live ghost. People say it happens, but you can live a long, long time there and never experience it. Furnace Creek is one of the few weather stations on earth to have in fact recorded zero humidity—no moisture in the air whatsoever—several times in the 1940s. Three percent is typical. To me, though, high humidity and temperatures in the nineties felt like a letter from home. I'd trained in humidity. East Coast steam had been my environment. Fighting to extract a good deep breath from the dense, moist—not to mention polluted—air of the Atlantic seaboard in summer was simply part of what running in the New York metropolitan area was all about.

But in the same way that a 17-mile downhill run from the edge of the park was not really Badwater, neither was New York steam. Maybe, I thought, Ulrich would boycott that anomaly, too, and wait for Death Valley's meteorology to go back to normal. What would his highly honed measures of purity say about this? Would he perhaps pick a fight with the air we breathe?

Along the road, runners and crews sat beside their vehicles in completely phony postures of relaxation. No one could really unwind—or, even less likely, sleep—and yet, at the same time, everyone also knew that it was the last chance to try for a very long time. The flow of time felt suspended. The clock that had ticked for months relentlessly toward the Badwater starting line had stopped, and the world itself seemed to be waiting, on pause, for the natural progression of events to resume. The soldiers from Major Curt Maples's Marine Corps crew were stretched out on blankets, looking stiff and tense with their eyes closed, as though under orders. Other teams had music blaring. Some people jogged back and forth down the road clutching water bottles.

Being put on hold gave me a second chance with my wife. With the whole timetable now thrown out, she'd need to know that our news bulletin calls wouldn't be coming at the times and places she was expecting. So I walked up to the pay phones at the general store and called her just as she was getting to work, thinking how I wanted to be a better human being and husband than I'd been the night before. The washed-out road had presented an opportunity.

"I'm sorry about last night," I said, as soon as she'd gotten over the shock of hearing from me at a time when she'd imagined me somewhere out on the course.

Fran sighed and said she was sorry, too, that she hadn't been more thoughtful. We chatted about the false start at 3,000 feet and the humidity and what the altered time frame might or might not mean for my chances. But there was still a distance we couldn't entirely bridge: Too much had gone unsaid by then. Maybe she believed I'd become selfish and withdrawn. Maybe I thought she hadn't tried hard enough to understand my goals and dreams. Maybe we were still stewing about the failed conversation of last night. But when we hung up I felt once again that we hadn't fully connected. Like that day in the spring when she'd touched my arm, I was far away already, gone down the road again. It was not a good pattern.

At about 9 A.M., the signal finally came, and the caravan began forming up. Ben had told us, when we'd gathered around him for the last-minute briefing, that only one lane had been cleared, so we'd have to drive single-file down the Badwater road, led by the rangers. But that would still get us there in plenty of time. The race, he said, would start precisely at 10 A.M.

Driving the 17 miles to Badwater single-file quickly became scary, with so many wildly overanxious people all riding each other's bumpers. Wayne had to stomp on the brakes over and over as the line got ahead of itself, then suddenly slowed to a crawl. Mud washes were everywhere, on the shoulders and spilling across the uncleared traffic lane—evidence of the floods that had roared down from the Black Mountains. With no vegetation to stop or slow its path, the water had simply swept across the highway toward the lowest ground. And as we got closer to the bottom, we could see where much of it had ended up: the stagnant wastes of long-dead Lake Manly were laced with ribbons of water that glinted, blue and flat, out into the distance across the salt pan that the Spanish explorers had ironically called the Playa, literally, Death Valley's "beach."

At Badwater itself, everything was in chaos. One lane of road meant hardly any place to pull over and park, so the cars and vans and trucks of the crews were backed up far from the little elevation sign, 282 FEET BELOW SEA LEVEL, that marked the starting line. And my own confusion compounded everything. I'd had to pee so badly I jumped out after we parked and ran down to the bathrooms. Then I'd realized that both of the water bottles on my little fanny holster were empty. So I'd jogged back to the van, only to find it locked. By then the runners were being summoned to the sign for the traditional prerace pictures, so I jogged back down once more, fretting and angry and ridiculously worried, as though my bottles really had to be filled at that very instant to avoid some global calamity.

I was certainly not alone in my over-the-top energy spike. Standing there behind the elevation marker, people seemed ready to shake or cry or laugh or do all three at once. The constant jokes, the nervous shaky sips from water bottles, the sudden stretching and twitching that rippled through the line—every expression and motion screamed for a beginning or, perhaps more accurately, an end to this particular phase of the suffering.

By purest chance, I happened to end up next to Scott Weber, a legend of Badwater on a par, almost, with Ulrich himself. Weber had finished the race five previous times— including one of the famous "Runs You Don't Want to Try" that I'd discovered on the Internet. In 1994, he crossed Death Valley four times in a row, from Badwater to the top of Whitney and back to Badwater—*and then did it again*, for a total of 600 miles. He'd also advised hundreds of runners over the years about training for Badwater and other ultramarathons. In the tiny world of super-distance, "Coach Weber" was all you had to say.

I was just trying to work up the nerve to introduce myself when a runner I didn't know came bounding over.

"Coach Weber!" he said. "What's your advice?"

Around us, people who'd heard the question fell silent and turned their heads to look, as though we were all in one of those old E. F. Hutton television commercials in which someone brings the party to a halt by asking financial advice from a stockbroker. "When E. F. Hutton talks," the announcer would say, "people listen."

Weber glanced around to acknowledge his audience but

paused for only the briefest of moments. "I have one word for today—salt," he said. "One gram every hour and you'll stay out of trouble."

Almost immediately after that, the group broke up and I scrambled my way toward the van, neurotically obsessing over my empty bottles. They had to get filled right now! They had to!

By the time I found Pat and we'd raced up together to the van, everyone was gathering again back at the starting line.

"Salt," I said to Pat and Wayne through my short, struggling breaths of nervous energy. "That's the advice—gram an hour."

They nodded. Okay. Fine. Whatever. We were all so jittery that ordinary conversation was now impossible. We'd begun talking like Massanutten Bob. Adverbs and adjectives had been dispensed with.

As I jogged back down, Adam Bookspan, the racewalker and musician, had already started playing the national anthem, unaccompanied, on his trumpet. I tried to breathe, to settle back down, to absorb the moment and appreciate the spectacle. But everything seemed off balance and out of control. I'd imagined a slow buildup to the Badwater takeoff—an eternity of waiting and watching the clock—not some spinning, drunken stagger toward the starting line, full of last-second things that hadn't been done and now wouldn't even be remembered. Screaming felt like the only release possible, and I guess everybody felt pretty much the same way because when Adam finished, the roars were hoarse and loud, like overtaxed steam whistles.

It's a measure of my own still-fluttering, shallow insecurity, I suppose, that I looked around the group at that moment to see what everyone was wearing. I'd wavered, because of the strange humid weather, between my spandex running shorts and my head-to-toe desert suit, but I'd finally gone for the full-ride desert whites, and now I was relieved to see that perhaps a quarter of the runners were dressed as I was. Whatever happened, at least I would not stand out as Media Guy today. I blended in. I'd painted myself into the picture so completely that I even looked the part, more or less. I'd also lost the last vestige of my *Times*-ian objectivity. From this moment on, I saw, I would no longer be an observer of the scene, but a fully engaged actor. I was in Badwater too deeply now to see it from any perspective but my own. I'd become just one more numbered runner, milling about on the edge of a stagnant, blistered lakebed on an early morning in July at a temperature of 115 degrees Fahrenheit.

There were no speeches. No momentous exhortations or attempts at stirring rhetoric. We all knew why we were there, or at least we knew what we had to do. Nothing that anybody said could alter anything. It was too late for that.

Matt Frederick, the race director, simply asked if everyone was ready. He announced the time according to the official race clock, then paused a moment to let people synchronize their watches. I couldn't help laughing out loud. Synchronizing your watch meant you cared about knowing exactly where you stood in the race—to the minute. For me, I knew that rounding to the nearest hour would probably be close enough. But I couldn't help it. I was in all the way by then. So I synchronized.

Matt paused again, and then without warning began counting down from 10. It took on the nature of a chant as the rest of us joined in, and then there it was. Zero. No gun, no balloons, no crowds except the crews and a few cameras. Just zero. Start. The beginning. Searing hoarse roars and cheers erupted from everyone. Major Maples, standing near me, screeched, red-faced, like a warrior. I grabbed Pat for one last hug.

"I'm so proud of you," she said, squeezing me tighter.

If there'd been time, I would have argued with her. I hadn't done anything. I was just standing there with 135 miles in front of me. I hadn't even crossed the starting line yet. Save your pride for tomorrow or the next day, if there is one, I wanted to say.

For now there was only potential, only the future. But it was a bottomless kind of potential of the sort that only comes at rare moments in life when all that really matters is what happens next. The past had ceased to exist and so had the present. There was only the open road, the unanswered question of everything extending out before us. If we could remember being born, it would probably be something like this. Becoming a parent also has a bit of it—for a brief moment in time none of what we are matters, only what we will be. Anything and everything is possible. Life begins.

And then we were moving down the road.

The 41 people who started down the highway with me all had real lives somewhere. Eric Clifton, who was considered the front-runner, having won more ultramarathons than anyone on earth, was in real life a film projectionist for a multiplex cinema in Albuquerque, New Mexico. Nick Palazzo drove a truck, delivering linens on Long Island. Ephraim Romesberg was a retired nuclear engineer. Arthur Webb was an electronics technician with the U.S. Postal Service. Cathy Tibbetts was an optometrist in a small town near the Navajo Indian Nation. Jack Denness was a chauffeur for Lloyds of London. But now, with those first steps, we all belonged to Badwater. What we were before didn't matter.

I'd heard the concept of the "Badwater World" discussed before race day and I'd always scratched my head about it. I'd imagined that the definition hinged on some bizarre effect of heat or dehydration. But at the very moment we began, as the cheers and hollering were still rolling out over the salt pan, I suddenly got it. Badwater was now dictating the terms. With that one word, "zero," a partition had come down dividing the old reality I'd known from this new one. The ordinary circumstances of life had been suspended and walled off.

It was all very much like my little flashlight beam that night at the Boogie in North Carolina. I was inside the Badwater bubble now. I moved and it moved and I knew that for now and for the future that extended all the way to the farthest horizon, the bubble would define everything. Never would I see beyond it or be able to run past it.

I felt the impulse to speed up stirring inside me as the faster runners charged ahead down the road. Partly it was the classic racer's mentality taking hold, the competitive instinct to catch the guy ahead of you and pass him and beat him if you can. But there was also something else. Out here, falling behind meant being alone. I could feel that already, only minutes from the start. And I knew from my experience at Telescope Peak in May how deep that loneliness could get. Where we were going there would be no crowds, no stores, hardly any cars, probably no wildlife and nobody to talk to but your crew—and only then for a moment or two when you'd stop by every half hour or so. The temptation to go faster—to throw away all that's been hammered into your head about pacing and the dangers of heat prostration—was hard to resist in part because you think that by giving in you might not feel so exposed under that vast sky. There might be shelter, of a sort, in numbers.

Now the lead runners were already becoming white dots, just as Ben had warned me they would back in May. I'd gotten a last glimpse of them at about five miles out when I'd seen them going up a long hill on the distant horizon. Then they were all over the top and gone, like mirages. I doubted I'd ever see them again. Ben had known.

I repeated his words to myself now and tried to hear his voice as I pushed my pace back down toward the slow rhythmic jog I hoped to maintain through the first day's heat. *Let 'em go. Just let 'em go. You'll never see them again, but that's all right.* I breathed and tried to jettison all the worry and fuss that would siphon off the precious energy I'd need today and tonight and tomorrow and the next night—on and on in a chain that had no end. I tried to reach out with my mind to touch the walls of the place I'd entered.

It's one of the more strange and appealing things about running that the world around you becomes transformed by your very motion through it. As we jogged out and up from the bottom of the hemisphere, the barren, moonlike terrain of the Badwater basin became instantly alive and vibrant. I was in Death Valley—and part of Death Valley—in a way that I hadn't been before. All my senses were sharpened. I could smell the brackish chemical muck of the salt. I could feel the slight morning breeze on my hands and face. The sun, rising higher by the minute over the Black Mountains, was like the pulse of life itself—warming every surface.

Images and sensations were pouring through me in those early moments of the race as though a floodgate had been opened. Things had been built up so much, for so long, that the release of pressure—the astonishment of finally being under way and heading down the highway—had created a kind of a vacuum into which pieces of the world were being sucked away, as though my life itself had sprung a leak. My wife and sons back in New Jersey, my work, my brothers and sisters, my mother—all the touchstones of what I'd been began flickering by in breaths and strides, 100 yards at a time.

And then all those images and thoughts were gone, too, drained down and washed away. The Badwater matrix—the collective assumptions and demands of the Badwater World—was going up. What I'd just seen was a last glimpse as the door closed.

I certainly thought about the things of real life—especially my family—as the race went on. But already it seemed that the world beyond Death Valley was somehow oddly *outside my universe*. In the same way that I'd previously only been able to think about Badwater as a concept, now ordinary life became the concept that I could only perceive dimly, if at all. Badwater had been a movie playing in my head for the last year, a continuously running newsreel fantasy of dread and redemption that I'd watched a thousand times. But now the chairs had changed. I was in the movie and my old life outside was the flickering fiction—a made-up world that was hard to quite imagine.

The parameters of a Badwater existence are basic, even downright stupid in their primitive simplicity. I had to worry about drinking enough liquid and not going too fast. I had to decide whether to run on the road and so take the heat directly from the pavement, or go off to the side into the dirt shoulder where the ground was a little cooler, but where I risked getting sand or rocks in my shoes that could trigger blisters. I had to worry about getting enough salt and enough sugar, enough carbohydrates and enough protein. I had to think about where to rest and for how long. And that's about it. Thought and motivation had been harnessed to the science of sustained forward motion—keeping my body cool enough and fueled enough to go on. Everything else—all the grand issues of the human condition—had receded into the distance. Just more white dots on the distant horizon that I might or might not reach.

It made me dizzy just to think of it: I was inside the beast at last. My head buzzed with the power of where I was, and the heat, which had climbed to 118 degrees as we pushed toward noon, and the exhilaration. *Death Valley . . . Death Valley . . . Death Valley.* It became a rhythmic mantra as I ran, a mnemonic broken record. Whole universes seemed to hang by that name, with its conjuring of history and horror, glory and greed, and they all seemed to spin before my eyes.

About 10 miles from the start, I passed a formation of salt and gravel deposits by the roadside that, for reasons I couldn't make out, had been grandly named the "Devil's Golf Course." It looked like random piles of rocks to me. The name, I knew, was all about context—this was the Devil's Golf Course because the devil was an image of death and we were in Death Valley. But it made me start to wonder how things might have turned out differently if death had *not* become the prevailing local motif.

According to legend, William Lewis Manly and his party of gold seekers in 1849, having barely survived their disastrous attempted shortcut to the California goldfields, turned as they were leaving for one last look at the place that had almost killed them. As they stood there, someone muttered, "Good-bye, Death Valley," and that was it. What was perhaps nothing more than an ad-libbed put-down immediately stuck. Death Valley it was.

But suppose that fateful mutter had included some other phrase, like "Wrong Way Valley" or "Oops Valley"—or anything but what it did. How would the world be different? The answer, I decided, is that I wouldn't have been there at that moment running by the Devil's Golf Course thinking about it, and that it wouldn't have been named any such thing that it didn't remotely resemble. There'd probably be no Badwater race and no 20-mule-team Borax. Ronald Reagan would never have become the host of a television show called *Death Valley Days*, and would thus perhaps never have been able to rejuvenate his moribund acting career as a springboard into politics. On a little mutter that someone happened to write down and repeat, the fates of the great powers had swung.

Oops Valley would have disappeared into the shallow short-term memory of the American West. It wouldn't have become the great symbol that it did—of hardship in a harsh and pitiless environment, of romance and survival, of nature's extremes and mankind's ability to endure. The valley would still have eventually been singled out by cartographers and climatologists as the lowest sunken land area west of the Dead Sea (another crucially named landmark) and as the hottest, driest place of human habitation on the planet. But without an image and an aura, it would have remained a geographic curiosity and probably not much more.

Death is what gave Death Valley life. The images and associations that could be conjured up by the phrase, and the collective mystique that were built around it, still resonate from that one moment of its naming. From the stock speculators in the 1800s who found that a gold or silver mining company with Death Valley in its name was worth a premium on Wall Street, to the tourism industry that still to this day packages Death Valley as a kind of netherworld theme park (a pitch that seems to work particularly well with German tourists, for some reason), Death Valley myth and Death Valley reality have become completely intertwined.

As early as the 1920s, a bus-tour company from Los Angeles was portraying the idea of a trip to Furnace Creek as a kind of journey to the dark side—so horrifying you couldn't help loving it.

"All the advantages of hell, without the inconveniences," the company's ads proclaimed.

The imagery of death had taken over completely by then, with every newly named landmark in the valley tilted toward an ever-heightened sense of doom. There's the Funeral Mountains and the Black Mountains, the Devil's Cornfield and Dante's View. There's Thirst Canyon and Starvation Canyon and Last Chance Canyon and on and on, leading us to Deadman Canyon and, of course, Coffin Canyon. Even names that were accidental eventually took on the local color. Furnace Creek sounds like it was named because it's the hottest continuously occupied community in the world, but the truth is not so devilish or creative. The place was actually named for a real furnace—built by a group of Mormons in the 1800s to test the silver content of some ore they'd found. Stovepipe Wells, which also does a good job conjuring up images of blast-furnace ambience, was named because a prospector marked the natural springs he'd discovered there with a length of stovepipe stuck in the ground so that he and other travelers through the area could find it again.

As I ran toward Furnace Creek in the early afternoon, I started to think, though, that maybe these Death Valley folks hadn't pushed their favorite metaphor quite far enough. If there can be something as silly as the Devil's Golf Course, why not the Devil's Tea Caddy, or the Devil's Bedroom Slippers, or the Devil's Belt-Sander? You want real death? How about Rotting Putrid Corpse Overlook? Pustule Point? Desiccated Flesh Drive? Drooling Dementia Rest Area? The surface, it seemed to me, had barely been scratched.

I suppose, on a certain level, I was letting my old suspicions about Badwater percolate back up to the surface. I wanted to bring Death Valley back down to size so that it wouldn't eat me alive. I needed to make the thing I was so scared of an object I could play with and laugh at. And it occurred to me that a similar impulse probably explains why the doom-and-gloom name did stick back in 1849.

If Death Valley hadn't existed, I think people would probably have invented it—or someplace like it—in order to put their own genuine terrors of death onto a more earthly, manageable scale. Palpably ridiculous tales about Death Valley were created and repeated—and apparently widely believed—because people wanted, and maybe needed, to think that such an outlandish place could really be found somewhere out there on the mysterious edge. They'd wanted to believe, just as I'd wanted to believe in Badwater.

In 1874, for example, newspapers around the world carried an item about the mysterious life and death of a man named Jonathan Newhouse. Newhouse was an inventor who'd supposedly built a mechanical cooling jacket intended to overcome Death Valley's torrid temperatures. The jacket, filled with water, was designed around the principle of swamp-cooler air-conditioning—essentially, that water cools as it evaporates. The wearer of the jacket would only have to pump water into the evaporation apparatus of the jacket to maintain whatever delightfully pleasant temperature was desired.

But as initially reported in the *Virginia City Enterprise* newspaper that summer, poor old Newhouse had designed his jacket a bit too well. He'd been found *frozen to death in the hottest place on earth*, the paper said. There was a small design flaw in the jacket, it seems—as is so often the case in such cautionary tales. The laces tying Newhouse into the suit were on the back where he'd been unable to reach them to make his escape. The story described with relish the horror of his frozen beard and the icy terror of a death in the midst of blazing heat. It was all a happy fraud, of course, created on a dull day by an editor with not enough to do.

But the real stories, like the saga of Charles C. Breyfogle, were just as wild. He was a prospector who staggered out of the sun one day around the time of the Civil War with the richest chunk of gold ore anyone had ever seen. What made him and his gold into legend, though, was that he couldn't remember where he'd found it. He spent the rest of his life searching in vain for the place where, in his heat-induced delirium, he'd found and lost a fortune.

That's one version of the Breyfogle episode, anyway. The other was that he was simply one more in the grand tradition of Death Valley liars, con artists and public-relations experts. The cynical spin on Breyfogle—substantiated by the fact that armies of prospectors looked for his lost El Dorado over the decades and never found a trace—is that he made the whole thing up. Breyfogle was in turn followed by the even more notorious Walter Scott, better known as "Death Valley Scotty," who became famous around the turn of the century essentially for being famous—a distinction earned by countless celebrities after him. In the dawning age of the media culture, Scott was one of the first masters of the art of shameless self-promotion. He lived for the newspaper headlines he could generate—about hidden gold, and secret mines in the desolate wastes, and enemies who wanted him dead—and whether they were true or not was secondary if not irrelevant. He was, in the end, a phony, but he got a good ride out of it while it lasted, and a mansion in the desert to boot, built by one of his backers in the

1920s. Scotty's Castle became one of the prime tourist attractions in the valley even while Scott was alive.

Death Valley thus became its own creation—a mixture of dread and hype, awe and hucksterism, desolation and clownish buffoonery, exaggeration and genuine peril, all in equal measure. What is and what only seems became the running thread, and indeed part of the mystique itself, from Scotty's era through television's *Death Valley Days*, and right into the race I was now running.

Death Valley is the crazed, skeletal figure crawling across the sands chasing a mirage of water that's never there. It's the skull and crossbones over the poison well, the blazing sun and the unquenchable thirst that bring on madness and ruin. In the Death Valley lexicon, great reward and grave threat are always conjoined. The valley offers much, but always demands just a little more—perhaps your life, perhaps your soul. It's El Dorado in hell, a promised land for the moral purist—the little bit of Ulrich in all of us—who understands that nothing comes without a price, and that sometimes the things that make the most sense make no sense at all.

On some of the bigger crews at Badwater, one person is typically designated the "pee monitor" for the course of the race—charged with the unenviable task of urine-nagging. Pee, as per Dr. Ben's ironclad rules about the bladder, is a key barometer of physiology in Death Valley. It should be clear and copious. If it's yellow, then you're not drinking enough, and if you're not peeing at all, then you're already well down the road to dehydration. Pat and Wayne and Travis and I had agreed in advance that we'd all pester one another about our pee and its various quantities and colorations. There weren't enough of us—fortunately, I think—for one person to get stuck being a full-time drudge about it.

Public urination is simply a matter of course at Badwater, no matter what the park rangers or tourists might think. When the nearest tree is 20 miles away toward the upper slopes of Telescope Peak, and the nearest real bathroom could be 12 hours or more down the road, and you've had it drilled into your head from every side to drink liquids constantly, peeing in public is what you do. It becomes, in fact, almost a matter of pride. Peeing a lot—say, every half hour or so—is proof of a certain moral character on the Badwater course, I felt. Frequent awareness of a full bladder meant I was topped off and staying within Dr. Ben's Rules.

I'd also read in one of my grubby little ultramarathon pamphlets that the stomach and bladder could be trained to be more efficient at processing liquid for absorption into the small intestine, and thus into the bloodstream. A better bladder had become one of my little side projects as I sweated out all those hours in the sauna back home. Over the months, I'd worked my way up to drinking almost a gallon of water in an hour without producing any urine at all—in a 160-degree sauna, the liquid just seemed to disappear into my body and out my pores. But that had been under laboratory conditions; now I had to drink even more because only by peeing could I know I was really getting enough.

To pee was to be in the Badwater matrix, part of the landscape: You're out there under a giant blazing sky, in the middle of a desert. There's about as much vegetation as there is on the moon, which is to say none at all, and there's no shade and no shelter unless you crawl into or under your support vehicle. A person is pretty quickly reduced in scale by those facts. You become an animal, just like Ulrich with his rickshaw—a creature of the road. You must drink and eat to keep going. And you must pee. And the difference between the fastidious and the crude boils down to a simple question: Do you go all the way off the road into the dirt to do your business, or do you do it right there on the highway? And if a car does happen by in midcycle, so to speak, do you turn away, or give a friendly little wave of hello and carry on with your work?

I couldn't quite embrace the wide-open public display of traffic-lane urination, as some runners were doing, and I was even modest enough for a while that I'd look back to see if a car was coming; if one was, I'd take a few more strides down the road. I was a moderate, I'd guess you'd say. I sure as heck wasn't going way off into the dirt just to pee. A few steps off the shoulder was plenty discreet enough.

An Inefficient Machine

My feet weren't right.

It took me a long time to actually say that—long after I knew the truth—because to admit it now, so early in the race, was just too much to face. Sore feet raised too many questions about the future and the miles ahead. So I tried denying it entirely and blocking it out. But as I passed the 12-mile point or so, the situation was becoming too glaring and obvious to ignore. What I felt wasn't pain, exactly, but rather a kind of vague and uncomfortable heat that seemed to fill my shoes until everything below my ankles seemed distorted and enlarged and exaggerated, as though some alien presence had crawled in there with me.

I hadn't felt anything like this in May when I'd done the first section of the course. Maybe it was the higher humidity. Maybe it was just the built-up atmospheric energy of July that was blasting up out of the pavement, despite the rain of the night before. My mind played over all the things that could explain and thus perhaps excuse what I felt. But

I still couldn't escape it. Almost from the first miles, when I should have just been floating along, blissfully free of all discomfort, I'd been very aware of the mechanics of my feet hitting the pavement. I was conscious of my toes and how they felt against the front of my shoes and I'd started to anticipate—and not entirely with excitement—how each footfall was going to feel. And I knew that was not a good sign.

I tried to keep up appearances. I took my salt tablets, or, as I thought of them, my Weber pills, every hour—or whenever we thought of it. And I tried to drink as much liquid as I possibly could suck down. Once when I came up to the van, Wayne dumped a whole bucket of ice water over my head that made me moan and shudder as though I were at the point of orgasm.

"Oh, my God," I said as the water poured down my neck.

"I haven't heard that for a while," Wayne said.

The next time I stopped, I told him the story of the spectrum, and my frustrations at being denied, at age five, the rainbow image of refracted sunlight through a water glass that he'd promised me. Wayne said he had no memory of that day at all, but I doused him with my own water bottle anyway and told him we were even.

I couldn't outrun the hard facts, however. Something was wrong.

The human body is not a terribly efficient machine in the heat. Of the energy that gets generated by a person running down a road, only about 25 to 35 percent actually results in forward motion. All the rest is the body's overall cellular excitement, a collective buzz of energy that raises the temperature in the tissues and has to be vented. That's one of the hardest, harshest truths about being on foot in Death Valley—your own body is your worst enemy.

A second source of heat comes from the ground. Badwater is run entirely on blacktop, which is surely one of the nastiest, most heat-absorbing surfaces ever invented. Temperatures as high as 212 degrees—the boiling point of water—have been documented on Death Valley's road surfaces. The third and most pervasive source of heat is, of course, the sun. The highest temperature ever officially measured in Death Valley, 134 degrees, was recorded in July 1913, *in the shade, of course,* by a thermometer five feet above the ground at the weather monitoring station in Furnace Creek. And Furnace Creek isn't considered the hottest part of the valley. Badwater, about 100 feet lower in elevation, is usually at least five degrees hotter, park rangers say. It's also several degrees hotter closer to the ground where your feet usually are.

Then there's wind. Wind, in the universe where most of us live, feels good. It cools you off. But not in Death Valley in the middle of the summer. Meteorologists say that when the air temperature rises above about 95 degrees Fahrenheit, the whole equation of airflow and heat absorption begins to shift. After that, wind increasingly *adds heat,* or at least compounds the difficulty of cooling down. By the time the temperature reaches a heat-index level of 122 degrees—typical conditions for the Badwater–Furnace Creek corridor in July—a wind gusting to 33 miles per hour, which is also not unusual for that time of year, can boost the apparent temperature by another 10 degrees, to 132 in the shade, if any were to be had.

By the time we hit 15 miles and the greensward of Furnace Creek was looming into view, I felt I could riff all day on heat and its various permutations. My head was filled with what I'd learned—too full, no doubt. But there'd been no other way for me. I was a runner of the mind, for better and for worse. I'd come to this place as much for the mental journey as the physical, and so it was perhaps only natural that I'd be haunted now by the sweaty scrim of my own education.

I was also consciously trying to distract myself. I was not a happy man by then. I was halfway to nauseous and I probably wasn't drinking enough because my pee-per-hour rate had dropped to almost nothing. Worst of all, I wasn't remotely having any fun. The general, vague awareness of foot mechanics that had marked my running an hour earlier had become actual, formal, undeniable discomfort that I could no longer rationalize as July heat or road radiation.

I'd tried running in the dirt on the side of the road, thinking that that might make a difference, then when I saw that it didn't I'd go back onto the shoulder. And it was getting hotter. Whenever I got to our van, Pat or Wayne or Travis would run out and spray me down with the misting bottles we'd brought. And every time I went by another vehicle waiting for a runner behind me, someone from that crew would almost always leap out and extend the same courtesy—a small gesture that was as soothing for its decency as the water itself was welcome. Now and then Wayne would drive slowly by with Pat's big stereo suspended out the van window, blasting me with the Melissa Etheridge song "Somebody Bring Me Some Water," a selection from my Badwater Tapes that had quickly become one of our anthems. I could usually lose myself for a few minutes in that crashing guitar chorus or, short of that, in the ridiculous sight of Wayne trying to drive while rocking out and holding a boom box all at the same time.

But like the cooling mist that would evaporate almost immediately, the fixes were temporary. I'd made a mistake somehow, somewhere. At 16 miles, I told Pat and Wayne to go on ahead into Furnace Creek and we'd meet there for a rest stop and some lunch. But by the time I got there myself,

I wasn't thinking about them. I wasn't thinking about anything but my feet. I chugged into the main entrance near the general store, sat down on a retaining wall and got my shoes off as fast as I could.

In my frustration and distraction, I hadn't even thought to ask where at Furnace Creek we'd find each other. Now the van was nowhere in sight. And so I sat there, feeling abandoned by my crew and angry because I was in pain so soon.

It had taken me four and a half hours to go the 17 miles to Furnace Creek, and I sat there thinking about that, too. I'd run 26-mile marathons in under four hours and not felt this bad. I'd run 42 miles in Death Valley over Memorial Day and not felt this bad. Was it really just the humidity? My shoes? My tape? I closed my eyes in the shade and started going through the bleak possibilities.

But I also found myself, in a strange way, enjoying the semi-celebrity status that came with being one among the Bunch of Crazies. Tourists walking around Furnace Creek who'd perhaps heard about the race were staring at me. Tourists who simply thought I was a freak in a white suit were staring as well, and I obliged them both equally. I closed my eyes on the wall and struck a pose of athletic languor. I was the warrior, out battling the elements—scarred and wounded in my repose.

By the time we all found each other, everyone was pretty thoroughly unhappy. Pat and Wayne had stayed on the road and had been waiting for me around the bend near the gas station, which was a perfectly reasonable thing for them to have done, I guess. And in my rush to get out of my shoes I'd ducked off the road, and now our initial awkwardness as a crew had become compounded by frustration. Everything was a tangle of missed signals and bad beginnings. I tried to eat a bite of the sandwich Pat had made and couldn't. I tried to apologize for the mix-up but it was halfhearted. I was angry at the world, and for better or worse, they *were* my world.

"My feet have swollen," I said. "I think it's time to try the larger shoes."

Pat fished through my stuffed suitcase full of running shoes and found the pair of brand-new size-12 New Balance 852s I'd brought along just for this contingency. They'd never been worn or broken in, of course—when and how could I break in shoes that were too big? And brand-new shoes are generally the last things you want on your feet in the middle of a race. But I felt that my choices were rapidly dwindling. Now that my feet *were* size 12s, I had to take what was available.

The change seemed to help for a while. I jogged out of Furnace Creek at about 3 P.M. feeling better—rejuvenated and more optimistic than I'd been for hours. The heat was getting worse—it had reached 120 degrees by then—but I was moving. Heading down Highway 190 past the road that leads down to the old borax mines, I even passed a few people who were walking, and that cheered me up briefly, too, in a shallow, petty kind of way. I told myself I was strong and tough and that I would hang on through this thing. But I knew even as I said it that that was also a sign of trouble. If I already needed a mantra to tell me I was okay, then it couldn't possibly be true.

I passed Chris Moon just about at that time, and his example kept me going as well. I'd seen Chris walk to the front of the room at the prerace meeting to pick up his packet of materials, and now, approaching from behind, I knew immediately who it had to be, even when he was just a distant figure ahead. He wasn't able to really run smoothly with his prosthesis the way that Dan Jensen could, perhaps because of how his injury had occurred from the land mine accident in 1995 that took his left arm and leg. Rather, it seemed that he propelled himself down the road through a kind of self-generated momentum. His whole body twisted in a corkscrew motion with each step as he swung his artificial leg around at a pace somewhere between a fast walk and a slow jog. The combination of twisting and lifting clearly demanded a prodigious expenditure of energy and a manifestation of strength and will that I couldn't begin to imagine in myself. My own paltry problems and discomforts were nothing, and as I passed him and we wished each other luck, I felt that I had no right to complain about anything again for as I long I lived.

That turned out to be a pathetically short-lived pledge. Within only a few miles of passing Chris, the pain in my feet reemerged worse than ever. My toes felt like they were on fire—squeezed from the sides and the top and the bottom all at once—and I finally faced the fact, about three or four miles past Furnace Creek, that I had to stop and see what the heck was going on. If I ignored the situation much longer and I had blisters that popped and bled, then I knew I'd really be sunk. Denise Jones had told me this at her foot clinic, so I knew it had to be true. Skin that goes beyond blistering to open and frayed laceration, she'd said, will only fully heal in open dry air. And ulcerated skin that remains trapped inside the steamy closed box of a shoe will only grow worse.

I thought of Bob Ankeney, the laid-back probation officer I'd met on the first morning of the clinic back in May, when we'd ridden together to the starting line in the back of Ben's old Dodge. Ankeney had been sprawled out on some boxes wearing a pair of busted-up old shoes and a scruffy shirt, and I'd been sitting there stiff and nervous next to him in my brand-new desert white Media Guy scrubs. And I heard his voice now in my head: "Death Valley doesn't allow mistakes. You make one mistake out here and it'll cost you, big time."

Ankeney's words echoed again and again as I made my way toward the van, walking by then and conscious of every burning step. *You make one mistake here and it'll cost you.* Well, Bob, I thought, wherever you are, welcome to my mistake.

So without ceremony or preface, I simply stopped. I told everybody my toes were hurting too badly to go on. Something wasn't working.

There's a certain level of guilt that comes from a surrender like this. I should be tougher. I should be smarter. I should be better able to endure. I should be more like Chris Moon. All the hard-edged old work ethic that I'd grown up with came bubbling back up through the ground as I walked the last few steps to the van. I'd failed. I wasn't worthy. I wasn't among the chosen.

Runners, I believe, are among the last great Calvinists. We all believe, on some level, that success or failure in a race—and thus in life—is a measure of our moral fiber. Part of that feeling is driven by the psychology of training, which says that success only comes from the hardest possible work output, and that failure is delivered unto those who didn't sweat that extra mile or that extra hour. The basic core of truth in that harsh equation is also one of the more appealing things about recreational racing: It really does equalize everyone out. A rich man's wallet only weighs him down when he's running, and a poor man can beat him. Hard work matters.

Now I'd fallen. And whatever this trouble was, I felt certain it was my own flaw or mistake that had brought it.

We didn't get out the folding chairs, being still optimistic that this would be no more than a quick pit stop. Rather, I just sat down on the step of the van, pulled off my shoes and socks and started unwrapping the toes that were giving me the most pain.

But then suddenly the whole world was swimming around me in a white, creamy light. It washed up like a tide as the pressure on my feet was released, surging into my head. I was underwater, unable to speak. If you're standing up and you get hit with something like this, you generally fall down. I swooned. My head felt like a balloon, tethered at the end of my neck, rolling around like it was floating in the breeze. I could hear Pat, right beside me, saying over and over, "Can you hear me? Kirk, can you hear me?" But I couldn't answer, and I couldn't feel anything—not her hands touching my face, not the cold towel that Wayne had draped over my head to try and cool me down and bring me back. I was too far under, submerged in the milk-white sea of semiconsciousness that swirled in front of me.

When my head finally cleared, I knew I was in real trouble. My feet weren't the only problem, and perhaps they weren't even the biggest problem. They'd distracted me and taken my focus off everything I'd known I was supposed to be doing. I hadn't been drinking enough, and I hadn't been able to eat anything for miles and miles. I was in a calorie deficit and probably dehydrated. Nearly passing out on the step of the van had revealed it all—I'd stumbled badly in only 20 miles. I'd screwed up.

I knew that I wouldn't be back on the road again anytime soon, if at all. I could see in the faces that still hovered in close how much I'd scared Wayne and Pat. They wouldn't let me go, I knew, until they were convinced I was mentally and physically stable again and wouldn't zone out and collapse somewhere on the highway out of their sight. Wayne pulled out a folding chair from the rubble and I sat down with a sigh. Pat began to unwrap the other toes.

The sight was about as bad as I'd feared. I had at least five blisters, some running the length of a whole toe. I looked up at the monochrome desert around us, and the sky that was beginning to darken from the west with the overcast glower of an approaching storm, just as it had yesterday afternoon, and felt suddenly and devastatingly depressed. It was over and this was the pitiful result. Death Valley had done this much to me in only 20 miles. I was wounded and floundering and I hadn't even made a whole marathon. Everything seemed to be in ruins.

Getting out of my shoes and socks and being freed from the pressure of my tape produced such a wave of relief, however, that I felt my other senses waking up, and I realized that I did have an appetite despite what I'd felt out on the road. Wayne suggested tomato juice and boiled potatoes, heavily coated with salt, and at that moment, such a meal sounded just right.

Tomato juice. Of all the things to want to drink. As Wayne fetched a can from one of the coolers, he started talking about how much he loved the stuff.

"I drink it hot, sometimes," he said. "Just heat it up in a mug, like coffee. It's wonderful."

I thought of Mick Justin the ultramarathoning accountant and his tomato juice advice. I'm drinking juice, Mick, wherever you are! As if it will do me any good now! I dumped salt bitterly on the potato Wayne handed me and thought of Scott Weber, so long ago back at the start, and Ulrich, who was no doubt charging across the desert at this very moment, unstoppable as always. I wanted to shout out into the wastes around us: I'm eating salt, Scott! I'm being good, see?

Salt. I stared at it intensely there on my cold potato, as though I could draw some meaning or solace from it. Salt has weird consequences for the body when it becomes out of balance. Too much and you retain water. Too little—by far a greater concern on a day like this—and the stomach doesn't empty of the liquids you drink. You start "sloshing," as it's called, and that can lead to nausea and worse. But all that I'd studied and learned seemed like a joke to me now. What good would salt do if I couldn't get back on my feet?

I watched, detached and distracted, as Pat began to work on my blisters. They weren't mine at all, it seemed. Those things way out there at the end of my legs were part of some other being, a foreign invader. The pain was distant and re-moved. I didn't care. I felt bad, for Pat, though. It was a ter-rible thing to have asked her to come all the way out here to this godforsaken place and do this. She had no experi-ence, and here she was with a pair of scissors trying to slice into my disgustingly enlarged toes to drain the liquid out. I pitied all of us—fools and phonies, duped and devastated losers. Who was I kidding?

I still didn't know, at that point, how I'd be able to keep going, or if I would at all. My only job, at that point, was to keep drinking and eating. But it was hard to maintain any remote shred of optimism. As we sat there, I watched all the people who'd been behind me—not that many, admit-tedly—go by out on the road.

They glanced over as they passed, probably with the in-evitable mix of horror and curiosity that makes us all slow down in passing a car wreck. There but for the grace of God go I, you think, and you keep going. They looked and they nodded and waved to me and then they were gone.

I gradually concluded that I was probably a victim of my own overzealousness. I'd been the good little student of Badwater who'd crammed for the exam, but hadn't done the lab work. I'd embraced the idea, as an intellectual concept, of taping my feet before the race. I'd even done it a few times, in shorter runs under less harsh conditions, and it had seemed to work well enough, and so in my prerace anxiety in Death Valley, I'd overtaped. That's what I decided as I sat there in my beach chair pondering the bleak hole into which I'd fallen. If a little tape had worked before, I'd figured, then by God a lot more would keep me blister-free when it really counted. My mummified toes had been squeezed with nowhere to go as my feet had swollen in the higher-than-expected humidity. I'd brought this on myself. I was still the fat boy who couldn't climb the tree. Every dark thought I could imagine was suddenly real and hanging over my head.

By the time Pat finished draining and squeezing and poking, and applying the special gel-pack burn dressings I'd brought, and had retaped my toes again, we'd probably been off the course for an hour and a half, and the central nagging question hadn't even been asked. What now? I was surely in last place, though I didn't care about that. What mattered was that I wasn't moving, and I had 115 miles to go. Could I even go five more? Ten? My feet felt better with the pressure reduced, and my head was clear now, but I'd yet to even try standing up, let alone running. The thought of trying to get back into my regular shoes—or even my size 12s—filled me with horror. I was repaired but still doomed. Badwater had done me and served me up quick, too. I'd been right to ask myself what business I had out here. I was a doddering fool.

The Mysterious Elixir

*T*oeless shoes. *Toeless shoes.*

One of the little pieces of Badwater intelligence I'd gleaned in my research was that some runners bring an old pair of running shoes with the toes cut out to wear on the steepest downhill sections of the course, where the grade reaches 9 percent or more for miles on end. With no toe box, they'd said, your toes wouldn't get jammed up into the front of the shoe from the force of your foot sliding down and forward as you ran. It was a blister-prevention trick, essentially.

So being the good little listener, I'd cut up a pair of my oldest, most beloved high-mileage shoes on the drive out from Salt Lake with Pat. Then it had been almost a joke, and a kind of homage to worn-out soldiers that had served me long and well. I felt like I was giving them an afterlife, a second chance at service. Even more important, it passed the time as I was sitting there on the passenger side with nothing to do while Pat took a shift behind the wheel.

But it occurred to me now, sitting there on my folding chair pondering the vast distance that still lay ahead on the Badwater course, that it might work the other way around. I'd already blistered, so maybe having no toe-box would take the pressure off and allow my feet to begin healing. I didn't imagine that cut-up shoes would provide a permanent solution, but it might get me going again, and that was all I could really hope for.

It was a moment that demanded improvisation. I was feeling physically much better, and in my head, where it really mattered, I wasn't ready to give up. I just had to find the physical mechanism—the one trick from the kit bag of things I'd assembled—that would ease me back out onto the road. I carefully pulled on a pair of clean socks while Wayne pawed through the suitcase full of shoes.

Partly, I was just trying to cut my losses. Every mile I could go on from this point would lessen the failure I'd have to swallow when The Line—the real, true end of the road—finally came. I didn't see the possibility of finishing at that point. There were just too many miles to go on feet already so brutalized. Wayne finally found the pair and handed them to me, and with nothing to lose—but with fear in every breath, nonetheless—I eased my feet into them and laced up.

They were ridiculous-looking, like half sandals with white socks protruding from the front. But because there was no toe-box, there was no pressure, either. I stood up.

"It doesn't hurt," I said, my mood brightening with every breath. "It doesn't hurt! I think this might work." I began to strut around on the shoulder of the road like a colt that had just learned to walk. I tried running a few paces back and forth. The shoes were a little floppy up front, where there was no longer any support, but I could now move without pain.

I strapped on my water-bottle belt and eyed the road. It was almost dusk by then and the dark cloud cover had moved across the valley, just as it had the night before at this same hour. Toward Stovepipe Wells, 20 miles away, the sky looked particularly forbidding. Occasional tiny sparks of lightning flickered from inside the heavy black air mass that hunched over the flat desert horizon. The wind, blowing from the west, was filled with dust and the smell of distant rain and a subtle taste of sage from the higher slopes somewhere up ahead.

I felt like I was starting the race all over, or starting another race altogether. Everything was different: I would move forward now into a gathering darkness on injured feet in altered shoes. I wasn't the same person who'd stood at the starting line and hugged his sister. Back then, my mixture of fears and exhilaration had defined me. Now I was back to earth. I was mortal, for better and for worse. The vague fantasies I'd harbored about doing really well, perhaps somehow even buckling, had been shattered, but so had some of my darkest fears. I'd glimpsed the edge of disaster, and now, standing back up on my feet again, refueled with potatoes and tomatoes—and even more crucially, relieved of pain— I felt good in a quiet and reasonable way that hadn't been possible before. Blowing out my feet at 20 miles, I saw, had been like a near-death experience, and I was feeling the survivor's high roll through me. Each mile I achieved from this point would be a bonus and a victory to be savored. My expectations were gone—they'd wandered off somewhere into the desert wastes—but I was still here.

Pat and Wayne remained worried about me, though. I'd seen it in their eyes after my little swooning spell and I saw it again now as I stood there by the van, feeling breathless and anxious like a kid on the high dive, checking and rechecking my shoelaces and my bottles. And maybe I was sending a message, too: I felt hesitant, afraid to take the first step that would mark my reentry into the race. Finally, Pat said she was going out with me.

She'd run with me a little bit earlier in the day, but I'd discouraged her from doing too much. I wanted her to be strong and rested, I said. I'd need her full energy and concentration tomorrow and the next day, when it would really count. But the idea of her joining me now seemed sweet and perfect and exactly right. In the transformed, postblister nature of the universe, all the old bets were off, anyway. I was ready for company, and maybe a little apprehensive about being alone, too. In any case, I no longer saw the point in asking her to conserve her energies. We'd get where we would get, and tomorrow would take care of itself—that was my new philosophy.

So we ventured out together, side by side, jogging very tentatively and lightly as I tried to gauge how hard I could push my feet and how much I could possibly allow myself to hope. And we were very alone. During the hours of my crash, the race had moved on. I was back on the course, but there wasn't a soul in sight in any direction as far as the eye could see.

Wounds are complicated in the way they can straddle the boundaries of mind and body and identity. As the van pulled away and Pat and I jogged toward the distant storm, I thought of the day a few months before Badwater when I'd fallen down on a morning run and bruised my ribs on a rock. It hadn't stopped me. But for several weeks after that, I'd run with a little ache in my chest, a deep-muscle pain near my right nipple that I'd usually become most aware of somewhere near the point of maximum exertion in my run, toward the final miles when my breathing was deepest.

The strange part of it was that I gradually came to *like* my little rib wound, or more accurately, the associations I could build around it, and the meaning that it held. It was a touchstone, a place I could focus on, where the physical regimen I was putting myself through could find its focal point. It was a chevron of achievement. I'd fallen in battle, or so I could imagine (when, in reality, I'd fallen because I'm a clumsy oaf and wasn't picking up my feet). And a little bruise was also not something that would stop me from running entirely, like a sore knee or a bad ankle. To the contrary, I felt it to be a kind of enhancement of the experience, as though preparing for Badwater had been given a greater gravity and earthly reality.

In his book *Iron John*, Robert Bly talks about wounds. He retells an ancient coming-of-age story in which a young boy is injured as he makes his way toward manhood. In the preliterate society in which the story arose, the boy's wound was seen in much the same way as I'd viewed my little rib injury—as a symbol of the long road through life, a marker that bestowed greater strength and endurance. Our wounds and the ways in which they heal are the wellsprings of our power, Bly says.

I only knew one thing. As Pat and I continued on together, I felt a toughness that I hadn't before—a hard, grown-up strength that was very different from the wild and immature excitement of the starting line. I would endure my wounded toes, and by doing so—wherever it took me down this road—I could claim a gift from what had happened. I wanted to sing into the desert afternoon: I've survived and I'm on my way. I've become a grateful runner at last.

Pat and I ran most of the next 20 miles to Stovepipe Wells together, at a pace and rhythm so steady that we often just waved and blew right on by the van as it sat waiting for us. Late afternoon turned to dusk, and evening into night, and ahead of us I began to see the taillights of other crew vehicles. I was back.

I should have known, or guessed, that Ben Jones would be there at the edge of Stovepipe, leaning against his old wooden wagon in the dark when I finally made it in, dragging up the rear of the race after 14 and a half hours through the bottom of Death Valley. He loomed up out of the darkness, lanky and languid, his arms across his chest, as I jogged into the parking lot at 12:30 A.M. Everything was closed up tight by then. We couldn't have bought ice or food or gas however badly we needed it. Everyone who worked and lived there had gone to bed, and everyone else in the race had already gone by.

I loved Ben at that moment. I loved his battered old "goodie wagon," as he called it, and the dusty old Dodge that pulled it. But mostly I loved the fact that he was there. I was in dead-last place. The glamour runners—Clifton, Banderas, Flores, Smith, the twins, Ulrich—were so far ahead by then that they might as well have been in a different time zone. And that meant two things: First, Ben had lots more interesting places he could have been at that moment, and second, he could only have been waiting for me. I was flattered and heartened and encouraged all at once, just by his presence. He had a room at Stovepipe, I knew, and he could have gone to bed, but he'd stayed up and stayed there to welcome even the caboose, trotting into the village lights alone, lagging behind the whole world.

He seemed to know all about my troubles, too, though I wasn't sure how he could have.

"Modified shoes, eh?" he said with a grin, not even glancing down.

I started to ask, but then I finally just shrugged and nodded.

"You're still all right," he said emphatically. "You've still got time."

When I'd first met Ben back in May, I saw him as a small-town doctor who'd found a purpose and meaning for his life in the odd doings of Badwater, and by the time I left, I'd even felt a little sorry for him that he needed to draw so much of his identity from this one thing. On his website, he's pictured trudging through the roiling sands as "Badwater Ben." Over Memorial Day, I'd seen him introduce himself as the "Mayor of Badwater" to a total stranger—a mystified tourist who'd wandered up to ask what the heck we were doing out there on the highway. Ben's utter devotion to the cause of Badwater had come to seem a little pathetic. Several times, I'd felt like telling him to get a life.

Now my perspective had changed. While it was still possible that this exotic little event on the outer fringe of American life was the centerpiece of Ben's universe, I no longer saw that as remotely pathetic at all. Ben was not a hanger-on who sucked life out of Badwater in order to clothe himself with its energies and mystique, but a father figure who breathed life into the race and by doing so gave it much of its aura of warmth and emotion. He really was the Mayor of Badwater. It wasn't an empty title at all.

Ben had no official role in the 1999 running. He wasn't crewing for his wife, Denise. He wasn't working for Hi-Tec in any formal way. In a race with no medical checks, he had no authority as a doctor except to offer advice and counsel. What he represented was hope and optimism and, to me at least, the crusading spirit of the plodder triumphant. He'd cruised by at least three times during the daylight hours, waving and hollering some encouragement, and now, just when I needed most to feel I was still in the race, he was there to tell me that it was all true, just as I'd imagined and hoped.

"I identify more with the middle of the pack and the stragglers," he told me at one point.

Ben Jones was what all the runners and crews had in common at Badwater; perhaps in the end, I sometimes thought, he was the only thing. When he pulled up and unfolded his tall frame from behind the wheel of his van, I always had to smile because for however long he was there, I belonged to something larger than myself. We were part of a community, however amorphous it seemed, and not just a guy and his brother and sister out struggling on some fool's errand.

Ben connected all the little white dots. In a race where as much as 50 miles or more could separate the lead racers from the stragglers like me, events that happened to one runner could seem almost incomprehensible to another, as though we were all on different planes of existence. Midnight for me meant Stovepipe Wells. Midnight for Eric Clifton, who was in first place and running a record-setting pace if he kept it up, Ben said, meant someplace so far away I couldn't imagine it. I would hit portions of the course in the dark that other people had crossed in daylight, and vice versa. The world was a tangle and Ben was about the only thing that held it together.

"Did you get caught in the storm?" he asked me.

I probably looked as blank as the tourists did when Ben would talk about being the mayor of a nonexistent town.

"It was a nice one," he added with his standard dollop of understatement.

Almost everyone, it turned out, had been hit by the storm that Pat and I had only seen in the distance as we'd gone back on the road. We'd been inside one reality, and

now, through Ben's eyes, I saw a completely different one.
The wind and sand had hit first, then the rain. The twins
had been seen dancing by the roadside, faces extended up
into the heavens as a brief, drenching shower blew across.
Other runners had huddled in their vehicles, waiting to re-
group. It sounded just like the little cloudburst fantasy I'd
had—and I'd missed the whole thing.

Three runners had also dropped out, Ben said, including
Curt Maples, the marine who'd been so full of fight that
morning. Maples had become so dehydrated heading
toward Stovepipe that his stomach had stopped processing
liquids. He hadn't been able to keep anything down and
had been forced to take fluids intravenously; under the race
rules, that forced his withdrawal. The others had quit with
foot or stomach troubles, though Ben didn't know much
more than that.

Ben's news from the front made me realize how isolated
and alone our little team was now at the tail end of the race,
but it also made me see how alone we all were. The Badwater community, I concluded then and there, was a lie, or at
best a gossamer wisp of truth. I thought of the Boogie, and
the invisible runners who'd floated by in the night, and the
spirits of endurance I'd seen on Massanutten Mountain,
padding through the dark woods with their bouncing flashlights. Those images seemed like pale reflections now. Just
as it did with every other measure of endurance, Badwater
and Death Valley took the runner's long-distance loneliness
to a new level of magnitude. Ben wasn't pitiful. The runners
were—all of us out there twisting and drifting in our soli-
tude, looking for connection in this least likely of places.
Ulrich, in his solo crossing, had exposed the truth.

In daylight, as I'd seen it in May and again before the
race, Stovepipe Wells was quirky and funky and splendid in

its isolation. Even if there isn't much there, the place is able to sustain the illusion of a certain bustling activity, if only from the cars driving through and the tourists squinting up at the big thermometer outside the general store to see just how hot it is.

Only now, under the blanket of darkness, did I really feel I understood what being in the middle of nowhere really meant. This was Johnny Quick's world.

Quick was a waiter at the Stovepipe Wells restaurant. I'd noticed him back in May on my first night in the valley as I'd sat there eating my salad and making up little fantasy stories about all the employees and the strange twists of fate that I imagined had delivered them to such a place as this. Quick, though, hadn't looked interesting enough even to make a story. He'd seemed utterly and profoundly unremarkable, a little man somewhere in his sixties, as colorless as the desert itself.

But then I'd overheard some people at a nearby table ask him how he'd come to be in Death Valley, and he'd said something about playing in a band. So when he got back to my table, I asked him myself.

"What kind of music did you play?" I said, expecting him to say something not terribly interesting.

"I played with Bill Haley," he said simply, with no flourish. "I was one of the Comets."

My jaw dropped, then froze open in midgape. Quick had to take another order then, leaving me to hold my astonishment until the next time he happened by. Our conversation continued on like that—in little packets whenever he had time to stop for a moment. He told me how he'd graduated from high school in Bayside, Queens, in the early 1950s, a footloose drummer who'd knocked around with some bands in New York but who in all probability was headed for a factory job. Then he'd heard that some guy named Haley was holding auditions down in Philadelphia for a new band. He took the train, he said, and got the gig. Soon after, the Comets went into the studio to record "Rock Around the Clock." Quick was nineteen years old, and he'd spent the next 30 years, he told me, traveling the world with the Comets until Haley's death in the 1980s.

Here, in the middle of Death Valley, serving plates of pasta and prime rib to tourists, was a guy who'd laid down the rhythm for the first rock-and-roll record ever to hit number one. I realized with a jolt how paltry and shallow my imagination had been in inventing the lives of Death Valley's residents. The world really was stranger than I could imagine.

Quick disappeared for a long time after that, taking orders and bringing out salads. When he came back, I was ready to ask him the question that screamed for an answer, the one I'd been leading up to from the very beginning. How did Bill Haley's drummer end up as a waiter in Death Valley?

Quick shrugged. A car accident in Texas killed his wife and children, he said quietly. His own arm was injured so badly that his drumming career was over, too. "I needed to get out of Texas," he said.

So he'd drifted around for a while and eventually came through Death Valley and found he liked it well enough. He'd been here for five years that spring, living in a dormitory out behind the restaurant with all the other motel and restaurant employees, working a split shift serving breakfast and dinner.

"They needed a waiter and I needed a job," he said without a trace of self-pity. "So I stayed."

Only later did I learn that no one by the name of Johnny Quick had ever played with Bill Haley, and that the drummer on "Rock Around the Clock" was a guy named Billy

Gussak who died in the mid-1990s, and that my waiter was in fact a prime topic of discussion in the small circle of Bill Haley–freaks who are constantly being compelled to deconstruct the rock-and-roll fantasy that spins out of the Stovepipe Wells dining room. Quick was the hero of his own Breyfogle story, wandering amidst his glittering illusions, or perhaps just having a good time at the expense of the gullible tourist crowd he could milk for tips.

Back in May I'd felt sorry for Quick that he was ending his days out here, so alone, in a place so dry and hard. I'd felt sorry, too, for the woman at the gift shop where I'd gone to buy hats and T-shirts for my kids. She was somewhere in her forties, married to a park ranger who'd been assigned to Death Valley, and she told me she wasn't sure how long she'd be able to take it.

"I sometimes dream at night about the smell of fresh-cut grass," she'd told me as I waited for my credit card approval to go through.

Now, in the silence and darkness of Stovepipe at night, I no longer pitied anybody. The woman at the gift shop and Ben—and even Quick, too, for that matter—were all out here living their lives as best they could. They were survivors and therefore deserved respect. Like Dan Jensen and Ulrich and Lisa Smith and my unnamed last-place heroine at Massanutten, they had the mysterious elixir of endurance. They were soldiering on and gutting it out. That's why we were all here.

And I was still here, too. That's all I could say about where I was in the race and in life at that moment, but it was enough. I was in the middle of Death Valley, in the middle of the night. I was in last place, already blistered so badly I couldn't wear regular shoes, and I was facing 93 more miles before a finish line that I could barely imagine. The next 17 miles through the night would be steeply uphill, from near sea level to the 5,000-foot summit of Towne Pass. We'd lost so much time that the 60-hour cutoff clock had begun ticking loudly in my head.

It was time to celebrate.

We were all starving, too. So Pat pulled out the folding chairs and Wayne set up his little propane stove. I dragged over a chaise lounge that was already in the parking lot, probably having been used by some other runner earlier in the evening. The lights glared down from the wall of the swimming pool shelter, near where we'd parked, casting everything into stark contrast, and the pool generator hummed and thrummed, but otherwise we felt like we were pretty much alone on the planet. Travis went off to look for ice.

I also drank another can of tomato juice, which I now strongly associated with every positive, magical thing that had happened since my crash near Furnace Creek. I'd eaten a potato back then, therefore potatoes were magic, too. Case closed. The truth was I didn't really know the formula of how we'd been able to get up and going again. We just had, that's all. And even if tomato juice and potatoes were not fully responsible, they'd surely played a part. And because Wayne had pushed tomato juice, he'd become embedded within the magic as well.

I'd said I was craving hot soup, but as Wayne began pawing through the food box, all he kept turning up were little cartons of instant mashed potatoes. I couldn't remember, at that moment, who might have suggested that I bring instant mashed potatoes to Death Valley. Perhaps it was something I'd thought up myself, like chopped-up energy bars in a freezer bag. In any case, I'd brought enough to feed all of us, over and over—all the mashed potatoes we'd care to eat, if we'd been so inclined. Wayne was totally grossed out.

"Jeez, who'd want to eat that?" he said, peering at one of the little containers, with its picture of a hearty, steaming white bowlful.

Something about all this—partly the idea of instant mashed potatoes in the middle of the night in Death Valley, partly Wayne's outraged disgust at the very notion of it—was immediately the funniest thing we'd ever heard. We all started laughing hysterically. Hot mashed potatoes! How ridiculous!

"It sounded good when I bought them," I said finally, wiping the tears from my eyes.

I felt a wave of bliss descending on all of us about the time the boiling water was ready. Everybody grabbed a chair. The night was silent but for the humming of the pool compressors and the low buzz of the lights. Wayne poured a cup of noodle-vegetable something or other and brought it over.

In the hard, cold light of the real world, the soup before me was probably not that good—a salty mix of overcooked noodles and reconstituted carrots in a polyfoam cup—but I felt when I brought it to my lips as though I were in the presence of the gods. Everything suddenly seemed right.

"This is about the best thing I've ever tasted in my whole life," I said.

It wasn't really the soup that had affected me so profoundly, of course, any more than hot mashed potatoes, in the real world, are particularly funny. I looked around our little sprawled camp—Wayne in a chair over by the stove, Pat near the van, the van itself, the way the lights from the pool building cast everything into extremes of brightness and shadow, my goofball toeless shoes resting by the side of my chair. I wanted to embrace it all, to swallow it, to seal it inside me forever—the light, the night, the food and especially Pat and Wayne, who'd gotten me this far.

"This is great," I said, though they probably thought I was still babbling on about my food.

But it was more than that, too. As we talked quietly there in the parking lot, I realized that without our even noticing it, we'd become a real team at last. The frustration and anger that had smoldered and divided us earlier, when things had started to go so badly around Furnace Creek, had evaporated and blown away. We'd been brought tighter by trouble, forged by our difficulties. We'd improvised and bounced back, and maybe we were better than we thought.

The 20-odd miles that I'd gone in my open-toed state had been strong and, for me, pretty fast. From out of despair had come hope. I was alone at the back now—that had been the price I'd paid. But I was also not alone in the way I'd been in those miles before my crash. We'd weathered a crisis, found a way through it together and now we'd reached our first major milestone.

I'd even begun to think that maybe in an odd way it was *better* that we were in last place, because back here, there weren't any other runners and crews around to compare ourselves to. Our effort was different and we were different, and now we could just be what we were. We weren't the Dream Chasers and we weren't the marines and now there wasn't much chance that we'd be reminded of it.

Sitting there in the parking lot in the flush of a warm meal and a few minutes of rest, I even began to get a faint feeling for the first time—in a flickering semi-cognizant way that I resisted putting into words—of actual confidence. The 42 miles from Badwater to Stovepipe we'd just completed had always been the section of the course that frightened me most, because of the heat. But we'd survived that, and now the 40-mile climb up and over the Panamint Mountains that would begin at this point would play to whatever small strengths I possessed. The months of leg presses and squats at the gym—three sets at 250 pounds every other day, week in and week out—had given my legs power, if not speed—enough, anyway, I believed, to carry me up those mountains. And going uphill would also push all my weight back toward my heels and away from the blistered areas.

If I could go 40 more miles, that would take me past 80. And if I could go that far, well, hell, I figured, I could just about see the end from there. What's 55 more miles when you've already done 80? It wasn't particularly logical to have any kind of elevated hopes at that point. But it felt good to be *able* to have them—to be in a good enough mood to have them, really—and so I sat there in my pool chair and let the fantasy ride.

At the back of my mind, however, was the inescapable conclusion, no matter what Ben had said, that the 60-hour race clock was now a real issue. It had taken me so much longer than I'd planned to make the first 42 miles that all our old thoughts about scheduling and possibly even stopping to sleep somewhere had been trashed. Even if my dream played out and I could keep going another 90-plus miles in silly shoes, and no other calamities descended on us, getting to Whitney by the cutoff would be a very tight squeeze. As terrific as I felt, I had to acknowledge that we'd been shoved right up to the margin.

Our delay had pushed the question of ice, too. It was too late to buy any in Stovepipe, where the only store closes with iron finality at 10 P.M. And the next closest place was 90 miles away, in Lone Pine. Without ice, we could be in bad trouble, and the six big chests-worth we'd packed that morning had entirely melted down to water in just one day's sweltering heat.

Ice wasn't just a fussy luxury, either. Ben had warned me

back in May that access to ice had proven to be a direct
corollary to his Death Valley Rule of Three. If you ran out,
he said, it compounded the difficulty of staying hydrated
because the body doesn't absorb warm liquids as readily as
it does cooled ones. The bladder begins to shut down.
Drinking hot water in very hot weather can also be a nau-
seating experience for the stomach itself, and if that happens, then two of your three systems are in stress and you're
probably going to crash.

We'd just begun to talk about the idea of leaving Pat and
me on the road with backpacks full of water while Wayne
and Travis dashed off at some point tomorrow into Lone
Pine for a breakneck run to refill the coolers when I looked
up from my chair and saw Travis walking across the parking
lot with three big garbage bags full of ice he'd discovered in
the motel's ice machines. He'd been discreet, he said with
a grin.

So we made preparations to embark. Wayne put away the
stove, Pat started stowing chairs and I went to the motel
bathroom, where I intended to brush my teeth, wash my
face and give myself the luxury of a shave. Every inch of my
body was encrusted with sweat and sunscreen and dust. I'd
smeared Vaseline into every possible crevice and point of
friction, from my nipples to my thighs and ankles. A clean
face, at least, would symbolize the fresh start I felt we were
making in moving on from here. But as I stood there, lath-
ered up and looking at myself in the mirror with my number 18 bib on, I froze, the razor suspended in my hand. Who
was this person? How had I come to be here in a public rest-
room in Death Valley in the middle of the night? I really felt
for a few seconds that I wasn't sure who was looking back
at me. What had I become? How could I possibly be in
such an exotically remote place as this, 42 miles into a
135-mile road race? It all seemed impossible and unthink-

able. I wasn't a person who would do this and never had been. What had happened to me?

I rushed the shaving and ran out the door. The road beckoned, and it didn't pose tricky questions about identity and reality. The soup had been real. The road was real. Tomato juice was real. Mirrors, though, were frightening and philosophically troubling, and I decided to avoid them for the duration of the journey.

Back at the van I needed to hug my sister. We'd come full circle since the morning, when Pat had hugged me there at the starting line. Now it was my turn to be proud. I wanted to say something about how much it meant getting to this point, and how moved I'd been to sit there in the parking lot with her and Wayne for that half-hour soup break and how grateful I was to both of them.

I didn't say any of what I was thinking, though. I was afraid of jinxing things somehow. There was plenty of time left for our team to unravel and plenty of road ahead on which the sibling bonds, however strong they seemed now, could be stretched to the breaking point. So I just told Pat I loved her.

"Thanks for everything back there," I whispered in her ear. I meant all of it—the blister repair, running with me, caring so much. "I wouldn't have made it here without you."

"Yes, you would," she said.

She squeezed me back a long time under the Stovepipe parking lights, and we both cried a little. To me there was a whole book in that hug. It said everything about us: our fears, our pride in what we'd done, our hopes. Neither of us wanted it to end. It summed up where we were, and who we were.

I took one last glance around as I jogged away, trying to press the memory of Stovepipe Wells–at–midnight into my mind the way I had the flower I'd picked for Fran back in

May. If we'd written a book back there in the parking lot, I now imagined building a shelf in my memory where that book would rest, and where I'd be able to retrieve it and read from it whenever I wanted for the rest of my life. Pat and Wayne and Travis were throwing things more or less randomly into the back of the van as I turned toward the road, and I loved that, too.

On summer days, car manufacturers from all over the world use Towne Pass as a place to test the cooling capacities of their vehicles. If a car is ever going to overheat, they figure, it'll happen here on this relentless upgrade through the desert. Signs warn drivers to turn off their air conditioners as the ascent approaches, "to avoid overheating," which surely must rank as one of the great oxymorons of the American highway system when the temperature is pushing 130 degrees: Bake yourself, the signs seem to suggest, so as not to get too hot. Radiator-water tanks are positioned every few miles. Elevation signs proclaiming each 1,000 feet of climb are prominently displayed.

The view is also spectacular as you begin to rise above the desert floor on a typically brilliant summer day. Each step reveals yet another vista of the white salt pan and the sand dunes near Stovepipe and the Funeral Range on the far eastern side of the valley and the roughshod Panamints ahead. It truly feels like you're climbing up from the bottom of the world.

I climbed in darkness. The landmarks that I'd noticed in driving up and over the mountain pass, and in hiking much of this section of the course over Memorial Day, were all gone. There was no moon and, after a few minutes, no artificial light, either—only the paltry glow of Stovepipe Wells, and that faded quickly. When I stopped and looked back,

the little settlement looked ghostly and unreal, like phosphorescent rocks hidden in the bottom of the sea.

I'd never been on foot in the middle of Death Valley at
1 A.M. I'd never been in any desert in the middle of the
night trying to cross it. Aside from camping vacations
when I was a kid, and some trips to the grottos of eastern
Nevada with my high school spelunking club, and my
jaunts into the southern Utah canyonlands in college
when the main priority had been inebriation, I didn't really
know the desert at night at all. To me, desert was defined
by daylight—it meant blazing sun and shimmering heat
waves and no shade. But all that was gone now, all irrelevant. Everything around me seemed to have been given
new form and meaning. The temperature had fallen as
well. Although the average overnight low at Furnace
Creek in July is just a few degrees below 90, it was cooler
than that already on these higher slopes—probably not
much above 80—and I'd switched to shorts and a mesh
shirt to better feel the breezes that were blowing down from
the mountain pass ahead.

It struck me as I walked the grindingly steady upward
slope that my blister crisis had been a godsend. As I felt the
power of my body, the push of my stride in the darkness and
the touch of the night breezes on my skin, everything
seemed new. The world was surprising and filled with eye-
opening wonder, and the simple act of moving through it
had become a source of joy. Above me, the sky was enfolded
from horizon to horizon with stars, more than I'd ever seen.
Meteors were as regular as metronomes, as regular as my
footfalls on the road, and the Milky Way, cutting a swath
across everything, was a road, too. The heavens above mir-
rored my little world below. I would follow the Milky Way,
or Highway 190, it didn't matter. All that counted was that
I was moving. That glorious phrase resounded in my ears. I

hadn't been stopped. I would go on. There was power in the night, and I had it in me and around me.

Perhaps I would have felt physically better and more whole without my blisters, but I also wouldn't have known, I think, the rapture of that night and the profound sense of rebirth that it represented. Towne Pass would have been a section of race and no more. I would probably have been looking ahead, thinking of what was to come. What had been taken away in my early physical failure, I felt, had been more than given back in my ability to appreciate going forward at all.

I felt like singing. I felt like shouting, really, but singing would do. So at the next van stop I pulled out a Badwater Tape and my cassette player and headset, hooked it up onto my water-bottle belt and punched the play button.

I was not prepared for the result. Powerful loud music in my head, under such a canopy of stars, surrounded otherwise by complete and total darkness, was a mixture of sensory deprivation and overload at the same time. The music was rendered more powerful by the night, the night more powerful by the music. When the chorus of "The Jean Genie" by David Bowie pounded into my head with its unrelenting, overwhelming bass line, I felt like the sky itself was shouting the music down at me and that the stars were pulsating with the beat. The night throbbed with the rhythm, and I had to move with it. When Steve Earle came on next with the hard East Texas oil-country rhythm of a song called "Telephone Road," I had to sing along as loudly as I could because that's what the night demanded.

The next time I stopped at the van, Wayne said they could hear me in the desert silence for perhaps half a mile. And Pat was climbing out to join me, and whether it was to keep me company or shut me up by making me turn off my tape, I didn't care.

The night owned me either way. Pat was back and we were climbing and the sky was singing loud enough that I didn't need to.

Rosebud

The hazy afterglow of our glorious night up Towne Pass lingered as Pat and I made it to the summit, and like some sweet hangover, it persisted through the break we took at the top. I'd gone nearly 59 miles from the starting line. At some unnoticed point in the predawn darkness I'd passed the old threshold of the farthest I'd ever gone in any race—50 miles—and now every step was in its own way a new personal record.

I think we were all feeling a little heroic, somehow, or just plain lucky, which is often the same thing. The adventure that had seemed so ready to stall out into disaster 18 hours earlier had been salvaged. We'd turned things around. The hard road out of Furnace Creek had broken us down, made us pay a price for being there, and then we'd kept going and it had all gotten so much better. The misery I'd felt, the worry on Pat's face and the way I'd seen Wayne look—hot and tired and unhappy, a lot like the angry teenager I remembered—seemed like scenes from another life. And we were still laughing together. Instant mashed potatoes in Stovepipe Wells had turned a corner there, too.

The air was cool and bright and brilliant at 5,000 feet, and I sat with my feet up and watched Wayne stake out what I was quickly coming to think of as his role: the chef. He set up his little green Coleman stove and made coffee that smelled like heaven itself. Then he began pawing through one of the coolers, only to find that the dozen eggs he'd brought had all broken in their box—a scrambled reminder to me of our soggy brown energy bar disaster—so he improvised. Pat had boiled some eggs before we'd left Salt Lake, and he chopped those up with some breakfast sausages that he had and some cheese that I'd picked up in Las Vegas on the drive out, and stirred them together in a frying pan.

"All the major food groups," he said as he cooked.

I'd thought, in playing the imaginary movie of Badwater in my head in the months before the race, that I'd probably be bone-weary and exhausted by the second morning, nodding off in my chair at every rest stop, but I wasn't. Instead I felt gripped by something beyond my own weariness—a jet stream of energy that was pulling me along and keeping me aloft. My body was tired and stiff and sore when I rose from my chair, but I was awake on a level that went beyond the mere physiological need for sleep. I felt embedded within the experience of Badwater, energized by the accumulated wonder and adrenaline of being there and propelled by something more than willpower, as though I were a small cog in a giant machine that was rolling down the road and taking me with it.

"Better than soup," I said as I dived into the mounded paper-plateful of food that Wayne handed me. That was high praise. Better than soup was quickly becoming, in the jargon of our team, the hierarchical peak of superlatives, a means of defining perfection.

In a way, all the old standards of pleasure and discomfort and joy and anguish were breaking down by that second morning at Badwater. We'd gone nearly 59 miles, or so our little checkpoint list told us. But mileage, I was beginning to think, was no longer the key measure of anything. We'd all journeyed together to a place that couldn't be told in miles, and the road had started to impose its own language and terms.

Ordinary, simple experiences related to the basic function of living, which I'd taken entirely for granted in the real world, had attained huge significance out here, filled with complicated nuances and unseen intricacies. And things that were complicated before had become simple, or entirely irrelevant.

Consider, for example, *sitting down in a real chair.* Is there a level of bliss that could possibly be greater in this life? I'd been reduced in my needs and wants by then to the point that I truly couldn't think of what might be better or purer or sweeter. A place to sit. What more *do* you really need?

And then it did get better. *Coffee. Scrambled egg-and-cheese slop in a frying pan, prepared by my brother.* Life seemed to reach one shattering crescendo after another in a symphony of things that were becoming too intense for ordinary words. Better than soup was the only way I could think to describe it.

But when a couple of guys drove up as we were eating and handed us a telephone, I was completely and instantly bewildered. Out of nowhere, like a scene from some absurd comedy or a Bugs Bunny cartoon, they'd walked over to us in our chairs in the middle of Death Valley—this least likely of places—handed us a telephone, jumped back in their car and driven away. What's more, they told us to use it, free of charge, as much as we wanted. They were planning an advertising promotion, they said. If their phones would work under these conditions, they'd work anywhere—that was to be their pitch. The technology was different, they said—not cellular, which was useless in Death Valley, but some kind of satellite connection.

I couldn't grasp what had happened. As much as I tried to comprehend the chain of events, and the motives of marketing that had produced a telephone there suddenly in our midst, I couldn't do it. My fatigue, like a creeping fog, was beginning to cloud over my ability to think clearly, despite the collective energy and momentum that was keeping me awake and moving. I kept pestering Travis, who'd spoken to our mysterious benefactors.

"And they just gave it to us?" I said.

"Yep," he said, for about the third time.

"And they said use it as much as we want, free?"

"Use it as much as we want, free," he repeated patiently.

"Really?"

"Yep."

I blinked and tried to get this thought inside my head. A phone-from-nowhere just seemed so ridiculously unlikely that I couldn't quite convince myself of its reality. The mystery of the phone's delivery was also compounded by the fact that it looked funny and didn't work like a regular phone. You had to keep the antenna, a bulky black thing as big as the handset itself, pointed directly up toward its satellite mother. Any deviation from the purely vertical, caused by bending over, looking down, holding the phone wrong, blinking too much—who knew?—and the satellite link would phase out with a little buzz and you'd once more be all alone in Death Valley.

So I called Fran on the hard-to-believe phone. I was standing on top of a mountain and she was just getting up, ready for work. I could see our bedroom, in my mind, another universe away.

"Fifty-nine miles," I said. She whooped and hollered and said how great that was. And then I told her about the magnificent night and the equally magnificent breakfast at the summit, the brilliant morning and the blisters and the toeless shoes. I omitted some things, like nearly passing out by the side of the road, partly for her sake but also because I was simply feeling too exhilarated to dwell on what already seemed like ancient history. I was rattling on by then like a runaway train through the station in my overcaffeinated euphoria. I told her about the astonishing joy of chairs and of eating . . . and then I must have turned my head the wrong way because there was noise like an overzealous bug zapper in my ear and the connection was gone. When I tried to redial, I got a recording telling me to try back in 15 minutes. I handed the phone back to Travis.

"Too complicated," I said.

I was entering the strange frontier of sleep deprivation by then—an element of Badwater I'd known would come but for which there'd been no real way to prepare. I hadn't slept at all in the night that had just passed, and the night before that had been the eve of the race, which meant I'd had four or five hours of sleep, at best, in the last 48. I was beginning to feel, in fact, a bit like our strange new phone—reality and perception kept phasing in and out. Things would be fine and clear and understandable, and then a moment later they'd be murky and incomprehensible and I'd be filled with the wildest sort of swirling uncertainty. To cite just one perhaps indelicate example, I had to take a bowel movement that morning and by the time it was over I felt like I just about belonged in the psych ward.

My first thought had been to use our portable toilet. But then someone pointed out that we'd passed, just a mile or so back, what looked like a ranger station where there appeared to be some real bathrooms. And then I was told that our toilet, or as it said grandly on the box, our "portable commode," had never been used. I'd have to set it up and break it in, so to speak. Everyone else so far had made do with the roadside.

A real bathroom, I said. Sounds great. So then the problem was how to get there. I certainly wasn't about to run an extra two miles—one back down the road and another to return—just for the luxury of a toilet I could flush. And so that raised the issue, for the first time, of my orange flag. If you leave the course for any reason, the rules say, you must plant your flag by the roadside. If a race official happens by and finds you missing with no absentee marker, you're disqualified as a possible cheater. So I jammed my fluorescent orange number 18 flag in the ground next to Wayne and Pat and Travis, who'd set up their chairs in the dirt, and climbed in behind the wheel.

Something about my little trip triggered a wave of deep and overwhelming anxiety that began as I pulled out onto the road and grew in force until by the time I got halfway to the bathrooms, I was also halfway to a panic attack. My breathing became shallow and rapid and my heart seemed to be trying to claw its way out of my chest. I felt like I was cheating, even though I was going the wrong way on the course and I'd followed all the rules. I thought that if anyone in the race saw me out there, they'd *think* I was cheating, and that would be about as bad as cheating itself. It would confirm, in their eyes, all the terrible things that I knew they all thought about me already: I really was the Media Guy. I wasn't real.

One of the runners I'd passed during the night, Jack Denness, an immensely amiable sixty-four-year-old Englishman crewed by his equally sparkling wife, Mags, with whom he'd stop periodically to take tea, had parked near the bathrooms, and in my state of deep weirdness, I didn't even want them to see me. I rushed in and out, ducked quickly back into the van and began racing back to our flag-planted spot on the road, feeling intensely guilty—even though I'd done nothing wrong. And then it occurred to me that dashing in and out like a criminal was about the most guilty-looking behavior I could have come up with, so I fretted over that, too.

Cheating would be extraordinarily easy at Badwater, and I'd been asked about it more than a few times over the previous months when I'd described to people how everyone in the race was more or less on his or her own, with no aid stations or checkpoints or formal structure of any kind.

"Don't people ever hitch a ride for a few miles?" a thirteen-year-old neighbor had asked at one point, with a smarmy little look that said, nudge-nudge, come on, now, you can tell me the dirty truth.

I said I didn't think so, that I thought it probably hadn't ever happened even once because it just wasn't that kind of race. I tried to explain that there'd be no point to cheating at Badwater, because in the end, you'd only be cheating yourself. Nobody except a tiny handful of runners at the front ever even think about winning, I told him, so for the rest of the field, it's a personal test—no more and no less. If you cheat, you fail no matter what. As Ben had said, it's just you against the course. I thought of Ulrich and his purity, and the sign on Gary's garage door about honor.

My little lecture failed miserably because, of course, I had no proof of anything I said. I didn't definitively *know* that no one had ever cheated. I really had no idea. But I desperately wanted to believe it. Even when my journalist's cynicism had occasionally flared up about Badwater and the ultramarathon culture, I never relinquished this particular point of faith. Badwater might not, in the end, be any kind of life-changing experience, as people like Ben and Ulrich constantly said it was. It might be smoke and illusion. But I refused to even consider that anyone would ever cheat. That seemed impossible and unthinkable to me.

My thirteen-year-old inquistor, a sports nut who lives for the intensely competitive world of ice hockey, shrugged and looked at me funny and I thought I knew what he was thinking: What kind of a race is it if you're not at least trying to win? And if Badwater is so tough, what makes you so sure there wouldn't be people who'd cheat just so they could brag that they'd done it?

Now, heading back down the road from the ranger station bathrooms, the circles that my mind was turning felt like they could spin completely out of control. I began to think that maybe I *was* a cheater. Had I really run and walked 59 miles? Might I have ridden in the van part of the way and blocked it out of my memory somehow? I shook my head to try and clear it of whatever was taking away my ability to think straight. I knew, when I could summon the strength for clarity, that I'd done nothing wrong. I could remember every step, every section and every mile. We'd signed our little sheets at the designated landmarks. Thinking this way was craziness—pure paranoid lunacy—and the scariest thing about it was how quickly it had come over me and how hard it was to get rid of once it had taken hold.

"Everything is fine," I said aloud to myself, gritting my teeth and gripping the wheel so tightly that my forearms ached. I reached my flag and crew and leaped out of the van into the sanctuary of the road as though our vehicle were haunted or plague-infested. "Everything is fine," I said. "Relax. Just relax."

The far side of Towne Pass is the section of the race I associated with toeless shoes. Heading past the 5,000-foot summit, the road goes steeply downhill for about 13 miles,

213

with a grade as high as 9 percent. If you ran it too fast, I'd been warned, you could burn out your quadriceps, or your toes, or your knees. But it was also an opportunity to make up some time after all that walking up the other side to the summit. For a runner, the allure of running fast downhill is like cheesecake to a dieter—you want it, you need it, you can hear the siren song of all that seemingly effortless joy calling out to you. And like the dieter who succumbs to cheesecake, you know you'll pay a price if you surrender.

A 9 percent downgrade was also a level of magnitude beyond anything I'd ever trained on. It reminded me of the drop-dead slopes Anthony and Paul used to construct in their room for their Hot Wheels cars when they were little. They'd stack things up as high as they could—books, boxes, toy chests, mattresses, whatever they could find—until the launching point propelled the cars hurtling down near to vertical. If a guy's car stayed on the track, he won. Survival was the test, not speed.

Ben had told me back in May that the strategy he'd developed for the downhill portion of Towne Pass, over his three Badwater races as a participant, was to try and run the slope as though it were flat, and I'd puzzled over that comment ever since, trying to figure out what the heck he'd been talking about. How do you pretend something is flat? Was it some power of the mind, or a force of self-delusion? Or had Ben just been pulling my leg? Was the advice just another piece of his bone-dry humor and I hadn't realized the joke? If you could pretend downhill was flat, why couldn't you do the same for uphill? It had all sounded like mumbo-jumbo to me.

What I quickly understood as Pat and I started down at about 10 A.M. was that pretending a downhill surface is flat essentially means running like a stork—full of stiff angles and funky twists that defy gravity. I tried about five different variations on Ben's idea—blocking out of my mind entirely the possibility that we were simply now at the extended physical-comedy punch line of his joke, and that he'd drive by at any moment honking and laughing at our ridiculous efforts. I tried to run a big loopy exaggerated gait with slow but long strides. Then I tried a gait that was somewhere halfway between speed-walking and running. Then I tried short choppy steps with my legs always flexed so the impact of my feet hitting the pavement wouldn't smash my knees. We probably looked as though we were just learning how to run at all. But early on a Friday morning in mid-July, there weren't any people to judge us, either. We could have yelled or screamed or run like fools and no one would have known. We could have stripped down and run Towne Pass as naked as that man had through the night at Massanutten and no one would have been the wiser. The world was empty.

That's partly what made it such a shock when Curt Maples and his crew of marines pulled up beside us in their van. They arrived like lightning on a clear day, as though they'd come out of nowhere, out of the very folds of my imagination.

I'd thought a lot about Maples through the night and into that morning. He'd been so full of ferociousness at the start of the race—a living, shrieking bulldog incarnation of everything I'd ever imagined about the Marine Corps. Ben had also told me how hard Maples fought to stay in, and how he'd resisted the consensus decision of his crew that it was time to withdraw, even after he'd vomited up the lining of his stomach.

Now he bounded out and across the road, looking just as fit and fresh and full of pepper as he'd seemed 24 hours earlier, as though nothing had happened.

He shook my hand. He was going down the course, he

said, stopping with every runner and crew to wish them well. All the other marines had trooped out by then, shaking our hands, uttering tight-lipped phrases of encouragement, hitting people on the shoulders just a little too hard.

"How are you feeling?" I asked him. Maples looked ready to run 135 miles right there in front of me.

"Fine," he said with a dismissive little shake of his head and a crooked smile that seemed somewhere between wry amusement at his own misfortune and shrugging acceptance. "My stomach reached a point where it wasn't taking in any liquid. But that's the thing about this race—you never know, anything can happen."

He shook my hand again and looked me right in the eye. "You've got a lot of guts," he said. Then he bounded across the road and leaped back into his van. Our little team suddenly seemed so unmilitary in its bearing by comparison to the crisp, hard-eyed group that had just swept through in their tight khaki T-shirts. Lisa Smith's team might chase the dream; these guys had looked ready to storm it with a full frontal assault.

We all just stood there staring as they pulled away and headed on down the highway. Here was a guy with his competitive juices clearly still in full boil, so filled with pent-up energy that he looked ready to pop. He had every reason to be raging at the universe in his frustration, but instead he'd become a coach and cheerleader, an ambassador of goodwill and sportsmanship. Maples had been unquestionably sincere in wishing me well, and that was a powerful thing in itself. He could have disappeared and headed home, or halfheartedly waved some bitter-tinged encouragement in my direction on his way. That's what most people would have done.

He'd stayed. He wanted me to finish the race, no matter what had happened to him. He wanted me and every other runner to keep going because that was the spirit he respected. It was the fuel that flowed through his own veins.

I was still insecure enough, however, that his parting words had rattled me a little. What exactly did he mean, "You've got a lot of guts?" I wondered. Was there a bit more emphasis on *you* in that sentence than there should have been? As in, "Boy, oh, boy, you *really* must have a lot of guts to be out here."

I certainly didn't feel as though I had a lot of guts. I was slogging along at the back of the pack. I wasn't a disabled runner like Dan Jensen or Chris Moon. I wasn't recovering from cancer like Louise Cooper-Lovelace. Those were the people with the courage Maples and his marines should have been celebrating.

True, I suppose I could have given up when my feet had first blistered out. But continuing on from that point had never been a matter of bravery. I was stubborn and I'd improvised. I'd figured out a way to keep going—that was all. I'd been smart enough to try a different thing when all the others had failed me. None of that had made me any kind of hero, even in my own eyes. To the contrary, I felt I'd shrunk over the past 24 hours. Perhaps in part because my wounded feet were so exposed to the world in my "modified shoes," as Ben had described them, I'd become more aware than ever how vulnerable I was—just a little human being on a big road in a vast desert, dwarfed by everything around me and everything ahead.

But I did feel special for having shaken Major Maples's hand. And I felt stronger and braver, too, just like that. I would persevere. I was really in a race after all. I found myself wanting to keep going in order to justify the major's respect, if nothing else.

My encounter with Curt Maples got me thinking all over again about some of the questions I'd been struggling with ever since Gary's death. What is the relationship of endurance and courage, or endurance and character? Or is there any relationship at all? I still hadn't remotely solved the mystery of why some people go on and others don't, but I felt that morning as though I'd received another clue.

I thought again of Mensen Ernst, a Norwegian I'd read about who walked nearly 5,600 miles from Constantinople to Calcutta and back in 1836, across terrain that was sometimes little more than a footpath. And I thought about James Saunders, who'd set a record in 1882, covering 120 miles in less than 24 hours. And I thought of Pheidippides himself, the young Athenian soldier whose long-distance run in 490 B.C. to proclaim a Greek victory over the Persians at the Battle of Marathon has become the modern symbol of endurance.

And I thought of the Pedestrians. They're mostly forgotten now, but right after the Civil War, they swept through England and the United States—a hardcore group of runners who'd defined the spirit of high-Victorian macho and helped create the first modern endurance craze.

I'd spent a whole day back in March in the periodicals room at the New York Public Library trying to chase down the Pedestrian spirit, scrolling through old newspaper microfilm, combing for clues about why super-distance running would suddenly have flowered as a passion, then just as abruptly died.

As the microfilm machines fluttered and clicked, I'd found myself falling into the Victorian Age. It was New York City, late February 1882, and the World Championship of Pedestrianism, the celebrated Astley Belt, which I'd never heard of, was at stake. A six-day, "Go As You Please" race had been announced. The contestants would run around a sawdust track at Madison Square Garden day and night and the man who covered the most miles in six days, from Monday through Saturday—running on Sunday not being considered proper—would take home the prize.

Day by day as the race approached, the pages of the old newspapers scrolled by in stark black and white. There were profiles of the favored stars, and gossip about their training tricks and a lot of canny public-relations spin—probably aimed at affecting the betting odds—about who was in top shape and who appeared to have gone soft since the last big competition.

Finally, race day arrived, and through the week of breathless deadline accounts that followed—complete with daily charts about the leaders and the laps they'd completed—I tried to imagine the runners and crowds and the newspaper readers who'd hung on these long-ago words. What had they all been looking for? Why did endurance matter?

As my time-travel-in-an-afternoon wore on, however, I'd found myself growing more and more disillusioned with the Pedestrians. With each passing day, running for the Astley Belt began to look like just another blood sport of which Victorian audiences were inordinately fond. The premium—what a later generation would call the "money shot"—was the collapse and breakdown of the runners, and if it involved vomit and gross debilitation, all the better. A reporter for the *New York Herald* described with relish the twitching, gimping, limping, haggard and tortuous final days for readers who couldn't be there. How would they keep going? Who would crack? Who had, in the jaunty sportswriter's tone of the day, enough pluck to go the distance?

"He had as much the appearance of a skeleton wrapped up in tissue paper as anything else," the *Herald*'s man on the scene gushed, describing a runner named George Hazael. Hazael, the reporter went on, "was a dismal looking piece of humanity. His cheek bones protruded in a ghastly fashion and through the loose neck of his brown shirt his collar bones could be seen standing out like fenders."

Hazael was also eventually the winner. He ran 600 miles over the six days. The top five finishers all did more than 500 miles. New York sports fans even got to find out what Hazael ate for his victory breakfast the next morning: tripe and eggs.

I returned my microfilm rolls just as mystified about the Pedestrians and the nature of endurance as I'd been when I'd started. I wasn't sure, as I walked out into the thrum of 1990s New York, whether super-distance running had simply been a freak show that wore out its novelty, a nostalgic glimpse backward at the quickly fading old physical lifestyle of the farm or something else entirely.

And now, standing on the roadside in the Panamint Mountains in the middle of Badwater, feeling I'd been touched by greatness from shaking the hand of a man who hadn't finished even a third of the race, I was more confused than ever. I'd finally come to understand that every runner had to find his or her own unique formula of endurance, and now I saw that the same was true for the harder question of victory and defeat. Maples had won Badwater. He'd returned with honor.

Just around a corner from where the marines left us, Highway 190 goes abruptly flat, stretching out onto a dry white lake bed that separates the Panamint Mountains from the little resort of Panamint Springs. The lake bed is an arm of old dead Lake Manly, the same lake that created the phenomenon of Death Valley as it settled and dried and died.

"Piece of cake," Pat said, nodding across the expanse to the green dot we could just make out on the other side of the valley. Panamint, a tiny motel, restaurant and campground complex that was really a resort in name only—the springs of its name gave it water, but you couldn't buy ice or gas or groceries—marked the 70-mile point on the Badwater course and had thus loomed up as a major landmark for us. If we made it there by 2 P.M.—our target—we'd have gone a little more than half the distance to Whitney in 28 hours. That would leave 65 miles still to go—including the two steepest climbs—and 32 hours left on the clock in which to do it. Not a huge cushion, because many of those remaining miles would be more like hiking than running, but enough, we figured, for a reward. We'd budgeted a 30-minute rest break—or perhaps 45 minutes if we felt flush. Hi-Tec had also reserved a bungalow at Panamint for use by the runners as we came through, and that meant perhaps a real bed to lie down on.

Ultimately, the dancing vision of all those rewards got the better of me. I knew from my visit there in May that Panamint had a few actual trees, something we hadn't seen for more than 50 miles, ever since Furnace Creek. Trees create real shade—and I began to fantasize about the delicious luxury of that, and the notion of being halfway through the race, until gradually Panamint began taking on dimensions that were pretty far beyond humble reality. Getting there became a journey in itself; the piece-of-cake four miles, an eternity. Panamint Springs Resort became a shimmering city on a hill.

The heat was a big part of our trouble. The Manly lake bed was white and ghostly and completely devoid of life, and as we went down, the temperature surged up in a way that shocked me and took my breath away. The lake bed air, blasting into my face like a hair dryer at close range, was as hot as anything we'd experienced the day before—a debilitating, withering kind of heat that quickly reduced our fairly jaunty pace down the mountain to a slow jog, and then to a walk. I began to feel weak and hollow and fragile, and then, like the onset of my panic attack earlier that morning, the physical manifestations of my fatigue abruptly became mental. Just like that, I was lost.

I looked around and I realized that I didn't know how I'd gotten there. I knew I was in Death Valley in a race called Badwater and that I was trying to get to Panamint Springs. But everything else was a jumble, as though the heat waves shimmering off the pavement and out of the salt flats were disrupting some radio signal on which I depended for my navigation.

I thought back over the places we'd passed through— Badwater, Furnace Creek, Stovepipe Wells, Towne Pass— and found I could picture them all individually. I could vividly remember the sights, sounds, smells and sensations of each. But I couldn't connect the dots. I couldn't remember how we'd gotten from one place to another in any linear, logical kind of way. The line that extended from Furnace Creek to where I stood now seemed unfathomable. I knew that about 28 hours had elapsed since the race began, but the meaning of that number was unraveling around me, too. Was it really only yesterday that we'd started at the Badwater sign? It felt like a whole lifetime ago.

When I told Pat about my confusion, she just shrugged. "We'll rest at Panamint," she said, nodding her head the way you would at someone who'd just slobbered all over himself. But I suppose saying "we'll rest" is probably about as good a response as there is when someone tells you he's lost his short-term memory. It's not like you can go back and look for it on the road. You just have to hope it'll turn up somewhere.

In the midst of my haze, I suddenly thought of poor Patrick Hodge. If ever there was a victim of the desert's ability to trick the mind, he was it. And the lake bed that fluttered around me now in its iridescent incoherence was just like the one he'd seen.

Hodge was a young man with the grandiose dream of hiking lowest to highest within Death Valley National Park—Badwater to Telescope Peak, going off-road across the Playa itself and filming the whole thing with his video camera as he went. He'd apparently looked up from Badwater one day in the summer of 1991, determined by an eyeball assessment that the park's highest point was not all that far away (in truth it was more than 20 miles), and simply taken off without enough water or planning. The narrative he dictated as he marched is dense and creepy—especially when you know how it turned out—with quotes from Herman Melville about entering the "jaws of hell," and an organ-music sound track supplied by a cassette player that Hodge carried with him.

On the video, which floats around in Badwater circles almost clandestinely, like a snuff movie, Hodge comes off as a fool and dreamer, precisely the kind of Death Valley romantic that the locals hate so much. You see his feet sinking into the brown mud of the eternally drying salt bottom, sometimes up to the middle of his shins, and you hear his hard breathing from the exertion of lifting his legs back up and out as he went on. But I think that for Hodge, challenging Death Valley in this way *was* just like a movie, and he was the star. He used the camera to show us what he saw and felt. He panned down to the mud as he walked, then up to the horizon, then to 12 o'clock and the blazing sun that was baking him and killing him even as the film rolled.

Hodge only brought a couple of small bottles of water with him and he turned around when he realized he was in trouble. But it was too late. His body lay undiscovered for almost two weeks and was found, by coincidence, just as the Badwater race was getting underway. He'd made it back to within a few hundred yards of his vehicle before collapsing, and he'd left the camera on until the end, though the batteries had already failed. Ben Jones, who'd been running the race that year, was brought by the state police back to Badwater to conduct the autopsy.

I felt I understood Hodge a little more as I went across the Panamint lake bed. Images, memories and notions began tumbling into my head just like they had into his, tossed by the pell-mell flow of a half-baked mind. Thoughts tripped over the furniture, cursing their own dull, heavy-footed clumsiness. I felt I'd become a witness to my own peculiarity: a stranger to myself, walking as fast as I could across a desert and spraying myself over and over in the face with a misting bottle, thinking of a bed and air-conditioning, thinking of anything and nothing at all. I felt empty and full all at once, flat and round, short and tall, dimensionless and adrift. The effortlessness I'd felt only a few hours before was gone. There was just me now—not the image or the alter ego—bedraggled and dragging my tattered baggage behind me, suitcases spronged and hinges hanging.

I had no answers now to anything. I barely had questions. With Panamint beckoning me, images and thoughts were like startled pigeons, fluttering away with the next breath and the next stride and the next wave of heat from the valley floor. Everything was ghostly by then—Hodge, Gary, the Pedestrians. Nothing had enough material reality to hold my attention for longer than a few steps.

There were real people eating lunch underneath Panamint Springs' shaded restaurant awning when we finally walked in, and I became abruptly self-conscious in a way I hadn't been since the start of the race. These diners weren't Badwater people. They were from the real world— normal everyday tourists, minding their own business—and my appearance out of nowhere, out of the desert itself, had confronted them with something that was almost certainly beyond their comprehension. I realized with a jolt in seeing myself through their eyes that I'd become—certifiably and unavoidably—one of the "crazies." I was an obsessive, addictive, maniacal, masochist freak trying to run across Death Valley in July. I was the entertainment over lunch, someone to keep an eye on just in case I did something spectacularly nutty.

But then, just like that, I didn't care a whit what the Panamint tourists thought of me. Caring took too much energy. So I walked past them and slumped onto a full-length lawn chair that was sitting in the shade under a palm tree right in front of where they sat, as if the spot had been prepared specifically in anticipation of my arrival. I closed my eyes and felt I didn't want to move at all, ever again. I didn't want to twitch a muscle even to brush away a fly, because even that minimal motion would be a waste of precious time and energy. If we had 45 minutes, then I wanted complete and utter immobility. I wanted paralysis. I wanted to lie there until the clock required me to get up. Maybe there was a room and a bed somewhere, but I couldn't be bothered to find it because that would mean rising somehow from this lounge chair that called out to every fiber of my being. I loved that chair like Charles Foster Kane loved Rosebud, like Linus loved his blanket, like Elvis loved his mom. It was a pathetic, bottom-dragging kind of love, but it was all I had at the moment.

Perhaps, it occurred to me, my abject chair worship indicated the arrival of my Badwater alter ego, in all his stripped-down simplicity. I needed to be horizontal now—that and nothing more. Everything else I could think of in the world was a luxury that no longer mattered.

Travis came back a moment later to report that the runners' room was really right around the corner. "It's cool and nice," he said, with the tone of voice one uses to convince children and the mentally infirm. There was a real bed, he said. I roused myself and followed him.

Travis was right. Like soup, and like the night stars over Towne Pass, and like so many other tiny things that had attained titanic significance on the Badwater road, the bed at the Panamint Springs motel was a sonnet and a tribute to everything about beds that could possibly ever be true. It was, astonishingly, even better than the lawn chair with which I'd just intimately bonded. From the moment I sat down and felt the cushioned pressure of the mattress against my aching legs and butt, I knew that I was about to partake of one of the singular experiences of my life. The bed was soft, and it was flat. And those were the only two traits it needed to have to achieve complete and utter perfection. I took off my shoes and lay back on the bedspread, putting my head on the dingy pillow that some filthy, disgusting runner before me had undoubtedly used. I was a deadweight falling to the center of the earth and a weightless free-floating astronaut at the same time. Everything was draining out of me, down into the bed, which was capturing my very soul. The bed owned me.

It seemed barely a few seconds later that I was jolted awake by the sound of moaning.

The noise was coming from behind a door at the foot of the bed—the bathroom I'd seen when I came in. I got up and went closer, partly to make sure in my own mind that I'd really heard what I thought, and then to consider what I should do about it. I pictured myself bursting through the door, where some poor bastard would be lying in a fetal position by the toilet, done in and dying, and I'd . . . well, I didn't have a clue what I'd do, exactly, but I knew I couldn't just ignore a cry for help and walk away or go back to sleep.

Never mind the ridiculous fantasy that I could ever burst through a locked bathroom door.

As I got closer, I could hear water sloshing around in the tub. More moans rolled out. "Oh, God . . ." the voice said. "Gaaaawd . . . Ohhhh . . ."

It wasn't pain at all, I realized, but pleasure. Serious pleasure. So deep down that pain was probably a very close cousin. The moans and groans of this runner's joy seemed exactly right somehow, and fitting. Hadn't my own little nap been just as close to the frightening edge of heaven? And this morning's coffee at Towne Pass? And the love I felt for my sister who'd walked all night beside me up the canyon?

Perhaps a bath was Panamint's payoff for this anonymous runner—being reduced in his needs and enlarged in his senses so much that soaking in a tub (maybe his feet, maybe his whole body, I couldn't tell) could produce such heights of bone-shaking, mind-blowing ecstasy. As the bed had owned me, the tub now owned him.

I smiled and gave a little salute. Carry on, my good man, I thought. You've found your soup, and I headed for the door.

Just outside the room, I discovered Wayne—stripped to his cutoff Levi's and sneakers and spraying himself down with a garden hose. Pat was just coming up the walk to the bungalow, and we stopped and stood there, watching him and laughing. He struck me at that moment as the perfect natural man—ignoring us and anyone else in the world who might or might not stop to gawk. He looked joyous in his wildness, shooting the water onto his head and up under his armpits and whooping loudly. It seemed right and fitting.

"I think I slept," I said to Pat, before she could ask.

She peered at me for the briefest of seconds. "Liar," she said.

Kirk Johnson

I never got the chance to ask her why she was so doubt-
ful and distrustful. Maybe I still looked like hell. Maybe she
believed that I'd become too much of an obsessive to ever
relax enough to actually fall asleep. And she also well knew,
I think, in all our subtle posturing around the question of
The Line, that I'd very much want her to think I was entirely shipshape and going strong, and that I was probably
capable of lying in order to make my case stronger. In any
event she told me they'd only left me in the room 20 minutes earlier, so however much I'd rested, it couldn't have
been more than that.

I nodded. Fine. Whatever. I took her word for it. I'd long
since abandoned my own watch by then. It was somewhere
in the van, still absurdly synchronized to the minute to
match Matt Frederick's official race clock, and still an-
nouncing its presence with occasional chirps and beeps.
Watches had become like mirrors: I'd found myself thinking
about them too much—how weird they were and how
strange it was to go around with one strapped on to you—
until I finally just had to take mine off with a little shudder
and put it aside. I was a directed being now, happy to be told
when I could stop and for how long.

"Well, it seemed like sleep, anyway," I said to my sister.

White Line Tapestry

Getting to the top of Father Crowley's turnout, at the 80-mile point in the course, should have been a positive experience, a milestone and a cause for celebration. The second of the three big climbs was now finished. The worst heat of the day was over, and as we reached the summit at about 6:30 P.M. on Friday, 32 and a half hours after the start of the race, a gusty wind had picked up, making it feel even cooler. The road ahead would be up and down but mostly flat now all the way to Lone Pine, and we'd be crossing the Owens Valley, which people had told me could be almost as hot as the Badwater–Furnace Creek corridor, under cover of darkness. Tomorrow, if all went well, we'd be in the Sierra Nevada. Death Valley's heat was over.

So I should have been able to holler and whoop something about Badwater being all downhill from here. Let's go, baby, and let 'er rip. But it wasn't in me. An emptiness had settled over us all, I felt—a heavy, blank, dull and leaden hollowness of the mind. During the steep eight-mile climb from Panamint Springs, I'd sometimes felt as though I'd lost touch with my body, too. Like the layers of sunscreen and sweat that coated my skin and the thick matting of dust and sand that filled my hair, there was a blanket somewhere inside me blocking my connection to the world. Nearly every part of my body ached in some small or large way by then, but the pain was filtered and refracted, full of murky echoes and ghost images. I'd become numb. At one point that afternoon, for example, I stopped at the van and grabbed a glob of Vaseline to smear on the inside of my thighs to ease the chafing. I'd then gone on my way and it wasn't until I stopped to pee perhaps a mile later that I realized I'd left the big rectangular lid of the Vaseline jar *down inside my jockstrap*. I hadn't felt a thing, though I knew when I saw the lid clatter to the ground that in the real world what I'd experienced for that last mile was surely uncomfortable.

I told myself that what we were all experiencing was just old-fashioned fatigue and sleep deprivation—we were dragging a bit, that's all. But a small, nagging voice kept saying it was more than that. Things felt frayed somehow, as though the seams that were holding us all together were coming apart.

Wayne called his wife Mary on the satellite phone from the Father Crowley parking lot overlooking the Panamint Mountains and the salt pan of Death Valley to our east, and as they talked, Mary went on-line over the Internet with my sister Wendy. It was an extraordinary thing, really, that we could be linked together like that from such a remote spot, but then Wayne asked if I had anything to pass through the network and I felt blank and stupid. I finally said to tell Wendy that she was there with us in spirit, and Wayne said that he could hear Mary typing it, and that Wendy had written back, and that both women were crying. I knew I should be touched by this, and that those tears were being shed out of love and support for the three of us there on that mountaintop, but it all felt so far away—as though our connection with reality were breaking up into static. It couldn't reach me somehow. I was already down the road, far away. I got up and refilled my water bottles.

Pat and Wayne, I'd decided, were beginning to burn out. They'd sat heavily in their chairs at the top of the pass, looking exhausted as the wind blasted around us, and they hadn't pushed me to get started again after our rest break—no nagging, no jokes, no anxious calculations about the 60-hour clock. They'd been terrific for 36 hours now, which was a hell of a long time for anybody, and now they'd reached the end. They wanted the race to be over.

One of the Badwater veterans I'd spoken to had told me that that's what had happened to him, so of course I now became convinced it was happening to me in just the same way. His crew, he said, had gotten a bellyful of Badwater long before Lone Pine and Mount Whitney. They'd given up and gone to sleep on his second night. He'd had to rouse them over and over—banging on the side of the vehicle and yelling at every stop so they'd wake up long enough to drive another few miles down the road to wait for him. That's the place I was thinking I'd come to. Pat and Wayne were retreating from the frontier. We were no longer a team. The joy with which we'd bonded back at Stovepipe and through the first night up through Towne Pass had been spent.

There was no one else on the road at that hour—no other cars, no other runners, not another soul in the world, it seemed, except me there going down California State Highway 190 as the last of the daylight petered out. And that feeling of isolation was like acid: It ate through the thin shell of my confidence and my resolve and my ability to even think straight. Part of the problem was that this stretch was different from anything I'd faced before. Through all the other sections of the race, I'd been able to visualize the discrete segments—Badwater to Furnace Creek, Furnace Creek to Stovepipe, Stovepipe to Towne Pass, Towne Pass to Panamint, Panamint to Crowley. The longest stretch had been 24 miles, from Furnace Creek to Stovepipe Wells, while the shortest was the one I'd just finished—the eight-mile climb from Panamint.

But now as I went on and dusk began to fall, I realized that I had no such concrete and measurable sections ahead of me, only a vague and oppressive gap of road. It was more than 40 miles to Lone Pine, where the 13-mile Whitney Portal Road to the finish line would begin, and there was nothing between here and there that I could fasten my mind on to as an intermediate goal. I simply had to go all night and I still wouldn't be there. I had 55 miles to the finish, and that number began to take on monstrous life as the shadows deepened, like a beast on my shoulders, bearing down with all its weight. I was alone and I'd soon be even more so as the darkness grew complete, and I feared I'd stumble on through that darkness without end forever and ever, amen.

It helped me for a little while to think about the Boogie. I'd found a way to get up and get going again that night, through my 4:30 A.M. crisis of the mental mine shaft. So now I tried to reconstruct exactly what had transpired under those North Carolina stars. I wanted the details; I wanted to drag them inside my head, and into my bones. I tried to remember exactly how it had felt to stand up on the roadside that night, and how I'd stretched my aching quads, and then how I'd managed to start running again, and what I'd felt when I made it to the final aid station, with only five miles left. Then I pictured how I'd stood at the aid station, leaning over, hands braced on my knees, staring down at my shoes under the stark white lamps.

I'd found Don Juan's rock that night. I'd dug up from somewhere a vein of ore, a strength. Sorting through those memories also made me see something that I hadn't back then. Getting up from the side of the road at 43 miles had been an act of pure faith—I didn't really know how my crisis would end, but I'd believed an answer could be found. And that faith was, in turn, what had created the answer itself. It was another paradox of the ultramarathon: By moving, you find out how to move. By believing that an untapped source of strength exists, it becomes manifest. Act as though you are among the elect, and perhaps you will be.

Gary had a visualization exercise he'd once told me about, and I found some comfort in that, too, and in the memory of the night he'd described it to me, about three years earlier, on a visit to Salt Lake City. We were in Pat's backyard—everyone by her pool, my kids and her grandkids all splashing together. A cool breeze was flowing into the yard like a tide, descending from the Wasatch Mountain peaks, laden with the midsummer evening essence of pine and glacier. A big family group had gathered, raucous with old stories and laughter, but the conversation I remembered was between Gary and me alone. We sat close. He lounged like a cat—languid, relaxed and composed—with one leg hanging over the arm of his chair. I remember looking at him and thinking how complete he seemed, how unified and coherent.

I don't know how the conversation arrived at this particular topic, but he began to tell me how he'd sometimes wake up, sleepless in the middle of the night, and work on his golf swing. Lying there in bed next to his wife, he'd analyze every movement, looking for flaws in the position of the club head and the angle of his elbows and the arc of the follow-through. He'd be able to see it all, he said, as though he were standing outside himself. He could also stop the action at any moment, for closer scrutiny of any individual frame. And then he'd take the shot. If the ball went true and straight and long, his reenactment had been a success. If it sliced or hooked, he'd go back to the beginning and start over.

I wasn't sure whether Gary used middle-of-the-night golf as a device to lull himself back to sleep, or whether it really did sharpen his game. I didn't ask back then. I didn't want to break the rhythm of the moment, or lose the vision he'd planted in my head with such vivid detail. Gary found peace in seeking the perfect golf swing. That was all I really needed to know. Through the movement of his body, and through discipline and practice, he'd created a tunnel he could crawl through to glimpse something beyond the darkness. Now, trotting down the road toward the vast Owens Valley separating the Panamint Mountains from the Sierra Nevada, I sucked on that memory like an old bone for its marrow. Midnight golf seemed important, somehow—a thread to hang on to, a chunk of some orderly universe that still might exist out there somewhere, a particle of hope.

Most ultramarathons in the 100-mile category are long since over by the beginning of a second night. They typically start at dawn or earlier and are finished the next day, 30 to 36 hours later, before sunset. The tiny handful that are hard enough or long enough to go beyond that into another night comprise almost a special category, notable as much for their physical exertion as for what might be called their temporal displacement.

The Hardrock 100-miler, for example, held every year on the western slope of the Rockies in Colorado, is another two-night race. Hardrock has a 48-hour cutoff and, like Badwater, an almost religious following in the ultramarathon culture. Whole websites exist for no other purpose but to talk about what Hardrock means or doesn't and what its particular second-night manifestations reveal or do not.

One runner I talked to who'd done both Hardrock and Badwater described the second night of an ultramarathon as a time when "it's always four A.M." Every decision and action and effort occurs, he'd told me, in that middle-of-the-night space when the body and soul have dropped the last of their defenses.

So I was prepared for the prospect of a great testing as darkness gathered. I was anticipating a night that would settle the question of whether I'd make it to Whitney or not. If I was still moving when the sun came up, I figured the answer would probably be yes—I'd consider myself a survivor. Perhaps even more than the finish line itself, which I could still not quite imagine, I was expecting a climax of Badwater, a culmination of the process that had begun two years earlier when I'd taken off from Pat's house during the week of Gary's funeral and run 10 miles for the first time in my life.

I imagined that, for better or worse, the real me would be exposed during Badwater's second night, if only because, at some point, there'd be nothing else left. The old narrator of my life would be brutalized into silence, and I would stand, for once, simply for who I was. I imagined a golden ray of light that would shine down, and I would spread out my arms into the glow and say, "I have arrived at what I am— this man, standing here at this moment in time—no more and no less." I would be burned clean.

* * *

Just before sundown, I realized that I could see things. In the twisty twilight mix of subtle shades and shadow, I found I could see, in fact, almost anything I wanted by just looking at it long enough. The little white line in the road that marks the shoulder, for example, had been plain old paint up until that moment. For more than 80 miles I'd stared down at it and never once had it changed. Now it became a tapestry: Every crack and spot and imperfection took on life. I saw skulls and devils and monsters and animals of all sorts—especially rabbits and skunks, it seemed, for some reason—all flowing past, embedded within the line like a comic strip.

Badwater is legendary for its hallucinations. Some of the veterans I'd spoken to before the race had used the word *magic* to describe the forces that can arise after hours and days of pushing and prodding at the limits of the mind and body. Others had laughed off Badwater's visions as mere trickery—a chemical and psychological sleight of hand no more meaningful than the average doodle. Runners have been known to see cruise ships and flying sheep, dematerializing bicycles and ghost wagon trains that rumble by through the night in vivid and memorable detail, right down to the plodding oxen and grim-faced pioneer men. One man in 1997 ran across the Golden Gate Bridge, which had been mysteriously transported—plausibly enough, so it seemed to him at the time—to the dark empty wastes of Owens Valley. Another man became convinced that the road itself had been turned into a giant semiconductor chip.

Bob Ankeney, the laconic juvenile-probation officer I'd met in May, told me he'd been drawn to Badwater the previous year by the prospect of the hallucinations, and perhaps enlightenment, that he hoped could result. But he hadn't found what he'd sought, he said, and part of his reason for coming a second year was to continue the search.

Mick Justin, on the other hand, the Minnesota accountant who was making his fourth journey through Death Valley, regarded hallucinations as distractions that could burn up precious mental energy and were therefore to be avoided. He'd told me he planned to keep his head down, eyes front, through Badwater's second night, the better to concentrate on his running.

One of Badwater's unwritten rules is that the hallucinations are perfect. In other words, don't expect trite mirages like shimmering lakes and such. Expect visions. Expect the Sistine Chapel, with every detail down to Michelangelo there on his scaffold; expect people from your junior high school English class to wander suddenly and impossibly out of the desert and say hello; expect, some people say, to see God. Or the devil, for that matter, who was spotted—in running shoes, competing in the race—in 1995. Expect the cacti to begin singing to you at 1 A.M. from the bottomless darkness of the roadside near Lone Pine, as they did to a man named John Radich in 1996. Radich was so lulled by the music that he sat right down where he was in the middle of the highway, oblivious to all else.

In my moments of idealism that spring, I'd thought of Badwater as a search for the kind of thing that had captured Radich—something larger than myself, more pure and more beautiful. Hallucinations, from wherever they arose—a fevered mind, or perhaps from some greater place—could be a window, I thought. Like dreams, they must contain some meaning.

But the doubts never entirely fell away, either—the reporter half of my identity wouldn't allow it. As much as I'd tried and wanted to believe in the purity and inviolate spirituality of the second-night endurance experience, the tiny voices in the back of my head, like the carping of the Badwater bartender, kept whispering not to trust too much. Badwater was about nature, but it was also about human calculation. Crossing Death Valley on foot required a journey to the outer edge of endurance; doing so in a race meant participating in a deliberate and artificial construction of elements that had been made harder for the very sake of making them harder. The mind can make itself believe anything it wants, and see anything it wants, the voices said. The chemistry of exhaustion holds no patent on truth and probably should make one even more skeptical of anything that is revealed.

The white-line tapestry scrolling past me now was not a true hallucination by all those standards, because I knew all the time that it was just a line of paint in the road. I could turn it off if I wanted to, and that was fun for a while, too. "Paint," I'd say, feeling like Samantha Stephens from *Bewitched*, and once again with just a little squint of concentration, the line would revert to its flat, white, prosaic form. Then I'd relax my mind and it would all come right back, like a door that creaks open with every odd wind and can never quite be closed. There was a willful child inside me, and unless I stood fast and guarded the door, he would skip out into this twilight world to play.

After a while of this I looked to my left and saw to my surprise that someone had apparently come by and put down a fishing net of some kind, just off the shoulder of the road. The net had been laid onto the dirt and was holding up all sorts of different things, especially, for some reason, cups and saucers and china of various sorts. I ran past whole tea sets that had been set up there on the net. I knew that this was a fairly ridiculous thing, more or less, and that it was almost certainly not what it seemed. But I was also far enough into my dream state that I could begin to rationalize why it *might* actually be true. Maybe the stuff was for sale,

I thought—perhaps there was a swap meet of some sort out here. The netting was for efficiency's sake, perhaps: The sellers, when they returned to retrieve their unsold cups and saucers, could conveniently pick everything up with the net. No muss, no fuss. The items were also kept clean and out of the dirt that way and could be easily transported to the next point of sale. It all began to make sense.

The larger question, why anyone would ever actually think this was a good way and place to sell old china—laid out on nets in the middle of the desert 40 miles from the nearest town—didn't enter into my thinking. It just was, that's all, and it was up to me to try and understand it. Yeah, I could see why people might do this. A bit implausible, perhaps, but not entirely unthinkable.

I also ran for a while believing that the road had been enclosed on its right side by a retaining wall about three feet high, built of cement or cinder block, smack up against the edge of the traffic lane itself. And once again I didn't expend a lot of thought questioning the wall's reality—acceptance and rationalization were far easier and less demanding of energy. Perhaps, I thought, some kind of construction project was under way, or a new, experimental highway design. Only when I drifted over to the other side of the road was I struck by the truth: The wall was nothing more than the other white line marking the right shoulder. As I approached, everything that had seemed so solidly three-dimensional flattened out in a wink. I'd been pondering and trying to explain something that not only didn't exist, but would have made no sense whatsoever if it had.

I thought of Ankeney and Justin—both of them out there somewhere right now. Ankeney was probably peering into the shadows, seeking transport to some other state of being, even as Mick was writing it all off as fluff and nonsense, like an error on a debit sheet.

And I could understand both points of view. At dusk my hallucinations had been a plaything, a joke between my mind and the world around me about what was real and what was not. Now, as the darker, longer shadows settled in, things were taking on a more sinister edge. The goofiness of tea sets, sailor's nets and fake walls gave way to more amorphous and frightening shapes that seemed to be off to the side of the road. There were big things out there in the rocks and bushes and cacti, and I felt like I didn't even want to look sometimes because I feared what my mind could make them become. Just as I'd created an imaginary world of paint-line comic strips and middesert swap meets, I realized that I could all too easily create an army of monsters in the boulders and scrub vegetation off the highway. There were creepy shapes out there—things I didn't want my mind to play with because with every deeper moment of darkness, I was less and less in control of the situation.

My mental fatigue was also making it harder and harder to move. When I tried to run I could feel too well how my lower back muscles were gripping the hamstrings in my legs, like hawks with their talons into a rabbit, and then how my hamstrings were yanking and pulling on my calf muscles, then how my calves were twisting and torquing the tendons and muscles of my feet. Every square inch of my body felt connected by misfortune to the square next to it—a cascading network of overuse and abuse that compounded the fatigue and soreness of any one particular spot. I could still make myself move forward, but in the twilight of a fevered second night, it was as though I had to think about how walking or running was to be done, and that sharply escalated the amount of energy required to do it. The best I could muster was a very slow jog of small mincing steps that was, in truth, not much faster than a walk.

A strange idea was also beginning to gnaw at me: The taillights of our van—two round red circles in the distance—were really eyes. The notion had started innocently enough, like the white line of paint. But then, unlike my jolly little comic strip that I could turn off if I wished, the eyes started to take control. They asserted the reality that they *were* eyes and not lights at all, no matter how much I might want to think otherwise. And they weren't the eyes of some friendly being urging me on, but rather the red glowing-ember eyes of a bird of prey or a scavenger waiting for me to go down and not get up—eyes without mercy or good intentions.

My state of mind wasn't improved when the taillight-eyes became three-dimensional and started moving, either. One second they were flat red dots in the distance, and the next they'd developed long conical bodies and were zooming right toward my head. It was still just an illusion, I knew, but real enough that I flinched.

Everything by then was becoming more than it was supposed to be and also at the same time less. I was beginning to feel as though I couldn't trust anything I saw, or anything I felt, either. The disturbing image of taillight-eyes made it hard for me to feel comfortable even looking at our van anymore, however much it had been for all these hours and miles a symbol of home. I felt like my family was no longer there for me, either—as night settled in, both Pat and Wayne had gone to sleep, leaving Travis to drive the van. I felt completely alone, wrapped up in my riddles, trapped in an untrustworthy world.

My feet were also beginning to hurt again. My toes, the weak link in everything I'd done, were feeling pinched and hot. That had meant blisters before and probably did now again, so I tried not to think about it. If my mind could perform so adeptly with the visions that were playing out before my eyes, then perhaps, I thought, I could deny the reality of blisters as well. I'd figured out more or less how to run downhill as if it were flat, hadn't I?

But as the full blackness of the night settled in, I began to panic. The weight I felt bearing down on me—from the huge distance ahead, the growing pain in my feet and the psychotic games my mind was beginning to play on me—was becoming too much to bear.

I was failing, sliding and slipping. I wanted to lie down by the side of the road, and at one point, with the van far away and the deathly desert silence wrapping itself around me, I almost did. The shoulder looked so nice and flat and comfortable, a soft bed that would be as perfect as anything at the Panamint Springs motel. I wanted to quit, to give up, to wallow there in my isolation, to abandon everything—all my goals and dreams. I couldn't go on. It was too far and too hard.

So why not lie down? A small voice in my head began to ask the question and I had no answer. Why not? Why not embrace the empty darkness and let it take me? I'd surely find peace down there on the highway, or at least the bliss of unconsciousness. I would close my eyes and take the rest I so richly deserved.

But I couldn't do it, so I walked and cried instead—great pathetic sobs that wrenched up through my body until, by the time they got to my head, they were almost convulsions. I'd groan some sad and ridiculous lament, like, "Oh, God," and tears would squeeze out from my eyes and roll down my cheeks for a few seconds, then stop. I was like a towel being wrung out: A wave would sweep through me, twisting every muscle and emotion to a point of unbearable tension; then it would subside and I'd walk on, knowing that another wave was soon to come. I didn't cry for any particular reason, but rather for any and all reasons. I cried because it felt good to cry, and because I felt sorry for myself.

It occurred to me, after a while of this, that music might help. I'd recorded my Badwater Tapes, after all, with this second night partly in mind. And if ever I could use a boost, it was now. So at my next stop at the van, as Travis jumped out to see what I needed, I grabbed my headset and the tape that was on top of the stack. Then I walked back out onto the road and hit the play button.

The shock was instantaneous. Without warning—beamed directly into the jellied, quivering mound that my mind had become—was the duet I'd recorded from the first act of La Bohème.

I have to admit that I've never loved opera. A grudging toleration was about the best I'd been able to muster, despite repeated exposure. My wife had come from opera-worshiping roots, however, and for her La Bohème was somewhere near perfection. So in recording my tapes I'd included one brief selection as a symbolic gesture, a way to include Fran in the Badwater venture at a time when it seemed like I was shutting her out of so much else in my life. A little bit of Puccini was one of my ways of telling her she'd be with me in Death Valley when the time came. I hadn't thought much more about it than that.

Now I understood opera for the first time in my life. I understood my wife. I understood her father and her sister, who talked about opera performances like old love affairs. The music took me and owned me more completely than even the bed at Panamint or the soup at Stovepipe. From the first notes, rolling up and up into those glorious, aching harmonies between the two doomed lovers—Luciano

Pavarotti as Rodolfo and Mirella Freni as Mimi—I stopped being me at all and became simply a vessel into which the music poured, filling every space.

When their duet reached its crescendo, I felt that it might shatter me like a wineglass. I turned my face up toward the sky and shook as tears rolled down my cheeks, crying along with a whole world that seemed wrenched from horizon to horizon with the beauty of longing and loss. I was but a tiny boat riding a giant swell of emotion that I could no more control than I could the great wide sea. If it swamped me, well, then that was how it would be. I was without will.

I ultimately couldn't bear it. Maybe in some way I feared it really would empty me out and I'd cease to exist but for those harmonies. I'd become a hollow man, filled only with a stuffing of Puccini, walking down Highway 190 blubbering about Mimi and the cruel Paris winter and straining for a high C that I would never reach. I finally had to turn off the tape.

The opera had delivered me to a place where I knew I had to talk to someone other than myself. I pulled off the headphones, breathing hard. The red eyes were getting closer. My feet were in trouble. It was time to try and figure out how bad things really were.

When I got to the van, I told Travis we needed to unwrap the toes and take a look. In truth, my feet had become simply a symbol, a metaphor for the army of things that seemed wrong. Feet would be a place to start, though. I really needed to talk, to reach out and feel that another human being was there and that I wasn't sliding off the edge into some place from which I couldn't come back.

"It's my little toes," I said pathetically, like the child I was becoming.

Forty-eight hours before that moment, I'd never met

Travis Gray, and yet now I felt I'd known him forever, that we'd been here together on this road since time began. He'd become embedded into the Badwater universe. Pat, Wayne, Travis, the van—our self-contained little bubble was all there was and all there ever had been. He got a chair for me and I put my feet up while he sat on the van's tailgate and unwrapped the tape. There were, as I'd feared and suspected, new blisters—three or four big ones, again all on my toes. Even without toe boxes in my shoes, the pressure and friction of all those miles had continued. As he worked—puncturing, draining, applying new dressings—I began telling him my troubles.

"I feel like I'm sort of falling apart here, Travis," I said, biting my lip to avoid crying right there in front of him. He was a guy, after all. "And tonight is really the night when this thing is going to happen or not." I paused for a minute. Travis looked up but said nothing. "I think pretty soon you guys are going to have to take care of me in a way that you haven't had to . . ."

Travis just nodded and kept on working. And I felt very small and weak.

I knew, even as I spoke the words, exactly what I was doing and what the consequences would be. I was manipulating Travis so that he'd wake up Wayne and Pat. I felt alone and overwhelmed and close to the point of dissolution and in some petty, small, selfish and nasty way, I needed everyone else awake and suffering, too. I'd become the demanding, prissy, egocentric athlete I'd always hated, wallowing in my self-pity and demanding that everyone else share my experience because it was so precious and important.

I wasn't tough at all. I didn't have guts. I'd been too small and weak to tell Brian Manley to feel better that morning before the race, too pathetic to be honest with Ulrich, and now I'd connived against the people I needed and loved most in the world. My hopes about being burned into some state of inner unity or peace by Badwater were a sham and a fraud. There was to be no golden ray of light. I was not healed. I went back out on the road and cried again. I'd lost.

Rhyolite

When I got back to the van, Pat and Wayne were both outside, as I knew they would be. Pat was stretching, preparing to join me on the road just as she had after my first crisis with the blisters, and through the climb up Towne Pass, and across the eternal lake bed into Panamint Springs.

"Travis woke you up," I said, when we were out into the darkness. "I'm sorry about that . . . I . . ."

"I was just getting up," she said.

I glanced over at her briefly. "Liar," I said.

We walked for a while. But I couldn't hold it in very long. The cumulative troubles that had driven me to want to lie down on the road and bawl were mostly still there. I felt buried. "I'm losing it, Pat," I said. "I just don't see how I can make it all the way to Lone Pine." I was trying not to cry again, but my emotions were so close to the surface that it couldn't be helped. "It just seems so far . . ."

Pat didn't hesitate for a moment. "We're not going all the way to Lone Pine," she said. "We're only going as far as those taillights up ahead." She nodded in the direction we were walking.

I had to catch my breath. *The eyes!*

"Don't think about anything else," she continued. "Just get to the taillights. Then we'll do it again."

Neither of us spoke for a while, and that left only the sound of our feet on the roadway—a light crunching of gravel on blacktop that was amplified into greater significance by the profound stillness around us. I wasn't sure about Pat's suggestion, but when we came over a little rise a few minutes later and saw the van's lights there in the distance, I found that I could concentrate on them, and use them, however much they'd terrified me only a short while earlier.

As we grew closer, I found myself feeling stronger and stronger. This small moment in the middle of the night, in the middle of the desert—a few simple words between a sister and a brother—had turned a corner. Badwater might not purify me into some state of higher self-realization. I might not make it all the way to Whitney, or even all the way through the night. But I could get to the taillights at least once. And if I could do it once, I could probably do it again.

Pat, I decided, had put her finger on the very heart of the matter. Got mean old eyes after you? Hunt 'em down. That's what getting to the van meant. That's what running Badwater meant. Challenge the hardest, scariest thing you've ever heard of, and no matter what happens, you've achieved a victory—over your own fears, if nothing else. Propel yourself toward the worst thing in your field of vision and you lessen or eliminate its ability to harm by reducing it to your own scale, just as Death Valley does to the idea of death itself.

And it doesn't really matter whether you get there or not. In fact, you never do and never can. The demon taillights always escape, always hover out there in the distance, ready to attack again and again forever. The victory comes from the chase itself, beginning at that moment when you decide to go forward.

The urge that Barbara (or was it Angelika?) had described back in May on the slope of Towne Pass, "to see what is possible," and Dan's endurance philosophy of pushing past the point of failure were both the same thing. Search out the worst you can imagine and there you'll find the best that is in you. The light and the darkness are two sides of the same coin, inseparable and crucial to the whole.

I realized as Pat and I went on together that we'd finally reached The Line—our crucible place where my fate at Badwater was to be determined. The moment hadn't come as we'd thought it might, in some horror of physical torment where continuing on was a risk to my long-term health. It hadn't come on its own at all—instead we'd had to summon it. Just like the demon eyes, The Line wasn't something to be avoided, but rather a point of decision and resolution that had to be met and crossed as part of getting to the end. Pat's little device had given me a mechanism by which I could navigate the crossing, like the red square from Gary's old shorts that I'd stared at so intently on that long afternoon of my first marathon.

I settled down after that. Though I still couldn't listen to music and I was prone at any moment to some epiphany or other that felt like the most profound thought in the history of the world, I was moving again. That was the phrase that mattered, just as it had on that first night coming into Stovepipe Wells. I was walking, mostly, trying to maintain 16- to 17-minute miles, trying to concentrate on nothing more than going forward. I'd stopped thinking about Lone

Pine, or Whitney, or even about Badwater itself. I'd become simply a figure in the night, blank and empty and invisible.

Then, somewhere in the middle of that emptiness, I began to perceive shapes in the distance. At first I thought they were boulders or bushes of some kind. But as I grew closer, I saw that Highway 190 was approaching a town. A big corrugated metal building sat squat across the road straight ahead, with a car parked in front of it. An assortment of trash and machinery, including an old pickup truck, rusty and dilapidated, sat to the left. Fifty-five-gallon drums were scattered here and there, some of them sprouting weeds. The road went right up to the metal warehouse-style building and ended.

This was not supposed to be happening. There were no towns on the route. Something was dreadfully wrong. We'd missed a turn somehow and ended up on a dead-end road. *We were in Keeler!*

Of all the desolate desert towns I've seen in my life, Keeler, California, about 20 miles east of Lone Pine, is surely the most forlorn. In the real world, it's grim enough— a little community of rusting trailers and sheet-metal shacks plunked down on the edge of dry lake bed from which the residents eke out an existence as salt miners. Not only had we made a wrong turn, but we'd ended up here, of all places. We were lost.

I stopped, completely panicked, and turned around toward the van, which I'd left just a few minutes before. The headlights were coming toward me now, and Wayne stopped as he saw me running back.

"Did we miss a turn or something?" I asked. "I think we're on the wrong road."

Wayne looked at me blankly.

"What's the matter?" he said.

"We're coming into a town here," I barked, annoyed that he had to ask. Geez, it was right there in front of him. I immediately concluded that our arrival in Keeler was Wayne's fault. He'd missed a road sign somewhere in his exhaustion and screwed up. As much as I'd thought that he and Pat would need to take care of me, I now saw that it would be the other way around. I began spinning scenarios of how far back we might have missed the road, how much we'd have to backtrack and how much time it would cost us. A complication like this was the last thing any of us needed.

Finally, I sighed and turned back in the direction we'd been going. Maybe there'd be a sign or some other clue illuminated by the van's headlights about where to go from here. The thought of knocking on doors at 3 A.M. to ask directions in a place like Keeler was already giving me the creeps. I pictured shotguns and big dogs.

But the town was gone. In the glare of the high beams, there was nothing even to suggest what I'd seen—no boulders that could look like buildings, no cacti to suggest cars. Before me was a stretch of road as blank as every other stretch that had preceded it. The rusting ramshackle universe that had been so horrifyingly real a moment before was without material existence.

"Never mind," I said, and turned back down the highway.

It occurred to me, as I continued on through what would have been the middle of my little town, that perhaps I'd just seen the ghost of Rhyolite.

Rhyolite, Nevada, was a town that had flourished and died on the eastern edge of Death Valley, and it had haunted me ever since I'd seen the crumbling remains of it in May. As a story, the rise and fall of Rhyolite offered everything: audacious dreams and hardscrabble reality, hope and hopelessness, soaring ambition and inevitable doom—

the very mixture that had captured my imagination ever since *The Flight of the Phoenix*.

For a time just after the turn of the century, upwards of 12,000 people lived there. It had 52 saloons for its hard-drinking gold miners, a large and impressive bank building with properly august concrete columns in front and even its own stock exchange with 67 stockbrokers. And then the whole thing had vanished without a trace.

The day I visited over Memorial Day, the little bits of Rhyolite that remain—a few crumbling walls and the railroad depot, which had survived by virtue of being turned into a whorehouse as the town died—were attended by a sixty-something man named Bill, who lived there in a motor home with his wife, offering free tours as a volunteer for the United States Department of the Interior.

Bill told me that he and his wife had lived in Wyoming in their younger days, where they'd developed a rule of thumb for use in retirement. The rule had brought them to Death Valley.

"If we ever have to turn on the heat, it's time to go south," he said, grinning in a baseball cap. "We both had enough cold weather for one lifetime."

He spoke about Rhyolite the way you might about an eccentric, endearing uncle who'd lived a wild but charmed life and died while still young and uncorrupted. Rhyolite was about dreams, Bill said, as though he'd been there back when. The upward cycle peaked in 1906, as gold boomed in that part of the valley, and by World War I, the dream was over. The bustling, proud little parades and the civic booster clubs and the fantasies of future grandeur lived on only in the smudgy black-and-white photographs in Bill's brochures.

Rhyolite's demise came because mining technology had hit a wall. There was still plenty of gold in the mines that had given the city its life—the Montgomery-Shoshone and the Bullfrog—but the cost of getting out the ore and processing it kept inching higher with each year until, in the wink of an accountant's eye, the place was no longer viable. So it died. Many of the miners, who lived in semi-permanent shacks, loaded their homes onto wagons and moved on. And because lumber was so valuable and scarce, people cannibalized the town as they left, ripping apart the buildings to get the wood so that it could be carried off and used somewhere that mattered now that Rhyolite didn't.

Like a desert flower, Rhyolite had blossomed for a day, then wilted and dropped its seeds—in this case the skeletal frames of its buildings—as the raw material for another generation of dreams. It had functioned just as it should within the harsh ecosystem of Death Valley, and the dried husk of its glory had been very moving to me. The handful of partial walls and storefronts that remained are still there because they'd been built of concrete or steel-reinforced frames instead of lumber. Their builders designed them to be lasting or imposing or impregnable. And the irony is that they did last through the town's death agonies—only because they were built of stuff that nobody wanted to cart away.

In my imagination, Rhyolite the ghost town lived on. Looking at Bill's pictures of the Fourth of July parades and the crowded main drag, Golden Street, I'd made up my own little Breyfogle story about the place. The town didn't die at all. It just got lost, like old Breyfogle's gold. It drifted off into the desert, eternal in its undying and hard-bitten western hopefulness, down at the heels perhaps after so many years, but still there, a Flying Dutchman of the empty wastes.

I knew, as I walked on down the highway in the grip of

Badwater's second night, that with only a tiny amount of effort I could convince myself that I really had seen Rhyolite's ghostly edge back there and that I'd been on Golden Street again. But then after a little while I decided it might be best to leave the dead where they lay.

That morning back in New Jersey, Fran and the boys were preparing to fly to Salt Lake City where we all planned to reunite after the race, and I told her I'd call her at 6:30 A.M. East Coast time, just before they needed to leave for the airport. That little deadline, 3:30 A.M. in Death Valley, gave me something else to shoot for, another plateau on which to place some meaning. By coincidence we were also nearing the 100-mile point as 3:30 A.M. approached, which gave our planned rest stop an added measure of significance.

So at about three, shortly after my visit to Keeler-Rhyolite, Wayne and Travis said they'd head down a mile and a half or so, make coffee, get out some chairs and we'd all take a break while I tried to get through on the satellite phone.

The phone worked well enough. I dialed and it began to ring. Unfortunately, I was not functioning properly by then, however much I'd thought over the last few hours that I'd somehow grasped the true nature of the universe. As I waited for Fran to pick up, I found myself staring at the phone there in my hand. What a totally bizarre concept a telephone was—that I could be sitting here at 3:30 A.M. in Death Valley about to talk to my wife in our bedroom. How strange to even talk on a phone! How funny it looked with its clunky big black antenna, and how mysterious it had been that two guys would just walk up out of nowhere and give it to us . . .

"Hello?" It was Fran, and she was speaking to me, and

that was my cue to speak, too, I knew. But somehow it all seemed so difficult. What was I supposed to do now?

"How you doin', baby?" she said.

"I'm tired," I said. Then I said nothing else, which probably sounded ominous at her end. I felt I needed to say something, but I was having trouble finding words. "We just passed a hundred and one miles," I blurted, as though it were an afterthought.

Fran screamed her excitement in my ear and then paused to yell the news to the boys, who were probably upstairs in their room getting ready.

"You're almost there," she said. "You're really going to make it! That's only thirty-four miles!"

She went on and on after that, gushing in her enthusiasm. But I was having a very hard time keeping up. I asked her several times where she'd be that night when the race was over, or the 60 hours had passed. Her dad's place, she said, that's where everyone would be. Then I asked her again. Then I told her again I'd gone 101 miles. From a million thoughts all at once, I'd apparently been reduced to just two—I was tired and I'd gone 101 miles. I didn't seem to be able to hold much else in my head. The storm of seemingly brilliant insights about Puccini and mobile desert ghost towns and the nature of human motivation and endurance had all blown past like desert raindrops that fall and fall and never quite reach the ground. I asked again when her flight was, and when she and the boys would arrive in Salt Lake.

"Did David get ahold of you?" she asked. "He left a message here saying he was trying to reach you."

David. David Edelman. "Yes!" I said, like a game show contestant who's thrilled to have finally come up with the right answer. I'd spoken to David, an old *New York Times* buddy now living near San Diego, sometime yesterday—

then promptly forgotten the whole conversation. "He's going to meet us in Lone Pine or somewhere on the road," I said.

David and I had played a bizarre version of telephone tag through the previous day, as we'd tried to coordinate his plan to join our crew for the final home stretch to Whitney. I'd spoken to him once for about 30 seconds before the satellite phone phased out of range, and he'd tried to call us back using a cell phone that couldn't get through at all. Our resultingly vague plan was to try and find each other somewhere on the Badwater course at around midday on Saturday. I couldn't believe I'd forgotten it all. And now I fell silent for a long time thinking about that and looking at the phone again instead of talking into it.

"Okay," Fran said, clearly trying to wrap it up. "Good luck, baby, I love you."

"I love you, too," I said.

Pat took the phone away from me pretty quickly after that, rather like you'd take a sharp knife from a child. *Hey, careful there, you might hurt someone with that.* She held the phone up to her ear and listened for minute, all the while looking at me.

"No, he's doing great," she said.

I had the vague impression that I hadn't quite communicated "doing great" to my wife, and thus Pat was pronouncing my condition now so unequivocally, both for Fran's benefit and for my own as well. I sat and watched my sister as she spoke, and found that I was having a hard time even following half a conversation, let alone fully participating in one.

So I grabbed the Frosted Flakes and milk that had been set in front of me. Cereal I could understand. And a cup of coffee in the middle of the night. Those were tangible, hard realities that I could still get my head around. The coffee was blazingly hot and black and bitter, the cereal fiercely sweet and cold. Food was not too complicated to understand, like mirrors and watches and now, apparently, telephones.

I heard Pat praising me again to my wife, in cheerfully insistent tones one would use to describe a simpleton who's performed well at some small task.

But I didn't mind, because it was true—I had become simpleminded. I needed people to take care of me and I'd manipulated them into doing so with my little babbling tantrum back with Travis. I'd descended into a place where I could take huge joy or terror in the most basic of things. I knew that the coffee and the sugar and the carbohydrates I was consuming would soon do their biochemical work and I'd be ready to go back on the road again, and that was the only other aspect of my existence that I could have told you about. I'm tired. I've gone 101 miles. I have a cup of coffee. Life was quickly approaching a singularity. Soon, even those few thoughts might be too many to hold on to.

Sometime not long before dawn, I began to wind down again, like the machine I'd become. The glow and the rush and the magic of 3:30 A.M. on the phone with home and coffee and sugary cereal already felt like some other life—a faded memory of energy, an echo of some distant dusty past that I could barely remember. Maybe I'd been to Rhyolite, maybe I hadn't and now it didn't matter. I was back to earth. I was falling asleep on my feet.

So Pat and Wayne consulted their watches and our mileage chart. How far to Lone Pine, and what time was it? Those were the two questions that determined the rhythm of our lives. They were the iron bands that held the world together, defining what was possible, what was real and what was important. Everything else had become irrelevant, or lost somewhere back on the road.

Our deadline to reach Lone Pine was 2 P.M. at the very latest. That would give us eight hours to hike the final miles up the Whitney Portal Road, and even that might be pushing the limit. Four to six hours was average for that final leg of the race, but Ben had told us on one of his drive-by stops that a runner several years earlier had needed 10 full hours to drag himself those 13 very steep miles to the finish line.

It was now 5 A.M. Saturday, and we were roughly at the 106-mile point. Pat and Wayne conferred a little more. "Thirty minutes," Pat said, nodding. I could take a full half hour off and still be okay.

In the real world, a half an hour is nothing, a sitcom's worth of time, a cup of coffee over the newspaper, the wait at the Lincoln Tunnel going into New York. It's a blip on the screen of a day—a fart in a blizzard, as a friend of mine likes to say.

But 30 minutes loomed before me then like a giant chasm of time, a library of unread books, an unknown city, a vast space of rest and peace to be explored at my leisure. After we settled the time question, or rather, when Pat and Wayne did—I mostly just stood there, waiting for them to herd me one way or another—I felt rich. What an incredible luxury—to rest, and perchance to sleep, for a full half an hour! I felt like a Rockefeller. What greater bauble of the high life could there be? What more could a body and soul want? That I was climbing into the backseat of a stinky, rubble-strewn mess of a vehicle, stained and sticky with spills and socks and crumbs, didn't matter in the least. I could have been lying down on almost anything, anywhere, and still felt I was living the life of a pharaoh.

Pat, who was apparently just as prepared as I was to call

any kind of horizontal posture a new form of bliss, flopped on top of the ice chests. Travis was asleep in the front seat. Wayne said he was going for a walk.

And so I stretched out, my legs extending into the air past the open door, and tried to imagine my body sinking into some paradise . . . and I couldn't do it. Here I was, with my first opportunity for sleep in nearly 18 hours, and it wouldn't come. Pat was out almost instantly, sprawled in an uncomfortable-looking heap like a rag doll. Travis was breathing softly up in front. A cool morning breeze was blowing into the van from the dead-silent desert . . . and I couldn't sleep.

I'd begged and wheedled for this rest break. Out on the road, I'd felt close to the point of physical collapse, as though I could fall down flat on my face every time I closed my eyes. And now here I had my chance and all I could do was lie there and think, although thinking is probably far too grand a word for what my mind believed itself to be doing. The wild notions and images that fluttered through my head were too ephemeral or nonsensical to be called proper thought. It was more like an autopilot that couldn't be disengaged—cruise control run amok. I closed my eyes and felt as though I hadn't stopped at all. I was still in motion out there on the highway, still walking, running, staring into the darkness for the lights ahead, worried about the timetable and my pace and my feet and all the other small details that had come to define my Badwater life.

Several times, I thought of giving up and just heading back out onto the road. I was wasting my precious half hour, so I might as well toss it away completely. But then I found I couldn't face the thought of that, either—much better to just lie there and try and pretend my body was healing and resting. So that's what I tried to visualize: I pictured my imaginary golden light flooding up through the van's floor and into my aching legs. I visualized my muscles and my blisters, and then below that into the threshold of my cells, all being mended and soothed by the honey glow. I imagined my fingernails growing faster than normal and my beard and hair sprouting suddenly like germinating seeds as my endorphins repaired all the things I'd strained or wounded.

And finally I accepted things as they were. Who I was, what I'd been searching for in coming out here, my dream of touching the mysterious edge where we meet our own limits—I no longer knew what any of that meant. I was what I was and I was here and that was fine. I accepted everything that had happened and ever would happen. The desert breeze blowing in through the van's open door was what it was and that was fine, too. I saw that all my dark doubts earlier in the evening about Pat and Wayne's commitment to our adventure had been nothing but craziness. They'd never wavered—it had all been a fantasy. And maybe the insights I'd had about endurance and The Line that had seemed so smart and true had been a fantasy, too. But that didn't matter, either.

I felt like a blanket was being pulled up to my chin, a comforting cover of open-ended release—from the doubts about my family to the pretensions of my own supposed brilliance. This thing we were all so wrapped up in was Badwater's story, not mine. I was just a minor character in the opera, playing my little part. It was an image that eventually would have lulled me to sleep, when out of nowhere, Pat bolted up with a shout.

"Ah!" she shrieked. "What time is it? How long have we been asleep? Travis!"

I sat up and looked back at her. She was frantic and wild-haired amid the rubble, and while I knew we hadn't been off the road all that long, the deep sleep she'd fallen into had clearly disrupted her internal clock. She thought we'd been out for hours and blown our deadline. "Travis! Travis! Wake up!" Pat yelled again. "What time is it?"

Travis pulled himself upright and announced that it was almost 5:30—not quite half an hour from when we'd stopped. Everything was right on schedule. Except that now I actually had to go back out on the road. I had another marathon to do, and that was fine, too.

The Black Walnut Tree

The first rays of sun on the third morning of Badwater somehow brought forth a rebirth of energy: I started running again. I took off toward the Sierra Nevada, which I could finally see before me, sawtoothed and blue on the horizon. I felt, with the dawn, as though I'd climbed out of a box or emerged from a cave, and that the light was recalling me to life. The human mind can't tolerate emptiness of the sort that exhaustion and desert silence can conspire to create, and during the long night mine had worked feverishly to fill that space up—not just with hallucinations, but with a whole swooping roller coaster of crises and calamities, doubts and deficits I'd built to populate the darkness.

Now I experienced what I think our ancestors might have felt in greeting the new day—joy that I'd survived. The beasts that stalk the night had missed me in my little hiding place and I hadn't been eaten, nor had my loved ones. I was still moving. Maybe my fevered imagination had helped me, maybe it had cursed me and compounded my troubles, but either way, none of it mattered now. I'd been blessed with another opportunity to feel the sun on my face.

I was alive. If one sentence could sum up my state of mind at the astonishing sight of the sunrise that morning, this was it. The long journey through Badwater's second night had reduced everything down to a couple of simple declarative sentences. I'm alive. I go on.

And so I ran, and everything seemed possible again. I knew, even as the energy surged through me, that it couldn't last and that I wouldn't feel this good and this strong for another marathon distance. But that didn't matter and I didn't care. Just as life had been reduced to a single impulse, so had my running: It could be done and so it must be done.

But this wasn't by any means the pure frisky running of a young colt. You can't spend 45 hours on the Badwater road and still feel the boundlessness of youth—it's been spent. You've seen your own limitations and you've learned that everything that begins must also end. You're old by the time the third morning comes. Ancient. Used up. Keenly conscious of your own mortality.

And then you reject all that and go on. Rejection of one's inevitable demise is what middle age is all about in a way that most twenty-five-year-olds cannot yet understand, and the rediscovery of that fact can be a huge source of joy at 115 miles and two days out on the edge. I'd learned by then what it felt like to have the clock stop where it was "always four A.M." I knew what paranoid bitterness tasted like. I'd come close to lying down in the road. And now it was another day.

So I ran like an old man, acutely conscious of my failings and the grim corruption of time—and loving every minute of it, as though the world were new, as only an old person can.

The morning was as bright as the night had been dark.

Kirk Johnson

The air streaming down from the eastern slope of the Sierras had been washed clean and I could feel it flowing toward me and through me. The peaks ahead glinted and shimmered and the long shadows created by the steeply angled sun gave all the landmarks of the desert a depth and dimension that made them seem larger, deeper and more profound than mere scrub, sagebrush and creosote. Everything sparkled and pulsated with three-dimensional life.

I hadn't known when the sun came up whether I was in last place or not, and frankly couldn't have cared less. I wasn't running to catch up with anyone, or even to make a better time into Lone Pine. I was running simply because my body's declaration of life had told me that I should.

But as I went forward I began to make out a couple of runners ahead of me in the distance. And this time I decided to let my racer's urge go. I wanted to pass somebody now, I really did. I knew it was petty and ridiculous, but I didn't care about that, either. The time for analysis and temperance and measured expenditures of energy were over. I wanted to feel, if only for this moment, that it wasn't just me against the course. I wanted to be an athlete.

When I got closer I saw that one of the men was Scott Weber, walking now with a pacer or friend I didn't recognize. I felt an added pressure from that—to be more than I was, to be a runner that Weber, the coach himself, a five-time Badwater veteran, might respect. I tried to straighten up as I approached, to stiffen my spine and lengthen my stride as best I could in order to make a good impression. And so, with the sun behind me, I chased my own shadow west toward the mountains in all their monumental glory. And in a small and insignificant way, I chased my own self-image at the same time.

And then I passed him. The little fat boy who couldn't climb the black walnut tree actually passed, in a real race, a

264

man who'd done a "Run You Don't Want to Try." I felt small and silly, but also victorious—not over Weber, but over something in myself. And he was everything I could have hoped he might be at that moment, and that I'd heard he was, in a coach. He became my coach, in a way, right there and then.

"Good running, man," he said simply as I went by.

I thanked him and wished him luck and felt a pang of guilt for how damn good it had felt. And still the road ahead beckoned.

One of the great quirks and charms of the ultramarathon is that older runners tend to do better, on average, than younger ones. Super-distance running is also one of the rare sports in which women can often do as well as men their own age. Ultramarathons are occasionally even won by women, an unheard-of thing in every other running event, where male musculature and stamina invariably dominate.

There's a definite sweetness in this: The farther you go, the more the world equals out. The inherent advantages of youth and strength are diminished; gender equality becomes real and concrete. That point had been driven home to me particularly at Massanutten in Virginia, when the race director—a gruff old-guy runner—had happened by our aid station sometime during the night. He'd been cruising the course, spreading the race gossip, much as Ben did at Badwater, about who was in, who was out and who was running well. He'd told us that among the very first to quit on the previous day, near the 25-mile point, was an eighteen-year-old man, who was also the youngest person in the race.

"Eighteen-year-olds aren't tough enough yet," the race director said with a little spit onto the ground. Case closed.

Weathered and leathery beats strong and fast. Clint Eastwood trumps Brad Pitt when the going gets tough. I'd liked the sound of that. But then I'd stumbled onto another possible explanation of middle-aged endurance dominance that was somewhat less flattering: lower testosterone levels. Middle-aged men, according to a theory expounded in one of the grubby little books that had arrived in my mailbox, do better in ultradistance events because, well—there's no good way to say this—we're a bit less manly. Younger runners have their tanks topped off with testosterone, which often dooms them in ultramarathon running because the hot-rod mentality of male-hormone overload forces them to run too fast, too early. In short, they burn out. Female ultramarathoners are better able to hold a consistent running pace, my little book said, because they're not victimized by their hormones, and middle-aged men have the same general advantage. We've been given the great good fortune, in other words, of being able to run like women.

I would have been more than thrilled to receive a compliment like that by the time we were approaching Lone Pine if it meant I was running like my sister. She'd been at my side, off and on, for more than 60 miles of the race—much of that at night—and I was in complete awe of her strength. We'd become joined, in a way, equaled out in our strides, and often, it seemed, she was the one who'd been forced to slow down for my sake, and not the other way around, although she was twelve years older, with no experience on an ultramarathon course.

I felt I owed her everything. She'd been there when I'd crashed and when I'd recovered, and in the times between. We'd crossed Death Valley together and though she'd suffered a few blisters along the way herself, she seemed as tough and as beautiful to me as she was on the morning of the start, as long ago as that now seemed.

*　　*　　*

As I'd known it would, my surge faded. I'd lived a whole life, distilled and compressed between the brackets of a run. I'd been born with the sunrise. I'd matured. And then I died. Just like the effect of a spirit leaving the body, I was suddenly deanimated, my flame extinguished. I was just plain old me again, a very tired and sore forty-one-year-old man, unable to move forward at any pace faster than a walk. When I arrived at the van, I shrugged and shook my head.

"I could see you slowing down out there," Pat said.

Wayne asked what I'd eaten that might have made a difference. I shrugged again.

I felt by then, after so many miles, that I'd become a creature of that road, almost an extension of the road, as though the road's moods and states of mind were my own. Up, down, strong, weak, elated, depressed—every possible emotion or thought was simply a reflection of my path down Highway 190's breakdown lane. I'd moved so deeply into the Badwater universe that I'd become embedded into the very nature of the two-lane strip that had become my home. The road said crash and I crashed.

During the long night, everything had been hopelessly deep and complicated and tortuous and every thought and emotion had twisted itself in knots of mysterious or monstrous proportions. Now everything was simple. I was tired, and I was a biochemical machine. I was depressed because I'd run low on something. I'd drink some Dr Pepper and have another slug of my favorite new beverage, tomato juice, or perhaps a can of what I called my "old-man drink," multivitamin Ensure, and a handful of wonderfully soggy brown carbohydrate nubs from the cooler. And that would make a difference.

If my emotional state careered downward after my little morning run, well, then that was just the way of the world, baby. Get over it. Shit happens. When all else fails, there's still momentum—the built-up, pent-up pressure of all that has come before, pushing you or dragging you on past the point of impossibility. My momentum, I felt, would carry all before it. And as I stood there behind the van gobbling down a few hundred calories, I had to laugh to myself. I'd finally developed instincts. I'd been able to see what my body and mind needed because I'd stopped thinking about it so damned much. Don Juan was right after all.

As the sun climbed higher and higher and the outlines of Lone Pine came into view, even my instincts felt expendable. The Whitney Portal Road was up there somewhere. To be on the Whitney Road, with 13 miles left, was to be at the gate itself, and with every step back onto the road, that notion began to squeeze out everything else until there was only a kind of drone in my head, a white noise of empty monochrome blankness. Only two things existed—going forward and getting to the Whitney Road. I'd become an animal like Ulrich. I felt much better.

But my feet were hurting again. I tried denying it for a while, tried treating it as yet another expendable concept that I could do without. And I would have thought that any place prone to getting a blister would have done so by now. Travis and Pat had patched more than a dozen by then. But all the signs were there—the vaguely hot sensation in my toes and the gnawing awareness of my feet hitting the ground.

I didn't want to stop. I didn't want to see more blisters, or feel my sister cut and drain more blisters, or lose any more precious time that we might need in getting to the top. And there were only 20 miles left, for God's sake. *Only 20 miles!* The phrase clattered in my head as loudly as my 43-mile failure had in North Carolina. In the real world, of course, facing 20 miles on feet that hurt as badly as mine did would have seemed crazy. Feet like that would have been a reason to stay in bed. But in the Badwater universe, 20 miles was just the final sprint. Only 20 miles means you're almost there.

I finally accepted fate and climbed up onto a cooler while Pat unwrapped the tape. I was unfortunately correct—three or four big new blisters, all on the toes again. I'd changed shoes early that morning, switching to a newer pair with the front half cut out, but the process that had hammered me from the beginning was somehow still at work, even then. My toes didn't like Badwater—that was about as plain as I could think of it. The part of my body I'd worried about most—my knees—had held up better than I'd feared they might after the Boogie, and a part I hadn't even considered, the tips of my toes, had almost done me in.

Pat was at work with the pointed scissors when Ben pulled up, and I think we must all have brightened when we saw him, because he joked that we looked too darn happy. I couldn't help it: When he leaned his head into the van, I just had to smile. Seeing Ben, at that moment, was like seeing my father, like seeing the perfect father. He was my connection to the world.

He had news: Eric Clifton had shattered the course record for an A.M. start. He'd finished just after 1 P.M. on Friday—about the time I was struggling across the lake bed into Panamint Springs—with a time of 27 hours and 49 minutes. Angelika Castaneda of the Twin Team had set a new women's record as well, finishing just before 11 P.M. last night at 36 hours and 58 minutes, breaking Lisa Smith's old record by three minutes. Louise Cooper-Lovelace, the breast-cancer survivor, had done well, too, finishing early that morning with a time of 40 hours and 14 minutes. Ulrich had finished in sixth place at just under 36 hours, an astonishing feat given what he'd been through just two weeks earlier on the solo run. Ankeney and Justin had made it in sometime during the night. Chris Moon, the double amputee from England, was still on the course, about to start up the Portal Road.

And Dan Jensen had dropped out. I felt my whole body slump when I heard that. I thought of Great Bear Ski Lodge in Sioux Falls and the image I'd held in my head for so long of Dan and I wheezing to the top, giggling with dirt in our shoes.

"Oh, my God, what happened?" I said.

"Ninety-five miles, last night sometime," Ben said. "I don't know a whole lot more than that. His stump got too swollen to go on, apparently."

Ben asked how I was doing and I gave some vague answer. I was still thinking of Dan. If he'd been stopped at 95 miles, then I felt sure he'd gone a long way before that time in tremendous pain. He wouldn't have surrendered without a fight, and it was the fight I was thinking of—the 20 or 30 miles, or maybe the whole race—during which he'd struggled to ignore or evade the thing that finally halted him.

Then Ben had even more shocking news. Lisa Smith had dropped out as well last night, with only 10 miles left. His details were vague. She'd become dehydrated and feverish and had to take intravenous fluids at a local hospital, and had therefore been disqualified from continuing. More he didn't know.

The news about Dan and Lisa shattered the last little bit of conceit I might have had about my own athletic ability as an explanation for why I'd gotten this far. They'd been stopped, but I was still in. How was that really possible? They hadn't failed to complete Badwater, clearly, because they were less fit or less prepared than I, so the only response was a kind of fatalistic shrug. What will be, will be. You place your wager and you roll forward as best you can and the outcome is not entirely up to you. There but for the grace of God go I.

If I managed to travel those last 20 miles, it would mean I was lucky enough and determined enough to do so, not tougher or smarter or braver than those who didn't. I certainly felt proud of what we'd achieved in getting this far, but also now reduced in scale as well, as though I'd been given a vision of my own smallness on the earth. I was what I was.

I found now, for the first time, however, that I could actually say the words to myself that I couldn't before: I will make it. And with that I began to picture what the finish would be like, how the scene would be set and how I might feel. Step by step, I began assembling a kind of montage of the race's imagined final moments, and then those images began to grow and expand in my mind until the finish line seemed to be all that was left. As we went forward toward Lone Pine, my whole life seemed to have become a ramp leading toward an entirely arbitrary, artificial, two-dimensional plane drawn across a road in the mountains of California—a threshold that would mark the end of everything that came before it and the beginning of everything after.

Lone Pine was being torn up by road construction as Pat and I walked into town. Dump trucks, pavers and other complicated machines roared and pawed, filling the air with the dense smell of burning asphalt. There were no assembled crowds and no cheers, no volunteers with cups of water offered from the sidewalk—no recognition whatsoever of who we were or what we'd done or how close we finally were to our goal. We were just two more anonymous travelers straggling in from the desert. The construction workers we walked by stared at us with mild curiosity; if they had a clue why I wore a number 18 on my chest, they gave no indication of it. And I stared back at them, just as blank and mystified. After the silence and emptiness of Death Valley, downtown Lone Pine might as well have been midtown Manhattan—a blur of busyness and motion and noise and chaos. I felt like a hick all over again, awed and scared by the tumult of the big city.

One of my minor paranoid fantasies of the past few days, when I'd allowed myself to think of Lone Pine at all, was that we'd miss the sign for the Whitney Portal Road. The left turn toward the mountains was marked only by a small sign in the middle of town, and I imagined us going right by it and out the other end of Lone Pine and on and on somewhere forever. It was a little like my nightmare of hiding in bed on the morning of the race, but reversed: Now I just wouldn't ever stop. Matt Frederick and the other race officials would be waiting for us at the finish line and we'd never show up and they'd never know what happened to us. We'd become our own Breyfogle story.

But then, there it was before us—the road to Whitney. We'd reached the final leg of the race. What had seemed unimaginable six months ago, and merely impossible last night, was now real. I had to grab Pat's hand as we approached the corner.

"We're home," I said. It didn't matter now that we were facing the steepest climb of the whole course—an ascent of 5,000 feet in just 13 miles. Nothing mattered because I didn't feel now that anything could stop me, short of some physical restraint or act of God. I could barely even stand still. It was 11:20 A.M. We'd beaten our deadline by three hours, primarily because of my running spurt that morning, and that left us with more than 10 hours on the 60-hour clock.

The arrival of David Edelman, my old *New York Times* friend, provided the perfect antidote to the mental and emotional heaviness I would probably have descended into at that point. Too much had happened on the road leading to this mountain. There'd been too many miles, too much thought and too much sweat. The momentum of it would have consumed me, and I would have built the final climb into some tower of meaning that it couldn't hold. I would have stacked those miles with every question that had no answer and every mystery that I'd hoped could be resolved in the final reel, and the search that had taken me this far would have collapsed like a poorly designed building—too tall to support its own weight. David had come to us from the real world, and that put things in perspective.

Seeing him also brought a strange realization. Pat and Wayne and Travis and I had become, in a way, our own country over the long days and nights that we'd traveled together. We were exhausted, dirty, smelly and—speaking for myself, at least—mentally unstable, and everyone we knew was in that same basic condition. We lived out of a dirty metal box and had come to love it dearly. Wayne had just announced proudly to us that he hadn't removed his sneakers now for 60 hours. We were all a little crazy from sleep deprivation. Encountering someone who hadn't been through Badwater turned everything upside down. Normal had come to seem like us—funky and exhausted. David therefore seemed like the alien—weird because he was normal.

In the same way that the news of Dan and Lisa had reduced me in scale, David's presence also now brought the race itself back down to size—he saw our endeavor with fresh eyes, and that allowed me to do the same. Badwater, however much it might have come to seem like the center of the universe to the four of us on our little team, was still an obscure event on the fringe of everything. Whole worlds were turning out there beyond our experience, full of people living their lives in blissful ignorance of everything that had transpired over the past two and a half days. We weren't doing something that people would talk about for 100 years, and no one but us and a few people who read grubby little ultramarathon books would ever even know that we'd done it at all. We'd crossed a desert and now we were climbing a road up a mountain—no more and no less than that. I felt grounded again as soon as I saw him, so filled with joy that I just had to hug him.

David and I had met at the *Times* when we were both clerks in the newsroom in the early 1980s. He'd gone back to school for a Ph.D. in paleoanthropology and I'd slogged on through the grueling trial of proving myself at the paper. But we'd stayed in touch over the years—partly, I think, because we could always make each other laugh. He appreciated silly, stupid, surreal humor as much as I did.

But I knew as he left to park his car in order to walk with us up the mountain that the merely surreal was no longer a big deal for me. I'd passed through that country last night. With almost no sleep in four days, surreal had become my second home.

I'd arrived in those final miles at a place that I could only think of as the frontier—of my emotions and my thoughts and the limits of my body. Everything I felt was an inch below the surface, ready to bubble out, uncontrolled and unedited—laughter, tears, joy, despair—as though my whole inner life had been disemboweled and pinned to the end of my sleeve. Beyond the deep physical ache that seemed to be climbing up my thighs into my chest with every foot of higher elevation, I was exhausted inside somewhere. At any time, everything I was might spill out onto the road, like blood from a wound. I could cry myself to death or laugh to death or run myself into the ground and there'd be no real difference.

When David, for some unknown reason, mentioned the actor Hector Elizondo, I really thought for a few seconds that it might kill me. Elizondo pops up on television every now and then for an herbal product line. "I used to think all ginkgo bilobas were alike," he says. At 128 miles into Badwater and halfway up the Whitney Portal Road, Elizondo and his ginkgo bilobas struck me as the most hysterically funny thing I'd ever heard. *Hector Elizondo, for chrissakes! Ginkgo biloba!* Like all the world walks around not only knowing what ginkgo biloba is, but comparing various kinds of it. Even saying the name *Hector Elizondo,* by that point, could send me into teary, wheezing laughter that I felt could easily spiral into terminal convulsions.

The next moment, I was crying. At 129 miles, the director of the documentary film being made about the race drove by in his car, a boom microphone extended from the rear window, and asked me how it felt to be climbing Mount Whitney. I started to say something about the accomplishment and the pride I felt in my family—strings of perfect sports clichés were coming out of my mouth as though I'd practiced all my life. Then, abruptly, I was talking about Gary, and then I could barely talk at all. My face became a grim, clamp-jawed mask as the tears rolled out from under my sunglasses.

"I'm alive," I stammered, barely able to get the words out. "I go on."

The internal editor who might, in the real world, have held me back from exposing my deepest feelings had collapsed somewhere on the road and now it was just me, ragged and twisting with whatever impulse happened to wander up. I cried in front of the camera because crying was what I had left.

*   *   *

The section of the course we were on, called the Alabama Hills, is probably the most recognizable landscape of the Badwater race, even to people who've never been to Death Valley. In the heyday of the Hollywood western, going to Lone Pine and the rugged red landscape outside of town meant going on location. Though it was only a four-hour drive from Los Angeles, it looked a lot like the Wild West, or close enough, anyway. And for generations of moviegoers, the hills in turn defined what the mythical western landscape *should* be.

But I could also see, walking up the slope in daylight, why doing this final section of the course at night—a typical timetable for runners finishing in the 48-hour range—was often reputed to be a psychotic experience. The roadside was lined with wind-carved rocks and spires and sandstone chimneys and arches. Passing by such a landscape under the full effect of a second-night hallucinatory binge would allow the mind to produce almost anything. I began to think back fondly on my innocent little tea sets.

We hadn't gone very far, though, when we came around a curve and my heart stopped. Dan and Robin Jensen and their daughters were there by the side of the road in front of their truck. Just like Ben back at Stovepipe, Dan could only have been at that spot at that time for me, and I was honored beyond words and beyond speech. We cried and hugged as though we were brothers, which at that point we were. Though we'd spent barely a day together back in South Dakota, and though I hadn't seen him since the morning of the start, we'd been together here, under this sky, and I felt that that had changed everything.

And yet I couldn't stop, not even for this. I tried to say how badly I felt that he'd had to withdraw and how little sense it made that he was out and I was still in. I noticed the trouble he was having trying to walk, and pictured again how hard the final miles must have been. But the mountain was drawing me hard and I couldn't resist it. Gravity had been reversed, it seemed, and I was falling up toward Whitney. I had to go on because I had no choice. Forward motion had become an act of faith.

About five miles from the finish line, right where the Portal Road starts to get really steep in a series of switchbacks, Wayne joined me for the first time in the race. I didn't even see him until he was there, right behind me. He didn't say anything and I didn't ask why. We all just walked on, silent by then but for our breathing.

I'd come to depend on Pat through the miles that had come before, but now the torch had been passed—Wayne would be at my side when the goal finally came in view. I felt stronger for that somehow. I felt a new resolution in my step. Somehow a circle had been completed.

When I'd driven up the Portal Road with Ben back in May, he'd shown me the two giant trees, just beyond the trailhead to Whitney, that have become the traditional Badwater finishing point, so I knew what the final hundred yards would look like. The road, after all the curves and switchbacks, would come around a bend, and the full vista of the little box canyon of timber and shear rock that marked the end of the Badwater course would open up into view, and there we'd be.

And so the final mile passed, and as Wayne and David and I drew nearer and nearer, I began to feel that the air—both literally and figuratively—was growing thinner. Everything was getting stretched and blurred and distorted by a high-pitched whine in my head—the song of the finish line. Time and distance had lost their meaning. And while my mind rumbled with all the events of the past few days, my idea of the future had become compressed into almost nothing. There was the finish line, and after that it was almost as though there *was* no future. All concentration and effort and will were focused on something that was now, astonishingly, unbelievably within view.

And then the finish line began to crowd out everything that was left. I felt in the final quarter mile as though the whole universe could blink into nonexistence, and almost as though it had, and the line would be all that was left, still there floating before me. And then it swallowed me, too. It became a black hole that sucked down everything to become everything. My body and all its aches—my sunburned nose, chafed thighs, battered knees and wounded toes—had become mere footnotes as the physical world receded from view.

My alter ego was there. He would finish Badwater. Or maybe I'd endowed him with such strength and ferocity that he shoved me aside. I felt in a strange way as though he'd erased me, or killed me, as the two great trees approached. This was *his* triumph, after all, not mine. This was his crowning achievement, his glorious moment of becoming and ending. I was in the way. There was no room for me. Perhaps at the finish line I became expendable.

Or maybe it was simple justice and crude fairness. I'd created this entity within myself. I'd summoned him and shaped him and trained him and pushed him, and now that he'd gone where I built him to go and done all that he'd been asked, he had to smother his creator. It was right and natural. I had to die so that in the moments after the crossing I could be reborn.

Of all the words I've pondered and all the neat phrases I've tested to try and describe the end of this long journey, that's the closest I've come. I was reborn—not in the religious sense, but quite literally. I didn't really exist at the moment of crossing, and then, in the moment after, I burst back into life in a way that made everything new. My Badwater runner was gone. Maybe he died, too. But I like to imagine that in the universe beyond this one where the Badwater finish line exists, we were, at least for that one instant, able to come together and look each other in the eye and shake hands. I imagine us each nodding our acknowledgment of the other's strengths—mine as architect and engineer, his as primitive animal spirit and warrior—then turning and each going on our way into the mist. Perhaps he turned to look back at me one last time and I at him before we each disappeared.

When we came around the curve and I actually saw the white tape of the line stretched across the road, and the handful of people who'd gathered there to watch, I felt a little ripple of the racer's mentality that said I should speed up and try, one last time, to run and break the tape in the best form I could manage. Instead I walked. I was what I was and nothing I did now in these final few steps would change a thing. Badwater had shown me that truth, for better and for worse and for always: The story of our lives is the journey, not the destination.

Then the tape broke in my hands and I was across.

I called Fran from under the giant trees of Whitney, using a borrowed cellular phone. It was another little symbol that we'd passed through to the other side—cell phones worked again. We'd come out of the desert. We were back in the world. So I stood there surrounded by strangers and I heard her scream and shout and behind her in the background the house erupting with noise and I told her I'd finished and that it was all over.

Fifty-four hours and 26 minutes was the time on Matt Frederick's official race clock—five and a half hours under the cutoff. Nine of the 42 starters had dropped out, and I'd come in thirty-second place, about two hours ahead of Scott Weber, who was the last runner left on the course. I don't remember much else of what Fran or I said after that. I just stood there holding the phone to my ear and smiling, relishing the knowledge that I could now hear my wife and she could hear me.

Wayne and I sat talking in our room until perhaps 9 P.M. that night despite our exhaustion—me sprawled on the bed, him in a chair by the window, legs up. I'd reserved two rooms back where we'd started so long ago, at the Lone Pine Best Western—one for the two of us and one for Pat. But when we checked in after driving down from Whitney, we found that they'd given us rooms with only a single queen-sized bed each, not the doubles I'd asked for. Wayne called the front desk to see if anything else was available, but everything was full. I said it didn't matter to me, that I could sleep propped up against the door and not care. Then Wayne shrugged and laughed, too. It didn't matter. Nothing mattered now.

We recalled the moments that stuck in our heads—the crazy hallucinations, Wayne hosing himself down at Panamint, soup and tomato juice, the strange unstoppable momentum of the final miles, Maples and his men, Dan and Robin by the side of the Portal Road.

"I'm kind of afraid to wear this," Wayne said, glancing down at his official Badwater race T-shirt with the picture of Ulrich tooling down the highway. "I'm afraid I won't want to take it off."

He looked over at me. "But I'll wear it anyway because I can hardly wait for people to say, 'What's Badwater?'" he said. "Then I can say, 'Well, let me tell you about it.'"

We were silent for a while after that, just sitting there in the room together, thinking of where we'd been, and maybe a little bit about where we'd go from here.

And then we went to bed. There was no choosing sides this time, no baggage, no unresolved old family issues—Badwater had rendered them all moot, all irrelevant, all blown away somewhere across the salt pan. We crawled in, both in our white briefs—the last of the Johnson boys—and I found a position where my toes didn't hurt so much and turned off the light and the night took us like the wind.

And Everything After:
A Postscript

One of the major 100-mile trail races in the United States, called the Old Dominion—held every year in the Appalachian mountains of Virginia—has a slogan printed on its T-shirts that says IT'S HARD TO BE HUMBLE WHEN YOU'VE FINISHED.

Badwater shirts, I've decided, should say precisely the opposite. It's hard *not* to be humble when you've crossed Death Valley and come out the other side. Anybody who could make it through the empty, vast darkness of a second night on the Badwater road and then come down from Mount Whitney feeling full of himself about the accomplishment just didn't get it, I think. And it's the highest tribute I can offer to this race and the people who participate in it that nearly everyone does get it.

The ultramarathoners I came to know are certainly as full of failings and flaws as any other group of people. But I didn't meet a single one who'd been puffed up into arrogance by his or her accomplishments. The Badwater bartender and her boss were wrong. The park rangers were wrong. And I was wrong in my moments of doubt.

Badwater, by its power and majesty, puts everyone to the proper scale—some it brings down to size, some it raises up—until you can't escape being just what you are: a bony little stick figure standing upright on two legs under a sky that will swallow you whole. However strong and brave and true you are, in Death Valley you're also tiny and weak and very human.

And then, after breaking you down, Badwater forces you to realize that you're not alone. In every other race I know, the volunteers who give out food and water along the course exist in an anonymous blur. A runner may be gracious and thankful for the help along the way, but inevitably he or she moves on down the road or the trail where another set of volunteers awaits. And that makes it possible to run a marathon, or almost any other ultramarathon, and still maintain the illusion that it's your own strength of will and determination—the power of the individual triumphant—that carries the day.

At Badwater, a runner's crew is everything. And that changes everything. In a place where a solitary heroic athlete (leaving aside Ulrich for the moment) couldn't possibly be alone and survive for even a day—let alone finish a race—the puffed-up egotism of the marathon runner collapses upon itself. I will owe Pat and Wayne a debt of love and gratitude for the rest of my life for what they did out there, because I know that on a fundamental level I didn't really do Badwater—we did it, together. I learned that the greatest moments of bliss arise from the simplest of things, and that the list of what we really need in life is astonishingly short: We need each other. Our baggage, contrary to everything I'd imagined about the simplified life, is what gets us through.

My own real achievement in this year, if there was one, was in trying the race at all. That's what I'm proud of and that's the thing I want my kids to remember. Their father tried. If I hadn't made it to Whitney, if the blisters had stopped me at 25 miles, if my stomach had kept turning just a notch or two further into outright nausea and I hadn't had a sister and brother around on that long Friday night to coax me back into believing in myself, the triumph I could claim over my fears would still be just as sweet, I think.

None of that makes me a hero. I finished Badwater because I worked hard in preparing for it and because I was lucky in that the problems we faced were ones that could be overcome, and because I was just too stubborn to quit. That, in the end, is about all there is to say. If my blister crisis on the first afternoon somehow ironically saved me, by pulling me off the course and out of the punishing sun through its worst hours, thus leaving me the strength for the nights and days ahead, I can only credit the graces that are sometimes given to children and madmen.

Dan Jensen, to me, is a genuine hero. Lisa Smith, who went back and finished the final 10 miles of Badwater on her own after the race was over even though it didn't officially count, is a hero. Chris Moon and Louise Cooper-Lovelace, who both finished ahead of me despite incredible physical challenges, are heroes. Curt Maples is a hero of character. Ulrich is Ulrich, a singularity among the people I've met in my life—beyond classification.

I called Ulrich several weeks after I got back home. I wanted to hear what it was like crossing Death Valley twice within a two-week period, and to get his thoughts on anything else he wanted to talk about. But I think I was also putting another demon to bed. I was finally over my Ulrich terrors. I could call him now. I'd reached up high enough to at least peer over the hedge.

I was also still in what my brother-in-law Tony had called a "liminal state," a sort of threshold between worlds—halfway at Badwater and halfway back in the land of the living, but belonging fully to neither place.

For weeks I'd been dreaming nearly every night that I was still in Death Valley. And always it was to the same moment my dreams took me—into the darkness of Badwater's second night, at the point of lost hope. Lone Pine was too far and I was too tired. California State Highway 190 stretched on forever. It made me realize how deeply I'd journeyed into myself that a part of me was having such a hard time finding its way back.

So Ulrich and I talked for a long time about Death Valley, and spirituality, and the legacy of the desert pioneers, and then I told him about my dreams, and how my Badwater experience had been defined and shaped and given life by the love of my family.

"That's what made it happen for me, in every way," I said.

Ulrich paused. "Those people *are* my family, my surrogate family," he said, referring to the Badwater universe of Ben and Denise and the other characters who inhabit the race. "My own real family is sort of lacking and not very supportive. They think what I'm doing is a complete waste of time."

Maybe I finally understood Ulrich a little by the end, too. We were both after the same thing, just getting there by different routes, with different strengths and talents. Maybe we were more alike than not. Or maybe he's still a god; I'm not sure.

So did I find the wellspring of endurance? Did I uncover the secret of Poon Lim the Chinese sailor and how he survived at sea? No, I didn't, and I came to conclude that it's probably like old Breyfogle's gold, or those magic-eye three-dimensional images: If you look too hard, you'll never find it.

What I decided was that my search for endurance, in a strange and paradoxical way, had created it. By going down the road to Badwater, and thinking that getting to the end would answer my questions, I found that I'd distilled in myself the very thing I was looking for. I found endurance when I stopped asking, *What would Ulrich do?* and simply plodded on in my own clumsy way. Then, like a poof of smoke or a mirage, my creation disappeared at the finish line and it was just plain old me again, the former fat boy, feeling like I'd had a visitation of some sort—a blithe spirit that walked onstage for a season, then departed.

I'd been wrongheaded, too, about where endurance could take me when I did find it. Running Badwater wasn't about limits and boundaries at all, as I'd once thought, but rather about going on and never giving up. For all its imagery of death and the severity of its climate, Death Valley and Badwater are about choosing life.

And when I figured that out, I finally understood that I hadn't entered the race to get closer to my brother Gary or to honor him at all, as I'd imagined at one time, but rather for totally opposite reasons—to put some distance between us, and to refute the terror and uncertainty that his death had introduced into my life. Badwater exposed that fact—brutally and honestly and with no gauzy sentimentality. I go on. I'm alive and he's not. I'm not him, and that's as complicated and as simple as things get in this world.

But then there are times when I feel that everything about my brother's life was revealed to me in those days and nights in the desert, and that the whole venture was a reflection of his strengths. And in those moments I can almost believe that his spirit was there, because the race produced all the things he loved so much: a challenge, a reaffirmation of the bonds of family, a reexamination of what really matters in life. I'm not enough of a believer to say that Gary was somehow the architect of my Badwater year, but I know he would have smiled on it, and on what it produced.

Maybe those are obvious, even trite conclusions about suicide and life and death and survival that I could have figured out without doing Badwater if I was smart enough. But I wasn't and I didn't.

The imprint remains. What I experienced over those 54 hours and 26 minutes has become a part of who I am. I don't think I'll ever again be able to eat a cold boiled potato or drink a glass of tomato juice without being transported back to that road and those days and nights with my brother and sister. And some things can reach me even more deeply than that, touching me in places where I am completely naked and defenseless, where Badwater seems to have climbed inside and altered the chemistry entirely.

One Saturday night about a month after I returned home, Fran and I were fixing dinner. She went into the living room to put on some music. I said I'd pour us some wine. I was making corn bread. The boys were playing outside. It was an ordinary scene in every way. And then suddenly it wasn't.

She'd put on the Puccini. The Puccini, for God's sake! And with those harmonies flowing up and up, so full of love and pain and memory, I was liminal all over again. I was in the Owens Valley, on the road to Lone Pine, it was the middle of the night and I was staring up into the heavens crying.

I put down my wineglass and followed Fran into the living room, where we danced slowly in front of the stereo as Rodolfo and Mimi made love with their voices. I was back.

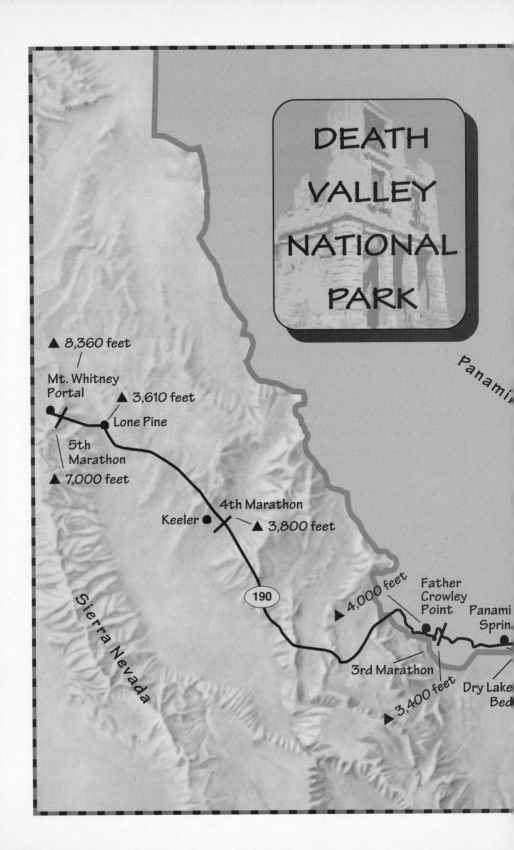

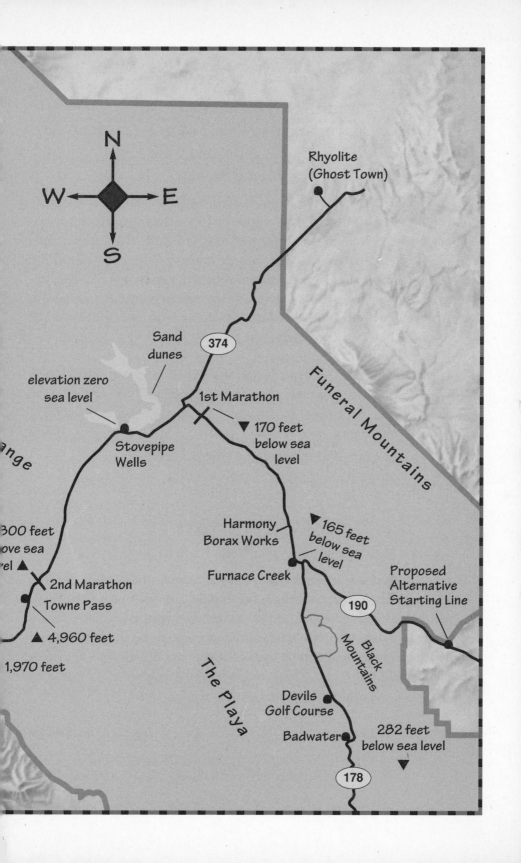

N
W   E
S

Rhyolite
(Ghost Town)

Sand
dunes

374

elevation zero
sea level

1st Marathon

▼ 170 feet
below sea
level

Stovepipe
Wells

Funeral Mountains

Harmony
Borax Works

▼ 165 feet
below sea
level

ange

Furnace Creek

300 feet
ove sea
el ▲

2nd Marathon

Towne Pass

Proposed
Alternative
Starting Line

190

▲ 4,960 feet

1,970 feet

The Playa

Black Mountains

Devils
Golf Course

Badwater

282 feet
below sea level
▼

178

BEYOND THE DEEP

The Deadly Descent into the World's Most Treacherous Cave
by William Stone and Barbara am Ende
with Monte Paulsen

Hidden in a remote region of southeastern Mexico is Huautla—possibly the deepest cave complex in the world. In 1994, an elite team of international explorers set out to go farther into the earth than anyone had before. Led by a larger-than-life, driven caving pioneer, the expedition faced some of the most severe, and most deadly, conditions ever encountered. This is their story—a white-knuckle epic of adventure, obsession, and danger that brilliantly illuminates the human desire to go beyond all limits in every way: to go beyond the deep.

"At long last, an epic to stand beside the adventure classics. BEYOND THE DEEP is *Into Thin Air* without the mountain, *The Perfect Storm* without the sea. Expedition leader Stone is Captain Ahab with a Ph.D., Columbus with a rope and dive tank."
—Jeff Long, author of *The Descent*

SEVEN SUMMITS

by Dick Bass and Frank Wells with Rick Ridgeway

Frank Wells was the head of a major motion picture studio. Dick Bass was an energy and resort entrepreneur. In middle age, both men left behind home, family, and successful careers to share an impossible dream. Facing innumerable dangers and obstacles, they set out to be the first team to climb the highest mountain on each of seven continents, from McKinley to Kilimanjaro to Everest. A breathtaking, exhilarating story of the human spirit, this is adventure writing at its finest.

"A hell of an adventure. A book for everyone who's ever dreamed of accomplishing great feats."
—Clint Eastwood

IN THESE GIRLS, HOPE IS A MUSCLE
A True Story of Hoop Dreams and One Very Special Team
by Madeleine Blais

They were a talented team with a near-perfect record. But for five straight years, when it came to the crunch of the playoffs, the Amherst Lady Hurricanes somehow lacked the scrappy desire to go all the way. Now finally, it is their season to test their passion for the sport and their loyalty to each other. This is the fierce, funny, and intimate look into the minds and hearts of one group of girls and their quest for success and, most important of all, respect.

"Beautifully written...a celebration of girls and athletics."
                                        —*USA Today*